The Modern Fantastic

The Films of
David Cronenberg

The Modern Fantastic

The Films of David Cronenberg

Edited by
Michael Grant

 Westport, Connecticut

Published in the United States and Canada by
Praeger Publishers, 88 Post Road West, Westport, CT 06881
An imprint of Greenwood Publishing Group, Inc.

English language editions, except the United States and Canada,
published by Flicks Books, Trowbridge, England.

First published 2000

Library of Congress Cataloging-in-Publication Data

The modern fantastic: the films of David Cronenberg / edited by Michael
Grant.
        p.   cm.
    Includes bibliographical references and index.
    ISBN 0-275-97058-2 -- ISBN 0-275-97059-0 (pbk. : alk. paper)
    1. Cronenberg, David 1943---Criticism and interpretation.
    I. Grant, Michael, 1940-

    PN1998.3.C75 M63 2000
    791.43'0233'092--dc21   00-029815

Library of Congress Catalog Card Number: 00-029815

ISBN: 0-275-97058-2 (Cloth)
ISBN: 0-275-97059-0 (Paper)

Printed in Great Britain.

Contents

Introduction
Michael Grant   1

An aesthetic sense: Cronenberg and neo-horror film culture
Ian Conrich   35

A body apart: Cronenberg and genre
Jonathan Crane   50

A(moral) monstrosity
Murray Smith   69

The naked crunch: Cronenberg's homoerotic bodies
Barbara Creed   84

Death drive
Parveen Adams   102

Cronenberg and the poetics of time
Michael Grant   123

The mysterious disappearance of style:
some critical notes about the writing on *Dead Ringers*
Andrew Klevan   148

Logic, creativity and (critical) misinterpretations:
an interview with David Cronenberg
Conducted by Xavier Mendik   168

David Cronenberg: filmography
Compiled by Michael Grant   186

David Cronenberg: selected bibliography
Compiled by Michael Grant   193

Index   212

Notes on contributors   218

For Katerina

Introduction

At one point in *The Fly* (1986), as his body is embarking on the horror of its mutations, Seth Brundle remarks: "I seem to be stricken by a disease with a purpose". Despite the fact that Brundle's body is taking on an intention and programme of its own, quite different from his conscious interests and strivings, he retains the wit and poise to give ironic expression to his predicament. He has, he tells Roni (Veronica), no wish to become just another "tumorous bore", prosing on about his symptoms. In his predicament and his reaction to it, Brundle is a figure who exemplifies much that is typical of Cronenberg's cinema, a cinema in which, as Linda Ruth Williams has argued, "death becomes simply the body's victory over individual agency, as it mutates into a dazzling variety of life forms in decay".[1] As she notes, the half-man, half-fly cannot die: he is trapped in a seemingly endless cycle, as mutation follows mutation. His death can come only when Roni gives it to him, blowing his head off as he gazes beseechingly at her, unable now to speak, and having lifted the barrel of the shotgun to his head with his claw. He would otherwise have been condemned to live on as a further appalling combination – of man, fly and telepod. The horror confronting him is that of the impossibility of dying, in which death is another form of life, and the degenerative mutation afflicting him simply that same life seen under another aspect:

Contemporary horror has specialised in making the inside visible, opening it up and bringing it out and pushing the spectacle of interiority to the limit to find out what the limit is.[2]

Williams' point receives vivid confirmation in *The Fly*, when one of Brundle's experiments goes disastrously wrong, and the chimpanzee he was attempting to transport from one telepod to the other ends up in the second device a quivering mass of flesh: the process of teleportation has turned it inside out, and yet it remains, in unimaginable agony, alive.

Modern horror cinema, inaugurated in 1968 with George Romero's *Night of the Living Dead*, is a cinema of the violation and destruction

1

of the body. This is body horror, and Philip Brophy, writing in 1986, has suggested that at its heart is a concern to play less on the fear of death than on "the fear of one's own body, of how one controls and relates to it".[3] He gives as an instance a scene from Dario Argento's thriller, *Deep Red* (1976), in which a compelling sense of bodily and physical presence is conveyed as a character's head is rammed repeatedly against the sharp corner of a marble mantelpiece. His mouth is open in a scream, so that his teeth are smashed on impact, an event rendered in graphic and explicit detail. The effect of impending and actual physical violence is created here, as elsewhere in Argento's work, by a signally brilliant and sophisticated command of sound, music, composition and editing. It is this mode of showing the horror, rather than telling it, that Brophy considers indispensable to the modern cinema's involvement in the destruction of the body. And Cronenberg, for Brophy, is an exemplary director in this field. *Shivers* (1976) is about an artificially constructed sex-parasite that transfers itself from body to body during intercourse, inducing sexual frenzy; *Rabid* (1977) involves mutation resulting from experimental plastic surgery, while *The Brood* (1979) deals with the bodily expression of psychological traumas and psychoses. Nola Carveth's body develops hideous grey sacs, which she tears at with her teeth, releasing a mutant brood of children through whom she embodies the overwhelming rage and hatred she feels for her parents and husband. *Scanners* (1981) is perhaps the ultimate example of modern body horror, as, in an early sequence, one scanner blows the head off another, in real time and in full view of the camera. (Something similar occurs early on in Romero's *Dawn of the Dead* [1979], where a soldier blasts the head off a zombie with a shotgun, an event presented explicitly and in real time.) This is in line with the view of Cronenberg developed by Williams, although her position has further ramifications consequent on her having seen the later films. For her, body horror is a form that has made a speciality out of the disturbance of the bodily interior – what she calls a "terrorism" of the blood and viscera. What is original about Cronenberg, however, and the feature of his outlook that differentiates him from a director such as Romero, is his willingness "to look positively from the inside out, asking 'How does the disease perceive us?'".[4] The result is that the interior of the body ceases to be a private space, and the distinction between what is inside and what is outside begins to break down. In *Rabid*, the phallic or vampiric projectile penetrating its victims from outside, in order to inject them with a virus, is an extrusion from the inside of Rose's body. Rose becomes the one who speaks for, and exists on behalf of, the virus, which thus finds in her its expression. The telepathic power of the scanners negates the separation between mind

2

and mind, brain and brain, as the scanner passes through skin and skull, entering the brain of the victim. No sooner is he there, a presence established within the other, than he explodes the very confines which alone have made the act of scanning possible. Having entered the other from the outside, the scanner finally "comes from within". For Williams, this transgression is all the more extraordinary inasmuch as it centres on the male body. The abject is evident in the bizarre bodily changes to be found in films as different as *Videodrome* (1982) and *M. Butterfly* (1993), both of which focus on mutating or deviant men. Cronenberg's work at this level achieves a rupture of the categories constituting gender difference: as Williams has it, in these films "mutation signals a more pervasive postmodern 'gender-fuck' at work: women conceive without men (*The Brood*), and men turn themselves into women".[5] In the "fisting" scene in *Videodrome*, for example, when Harlan thrusts his arm into Renn's vaginal slit, what he is attempting is a form of rape. However, the vagina dissolves his arm, and he is left with a bleeding stump, prefiguring the stump of a hand and dissolved ankle which Stathis Borans is left with at the end of *The Fly*. In *Crash* (1996), the complexities of this order of conceptualisation are developed further, as the question of the boundaries between the inner and outer, the private and the public, of which the male body has been the focus, finds in the automobile a new kind of expression. Vaughan's car, a 1963 Lincoln Continental Convertible, the type of car Kennedy rode in at his assassination, is, for Williams, an "interzone". It makes external the interior of Vaughan's body. At the same time, he rides in it, as do others, and its interior is a place where he and they have sex. The subversion of sexual boundaries and positioning is, therefore, inseparable from Cronenberg's treatment of the violation of the boundaries between the inner and the outer.

What this kind of argument points to is the fact that Cronenberg's cinema creates its narratives and fictional universe out of the systematic and knowing transgression of what Wittgenstein would call the "grammar" of our concepts. For Wittgenstein, language is both the source of our philosophical confusions and the only way we have of laying them to rest: "Philosophy is a battle against the bewitchment of our intelligence by means of language".[6] Philosophy, as he understands it, is a fight against the fascination which forms of expression can exercise over us. It is, in effect, a struggle against language by means of language. The kind of investigation he sees philosophy as being may thus be called "grammatical", and he describes a grammatical investigation as one in which "[w]e remind ourselves...of the *kind of statement* that we make about phenomena".[7] This is not simply a concern with syntax or the correct formation of sentences. As Marie McGinn makes clear, Wittgenstein's idea of grammar relates not to language considered as a system of signs, but to our use of words, "to the structure of our *practice of using* language".[8] He seeks not a systematic account of the rules that govern our use of words, but an evocation of the distinctive patterns of use that are characteristic of how we employ words in the course of our lives. It is these distinctive patterns of use that constitute the grammar of our concepts. By means of attention to them, Wittgenstein aims to clarify what the grammar of our concepts actually is.

The purpose of this clarification is twofold. Firstly, he wishes to make us aware of the conflict between our philosophical idea of how a concept works and how it is actually used. Secondly, he is attempting to get us to see the many differences in the patterns of use that typify the different regions of our language. Wittgenstein calls these differences in use "grammatical differences", and, as McGinn notes, making us aware of these differences is central to his philosophical method:

> When he speaks of our need to '*command a clear view* of the use of our words', he is thinking both of our need to uncover the conflict between our philosophical notions and the way our concepts actually function, and of our need to become aware of the grammatical differences in how the concepts in the different regions of our language are used.[9]

One crucial area that Wittgenstein opens to grammatical investigation is that involving the distinction between the inner and the outer, the subjective and the objective. The problem with psychological concepts and distinctions of this kind is that they encourage the idea that thoughts and feelings are "inside" us in a way that our behaviour is not:

> Look at a stone and imagine it having sensations. – One says to oneself: How could one so much as get the idea of ascribing a *sensation* to a *thing*? One might as well ascribe it to a number! – And now look at a wriggling fly and at once these difficulties vanish and pain seems able to get a foothold here, where before everything was, so to speak, too smooth for it.[10]

As McGinn puts it, the boundary between the stone and the fly is not an empirical one (we have discovered that stones do not have pains inside them, but flies do), reflecting an empirical relation between some physical objects, the bodies of flies, for example, and the special category of private objects, such as sensations of pain. It is a conceptual one, and "reflects the conceptual connection that exists in our language between sensation concepts and bodies of a quite particular kind: living human beings and what resembles them".[11] In other words, it makes no sense to say of a stone that it feels pain, but it does make sense when said of a fly. In this instance, the false distinction between the physical realm and the mental, which the misapplication of the bewitching picture of the "inner" and the "outer" tempts us to make, is replaced by the distinction between the living and the non-living, and this lies deeply rooted in our grammar. The section of *Philosophical Investigations* quoted above continues: "And so, too, a corpse seems to us quite inaccessible to pain". McGinn makes the point of this clear:

> The death of a human being does not leave us with the 'thing' half of the previously coexisting body and mind, but at death the human body *becomes* a thing, an object that is inaccessible to psychological description.[12]

What Wittgenstein is considering here has to do with more than the way we describe things. The division between the living and the non-living enters into the fundamental form of our life, into what it is for us to be what we are: "Our attitude to what is alive and to what is dead, is not the same. All our reactions are different."[13] These reactions are tied up not simply with what we say, but with all our ways of being and acting in the world. They are inseparable from the very form of our world, and "what the world is for us is shown by the fact that we can make sense of some things and not of others".[14] To adapt a remark of Wittgenstein's, were human beings not in general agreed about what is living and non-living, our concepts of life and death would not exist.

Similarly, our concept of pain does not describe a "something" that lies hidden inside the physical body. It ties in with the living body, in the sense that there is no gap between the concept of pain and the cries and gestures expressive of suffering. Just as we can see joy in a human face, so we can see pain and suffering there. Wittgenstein remarks: "But isn't it absurd to say of a *body* that it has pain?". We do not, for example, say that my hand feels pain "but I in my hand".[15] As McGinn indicates, "[o]ur psychological concepts are grammatically linked with the concept of a subject, and that subject is not my body but 'I'...What Wittgenstein wants us to see is that this move from 'the body' to 'the subject who feels the pain' (to 'I') is not a movement between entities, but a *grammatical movement*, a movement between language-games":[16]

What sort of issue is: Is it the *body* who feels pain? – How is it to be decided? What makes it plausible to say that it is *not* the body? – Well, something like this: if someone has a pain in his hand, then the hand does not say so (unless it writes it) and one does not comfort the hand, but the sufferer: one looks into his face.[17]

What Wittgenstein here is insisting on is that this is an issue to be decided not by introspection, but by reference to the grammar of our language-game. When we do this, we shall find that, in our practice of describing living human beings, "the human body enters our language-game, not merely as an object of physical and physiological description, but as an embodied subject: a unified centre of psychological ascription".[18] What might seem at first sight to be a shift between two different entities – a physical body and a soul – is, in fact, a shift between two language-games, a shift in grammar. In other words, what we become aware of as we consider these issues by reference to questions of grammar is *how we go on*: "And *how we go on* is a matter of how we think, and speak, and intentionally and socially conduct ourselves: that is, matters of our experience".[19]

Cronenberg systematically violates these "matters of our experience" – that is, he systematically violates the bounds of sense, the grammar of the inner and the outer. In *Videodrome*, for example, Max Renn's hallucinations are treated as inner objects which can be recorded, and so experienced by others. The film ascribes sensations to inanimate objects, such as television sets, and it overrides the fundamental division between the living and the non-living. Nicki Brand appears to Renn after what appears to be her murder. Flesh turns into a machine, as Renn's hand becomes a gun, while machines turn into flesh, as videocassettes are transformed into pulsating entities with a life of their own. At the end of the film, flesh bursts forth from a television set, after Renn has seen himself kill himself. In *Scanners*, similar violations of grammar, in this case that of self and other, are employed as the basis of the film, while in *Dead Ringers* (1988) the Mantle twins appear to be two bodies with a single nervous system. In *The Fly*, there is an imperceptible transition from waking consciousness to nightmare, as Stathis Borans takes Roni to the hospital to give birth to Seth's child – a huge, writhing maggot. Nightmare and wakefulness are knowingly confused. I would argue that these and the many other transgressions of identity to be found in Cronenberg's work are not only a matter of the breaking down of bodily borders and the boundaries of the individual. Throughout his career, from *Shivers* to *Crash*, his films have sought to sustain an onslaught on what Jonathan Lear has called (after Wittgenstein) "the perceptions of salience, routes of interest, [and] feelings of naturalness" that "constitute being part of a form of life",[20] a form of life which finds expression in the grammar of our concepts. Williams has noted how in Cronenberg's body horror a relationship is articulated "between organs in different bodies, despite the physical space or different identities which might separate them".[21] She clinches her point with a quote from a character in *The Brood*, who says of Dr Raglan that he "encouraged my body to revolt against me...I have small revolution on my hands, and I'm not putting it down very successfully". There is, in Cronenberg's films, a turning away from the immediacies of communal and social circumstance, a subversion of contour and legible order, in a paradoxical drive to what exists on the far side of humanity.

Maurice Blanchot is one of the more compelling exponents of this aesthetic. For Blanchot, language effects the death of things as things:

When we speak, we gain control over things with satisfying ease. I say, 'This woman,' and she is immediately available to me, I push her away, I bring her close, she is everything I want her to be.[22]

Blanchot is pointing to something he sees in the work of poets such as Hölderlin and Mallarmé, whose theme is the essence of poetry itself, involving a recognition of the disquieting nature of the act of naming. If I am to say "this woman", I must somehow take away her flesh and blood, and, in the act of designating her, annihilate her. As he puts it: "The word gives me the being, but it gives it to me deprived of being. The word is the absence of that being, its nothingness, what is left of it when it has lost being – the very fact that it does not exist".[23] When I speak, I separate myself from things and from myself: "I say my name, and it is as though I were chanting my own dirge".[24] In literature, understood as Blanchot understands it, nothing speaks: literature has nothing to say, and no way of saying that nothing, and yet it is compelled to go on saying it. This is what Blanchot sees as the first slope of literature, and one might illustrate it from poetry in English by reference to the "anti-master-man, floribund ascetic"[25] of Wallace Stevens' "Landscape with a Boat", who assumed that truth lay "like a phantom, in an uncreated night," and was to be reached "by rejecting what he saw/And denying what he heard". Like Mallarmé, he sought to reach his goal by a series of negations that would plunge him into an abyss beyond the abyss. "He had only not to live, to walk in the dark,/To be projected by one void into/Another".[26] The second slope of literature exists simultaneously with the first. Here, literature seeks to get back before the murder of the first moment, and to return to "this moment which precedes literature", the moment which precedes the giving of names. Literature wants the pebble as it exists, and, attempting to take the side of things, it seeks for what in the pebble man destroys by naming it, that which is "the foundation of speech and what speech excludes in speaking, the abyss, Lazarus in the tomb and not Lazarus brought back into the daylight, the one who already smells bad, who is Evil, Lazarus lost and not Lazarus saved and brought back to life".[27] It is here that Blanchot's ideas evince a similarity with certain aspects of Emmanuel Levinas' approach to the notion of what he calls the *il y a* ("there is"). It is towards the experience of the *il y a* that art tends, as it seeks for the Lazarus who smells bad, who is Evil, who is not spiritualised or redeemed by the concepts of abstract reason:

> In the night, where we are riven to it, we are not dealing with anything. But this nothing is not that of pure nothingness. There is no longer *this* or *that*; there is not 'something.' But this universal absence is in its turn a presence, an absolutely unavoidable presence.[28]

The "I" is itself submerged by the night, and invaded by it. The horror of the *il y a* is that which returns in the heart of every negation, like Banquo's ghost. A corpse is horrible, since it already carries in itself its own spectre, presaging its return. The horror of the *il y a* is the impossibility of dying, so that the haunting spectre, the phantom, constitutes the very element of horror, a horror captured in stories such as Poe's "The Premature Burial" (1844), in which the world of horror is an existence beyond death, "of awakening underground with nobody to hear you or your fingers scratching on the wood".[29] Levinas himself refers to Blanchot's novel, *Thomas l'Obscur* (1941), which opens with an exemplary account of the *il y a*:

> The presence of absence, the night, the dissolution of the subject in the night, the horror of being, the return of being to the heart of every negative moment, the reality of irreality are there admirably expressed.[30]

As Simon Critchley puts it: "What if the rope with which the suicide leaps into the void only binds him tighter to the existence he is unable to leave? What if there is something stronger than death, namely dying itself?".[31]

The horror evoked by Cronenberg's cinema is located here. Seth Brundle is condemned to an interminable series of transmutations, none of which ends in death. He experiences a fate worse than death, that of the impossibility of dying. At the end of *Dead Ringers*, after Beverly has separated himself from Elliot, he leaves the Mantle Clinic and telephones Claire. He is unable to speak to her when she answers, and returns to the dead body of his brother. He lies himself down across Elliot's knees, and remains there, unmoving. A blue light focuses on his eyes, which are open. Beverly is not dead. The death that would consummate their sacralisation of the car crash is not granted to either James or Catherine Ballard in *Crash*: the film ends on James' line: "Maybe the next one, darling... Maybe the next one". In *Naked Lunch* (1991), Bill Lee is condemned to experience in a world of his own making the same death – that of his wife – twice over. In *M. Butterfly*, after the death of René Gallimard, Song Liling is also brought to confront an existence beyond death, as he sits, staring blankly forward, on the plane that will take him back to China. To clarify what is involved here, I would like to consider a scene in *The Fly* which, in my view, epitomises in one poignant and difficult exchange of dialogue the quintessence of Cronenberg's vision. Brundle's teeth have begun to drop out, and they land on the keyboard of his computer. Brundle stares reflectively at them, as though considering the contrast they constitute (one typical of Cronenberg) between the sterility of technological hardware and the fluid mess of organic, bodily detritus. He then bears the teeth into the bathroom, now unspeakably filthy and defiled, murmuring to them as he goes: "You are relics...yes, you are...you can't deny it!". Finally, he reaches the medicine cabinet, the "Brundle Museum of Natural History", and when he opens it we have a brief moment in which to see that it is full of the organs that have fallen off him – an ear, something that looks as though it might be a penis, and other items, described by Brundle as "artefacts of a bygone era, of historical interest only". At this point, we hear the door of the laboratory/loft open, and Roni enters. Brundle tells her that his teeth have begun to fall out, and he offers to show her the exhibits in his museum, an offer which, not surprisingly, she declines. He asks her what she wants, to which she replies: "I came to tell you...", but at this juncture her courage fails her. She has come to tell him that she is pregnant with his child, and that she is intends to have an abortion. Unable to confront him with him with this, she says only: "I wanted to see you, before...", at which point she breaks off in distress. Brundle twitches in pain and says: "You have to leave now, and never come back here". This is a moment of severance whose meaning the rest of the sequence develops. The remaining dialogue is as follows:

Brundle: Have you ever heard of insect politics?
[Roni shakes her head. Brundle laughs.]

Brundle:	Neither have I. Insects don't have politics. They're very brutal, no compassion, no compromise. We can't trust the insect. I'd like to become the first insect politician. You see, I'd like to...oh *[he moans and twitches]* I'm afraid...
Roni:	I don't know what you're trying to say.
Brundle:	I'm saying... *[He moves forward. There is a reverse-shot to Roni, who steps back. There is then a cut to Brundle, who looks upward, as the music begins softly.]* I'm saying, I'm an insect who dreamt he was a man, and loved it *[a melancholy slow melody becoming more pronounced]* but now the dream is over, and the insect is awake.
Roni:	*[weeping]* No, Seth!
Brundle:	I'm saying...I'll hurt you if you stay. *[The music now begins to rise in volume. Roni turns, weeping, away from him, as the music becomes full and portentous. The camera stays with Brundle, who stands looking after her, until he hears the offscreen sound of the door closing. He bends over, holding his head in profound sorrow, gasping with emotion.]*

The dialogue is delivered in a halting, almost gasping, delivery which the music reinforces, creating an intense sense of desolation and loss. The dominant colour is blue, which serves to contrast with the brown, mutating body of the man-fly, and, at the same time, enclose him in a space, a zone, which is not that of other locations in the film, such as Borans' office or Roni's flat. It is during this sequence that Brundle finally flips over or transforms into the non-human. The sequence begins with his recognition of his own bodily redundancy as a man, a human being, delivered in an ironic tone, one that significantly alters when Roni enters and he speaks to her of "insect politics". It is here that he moves more definitively beyond the human, saying things to her which she can no longer understand. His reply to her incomprehension is emphasised by the plangency of the film's score: it seems to fill his words as he tells her that he was an insect who dreamt he was a man, and loved it, a statement whose truth we are able imaginatively to appreciate when we set it against the reality of his love for her. Cronenberg's finest touch comes in the way in which he handles the next remark: "now the dream is over, and the insect is awake". After a momentary pause, he cuts away to Roni, who appears confused, fearful and distraught. There is now a cut back to Brundle, who interrupts his train of thought (he abandons his repeated opening phrase, "I'm saying") to tell her, with what seems like brutal directness, that he will hurt her if she stays. There is here a momentary resurfacing of his old feeling for her, and his recognition of what he has become finds desolating expression in the manner of his sending her away. Brundle understands that the inevitability of her being lost to him coincides with his having to confront the further truth of his unbearable exile from the human condition. The interweaving and rhythm of the different elements in play here serve to create an extraordinarily realised and vivid sense of what is human, and how what is not human is nevertheless crucially and urgently intimate with it. Cronenberg creates in the figure of Brundle a dark radiance, a radiance deriving in part, of course, from the contrast between the horror of his appearance and Roni's still shining beauty, a contrast supported by the film's lighting, but this is not the whole of the matter. There is about him that which comes from within him, from within the materiality and the opacity of his mutating body, and the sequence emphasises this as it ends, centred on him, focused on the enigma and ambiguity that are his condition.

There is in *The Fly*, therefore, a suspension between the human world and what is exterior to it, and Todorov has seen this kind of suspension as characteristic of the literature of the modern fantastic. It is by virtue of this concern with the limits of the human that the modern fantastic differs from the fantastic of the 19th century, a literature of which Todorov has given the classic account. This latter form, exemplified by Jan Potocki's *Rękopis znaleziony w Saragossie* (*The Saragossa Manuscript*, 1804-15) and Henry James' *The Turn of the Screw* (1898), depends on the occurrence within the familiar world of an event that cannot be explained by the laws of that world. As a result, the character who experiences the event has to choose between two possible understandings of the situation. Either what has occurred is the product of an illusion of the senses, in which case the laws of the world remain as they are, or the event has truly taken place. In this case, the world is under the control of laws which are unknown to us. "Either the devil is an illusion, an imaginary being; or else he really exists, precisely like other living beings – with this reservation, that we encounter him infrequently."[32] The fantastic is, therefore, fundamentally temporal, since it exists only for as long as there is an uncertainty as to the appropriate form of explanation. If one opts for a supernatural explanation, one enters the neighbouring genre of the marvellous. If one were to opt for an explanation based on natural causes, one would have entered the uncanny. The fantastic exists only insofar as one hesitates between these two genres: "The fantastic is that hesitation experienced by a person who knows only the laws of nature, confronting an apparently supernatural event".[33] The basic strategy of Romero's *Martin* (1979) is based on this dynamic. The film has as its central character a young man, Martin (John Amplas), who may, or may not, be a vampire. In depicting Martin's state of mind, the film makes us privy to his inner mental images. However, we are unable to decide on this basis whether Martin is suffering from the delusion that he is a vampire, or whether he is truly over 100 years old. He is not possessed of fangs in the classic fashion, and he knocks his victims out with injections of sodium Pentothol, after which he cuts their arms open with a razor-blade and drinks their blood. Nevertheless, his elder cousin from the "old country" is convinced that Martin is genuinely a vampire, a "Nosferatu". His certainty is based on family tradition, and ultimately the old man does him to death in the approved manner. The film itself does not decide the question of Martin's real nature, and the viewer is left irresolute, hesitating between the marvellous and the uncanny.

Martin is a modern film that uses the 19th-century structure of fantastic hesitation, and there are other modern examples of this, notably Stephen King's short story, "Nona", published in *Skeleton Crew* (1985).[34] The modern fantastic itself, however, differs from the earlier form in one important respect – it no longer invokes the supernatural. The marvellous is closed off to it. According to Todorov, this is due to the irruption of psychoanalysis, which has had the effect of fatally undermining the credibility of religious belief. Kafka's "Die Verwandlung" ("Metamorphosis", 1915) exemplifies the new form. The earlier form of the fantastic began from a natural situation, into which a seemingly supernatural event entered, disrupting the established certainties of the world. In "Metamorphosis", the story begins from the supernatural event (if, indeed, it is supernatural) of Gregor Samsa's change into an insect. Over the course of the narrative, the metamorphosis becomes naturalised, until it seems not only a possible occurrence, but also almost a probable one. By this juncture, the story is far removed from the supernatural. In this context, hesitation is beside the point. Its role had been to suspend the reader between two opposing possibilities, but in Kafka's story the narrative movement is based not on uncertainty, but on what Todorov calls "adaptation". That is, the extraordinary occurrence is seemingly assimilated into the logic of our world, and the unintelligible treated as though it had meaning. The supernatural is acknowledged as natural. Todorov argues that in Kafka this comes about because the world he describes is as bizarre and abnormal as the event to which it affords a background. In the fantastic, we have a literature which postulates the existence of the rational in order subsequently to subvert it by posing the possibility of the supernatural and irrational. Kafka goes beyond this by creating an entire world that obeys another order of logic:

He treats the irrational as though it were part of a game: his entire world obeys an oneiric logic, if not indeed a nightmare one, which no longer has anything to do with the real.[35]

In Kafka, the assumptions underpinning our forms of life are disrupted. Men may turn into insects, motives become unintelligible, or, in an example from Sartre, coffee may change into ink. To see the significance of this, we need to recognise that, typically, our use of language is set within the horizon of significant, non-linguistic behaviour. This is what Wittgenstein calls our form of life, and it is built upon the regularities of nature. Measurement, for example, depends for its continued practice on the stability of the objects measured, while the way in which we employ colour concepts presupposes that objects do not continuously alter their appearances. However, things might not remain so:

> What if something *really unheard-of* happened? – If I, say, saw houses gradually turning into steam without any obvious cause, if the cattle in the fields stood on their heads and laughed and spoke comprehensible words; if trees gradually changed into men and men into trees. Now, was I right when I said before all these things happened 'I know that that's a house' etc., or simply 'that's a house' etc.?[36]

For Wittgenstein, one possibility is that an event of this order would take away his ability to make any judgments at all. Doubt concerning these matters would drag everything down with it and plunge the world into chaos. This is precisely what the literature of the modern fantastic undertakes to achieve. Todorov quotes Sartre: "if we have been able to give the reader the impression that we are speaking to him of a world in which these preposterous manifestations figure as normal behavior, then he will find himself plunged at one fell swoop into the heart of the fantastic".[37] Todorov goes on to sum up the difference between the classic version of the fantastic and Kafka's reworking of it: what, in the first world, was the exception here becomes the rule. It is at this point that we return to Blanchot, on whom Todorov bases his own ideas of the meaning of the modern fantastic, a point Todorov does not fail to make clear. For Blanchot, writing of this kind, and particularly the writing of Kafka, is characterised by the way in which it engages with the paradoxical status of literature. Kafka's writing, which, in this respect, is comparable with that of, for example, Wallace Stevens, T S Eliot and William Burroughs, is in contradiction with itself. Todorov sums up Blanchot's position:

For writing to be possible, it must be born out of the death of what it speaks about; but this death makes writing itself impossible, for there is no longer anything to write. Literature can become possible only insofar as it makes itself impossible. Either what we say is actually here, in which case there is no room for literature; or else there is room for literature, in which case there is no longer anything to say.[38]

It is this doubling movement of impossibility that is, I would argue, one crucial aspect of Cronenberg's cinema, as it is of the writing of which Blanchot is the advocate (symbolist and post-symbolist poetry, for example, or the prose of Beckett or Kafka). It can be seen in the way in which action and narrative event are realised in oddly hesitant, yet insistent, rhythms, as though the significance of the events depicted were being surrendered to the ambivalent and opaque. This is inseparable from the style of the film which, in a work such as *Crash*, seems intended to induce a sense of movement through space, while leaving the viewer suspended in time. This derives in part from the pace of the editing, which refuses the temptations of emotional expressiveness in favour of a more detached mode, in which shots are held for an appreciable length of time. The simultaneous concentration on composition and internal framing, a concern for composition reinforced by Cronenberg's careful disposition of colour within the frame and across the sequence, tends to emphasise the individual shot at the expense of the sequence as a whole. The result of this is to slow the film down, with a consequent loss of momentum and kinetic energy. Reinforced by the fact that sequences refer only minimally to the sequences that come before or after them, the constituent elements within *Crash* (the sequence, and the shots within sequences) tend in this way to draw attention to themselves, standing as units in their own right. It seems to have been Cronenberg's purpose to keep the parts of his film in some sense separate from one another, and to allow them a pronounced tendency towards self-containment. The order of sequences becomes thereby of less significance than it would otherwise have been had the film's narrative been more classically organised. By virtue of this kind of interrelationship, the film seems to go forward only hesitantly, feeling its way, as it were, moving this way and that. Instead of exhibiting an onward narrative drive, it seems to fold back on itself, constructing a pattern of complex temporal displacement, in which elements are less subordinated to one another than merely conjoined. It is a structure that aims at evading the demands of interpretation, inasmuch as the situation it constructs is essentially one of irresolvable ambiguity. It is an ambiguity that follows from the fact that such an evasion is finally

14

not possible: meaning must inevitably return, even if only as the recognition that meaning is lacking. *Crash* is a film that goes nowhere. The characters follow the roads that circulate around Toronto, but no linear development ensues. They are denizens of exile, of what Blanchot has called "the infinite migration of error",[39] inhabiting a world of endless night. There is a sequence, set at night, where Vaughan picks up a prostitute at the airport and has sex with her in the back of his car, while James drives, watching them in the rearview mirror. The camera is so positioned that a series of internal frames is created, including the windscreen, the car windows, the rear seat enclosure, the mirror, and so on. The effect is to break down actions, objects and persons into shifting nuances of shape, gesture and colour. The result is an intense configuration of elements, conveying a sense of something both dynamic and still. It is a mode of reconstruction evident also in other sex sequences in the film, most notably that in the car wash, and its purpose would seem to be to suggest more than can be said, or to mean something that is beyond saying.

The displacement of fictional time and space into ambiguity and migration characteristic of *Crash* is taken further in *eXistenZ* (1999). It is the first of his films since *Videodrome* that Cronenberg has conceived and written himself, and it returns to that film's emphasis on the systematic dislocation of narrative continuity. The status and nature of what is taking place remain unsettled – and unsettling – throughout the film. The relation between the events of the virtual reality game, eXistenZ, and those of ordinary reality, which at the beginning of the film seems clear, is by the end rendered retrospectively ambivalent. The film develops in a way that leaves the nature of what happens at the beginning as uncertain as what happens at the end. Amongst other things, the film's ending fails to resolve the question as to whether the characters have returned to reality, or whether they are still inside the reality of eXistenZ or that of a second game, transCendenZ. There is no point at which the film's action originates in an unambiguously established reality, and no such point to which it unequivocally returns.

I will give a brief synopsis of the narrative. The film is set in a period which may, or may not, be the future. Allegra Geller, the goddess of the world of virtual reality games, is appearing in what looks like a church hall before a group of enthusiasts to première her new game, eXistenZ. The players have to be wired up to the game via a bioport, a plug inserted into the base of the spine. A fleshy cable, like an umbilical cord, fits into the bioport and connects the players to an organic game pod, which delivers eXistenZ directly to the nervous system. As Allegra starts to download it, she is attacked by an assassin, who is trying to destroy her and the game. She escapes with Ted Pikul, a low-grade employee of the game's production company, Antenna Research. Allegra entices Ted into the playing the game with her, so that she can see what damage has been done to the pod during the attack. Ted lacks a bioport, so one is inserted into him by a dirty garage mechanic, Gas. However, Gas belongs to the enemy, and the bioport he inserts is infected, intended to destroy the game by destroying the pod. After killing Gas, Ted and Allegra escape to a disused ski resort, where they meet Kiri Vinokur, who has earlier worked with Allegra on the game's production. Vinokur replaces the infected bioport, and Ted and Allegra can at last plug in and play eXistenZ together. The game involves a struggle between the enemies of virtual reality games – the realists – and those who defend them. Although the struggles for supremacy are violent and bloody, neither side seems to win, and characters who appear at first on one side are later to be discovered acting on behalf of the other. A number of characters are killed, including Ted, whose bioport is detonated by Allegra, when she sees him as her enemy. At this point, the narrative returns to the church hall and it seems that the action has been part of a game called transCendenZ, whose creator is Yevgeny Nourish. However, Nourish is immediately killed by Ted and Allegra, who turn out to be members of the realists, the anti-games faction. They then turn their guns on another character, who played a Chinese waiter in eXistenZ, where Ted killed him. He asks them fearfully if they are still in a game. Ted and Allegra do not reply. The screen goes black.

To experience the film is to experience the shifting perspectives it opens up, and to feel one's way into at least something of how the boundaries between fantasy and reality, the inner and the outer, can be made to shift and alter. It is a movement from which the figure of Allegra Geller is inseparable. For example, while she and Ted are within the reality of eXistenZ, she comments at various points during the action on the dilemmas she and Ted face and what they should do next, and how. She also gives Ted instructions on how to get other characters to play their parts adequately, while remarking, in a critical spirit, on the inadequacy of the game's dialogue and its poverty of characterisation. However, the film later appears to deny Allegra's commanding position. She would seem to be – and it is only a matter of what seems to be – a character in another game, transCendenZ, apparently created by Nourish. This, of course, opens the possibility that transCendenZ is itself only a game within another game, and so on to infinity. Self-reflection and self-difference are basic to Allegra's role, and when she tells Ted that there is as much freedom in the game as there is in life – that is, just enough to keep things interesting, it is in keeping with this order of ironic self-displacement that she speaks. What she is talking about is a conflict between the unconditional and the conditioned that provides much of the imaginative dynamic sustained throughout the film. The characters blunder around in a world of uncertain significance, following rules of which they have no knowledge, perhaps not even knowing if there are any rules. They have no choice but to go on, discovering, or failing to discover, the meaning of what they do in the course of doing it. The rules governing what they do – if any – emerge only retrospectively. When Ted complains: "we are under attack from forces that want to destroy us, but that we don't understand", Allegra replies: "It's a game everyone's already playing". In effect, eXistenZ is based on a very peculiar – if not nonsensical – notion of rule, following one described by Wittgenstein as a "paradox". Where any course of action can be made out to accord with a rule, no course of action can be determined by that rule. If everything can made out to accord with a rule, it can also be made out to conflict with it.[40] The rules – if that is what they are – of eXistenZ seem paradigm cases of just such a "paradox". Are we, therefore, to conclude that eXistenZ is not a game – that it is only the appearance of one, a mere show? I would argue that the whole film is based on this kind of uncertainty, as we oscillate between what the characters know and what they do not know, between what makes sense and what does not, between self-creation and self-destruction, and I would suggest further that Cronenberg's purpose in this kind of oscillation is to give the issue of modern scepticism a new twist. In a recent interview, he says: "I'm talking about the existentialists, i.e. the game players, versus the realists...As a card-carrying existentialist I think all reality is virtual. It's all invented. It's collaborative, so you need friends to help you create a reality. But it's not about what is real and what isn't".[41] Cronenberg is attempting to oppose what is undecidable to dogmatism and rationality, and his way of doing this is to try to provoke his viewers, stimulating us to participate in his film by virtue of that very undecidability. Being thus drawn in, we are brought to collaborate in a mode of self-transcendence that Blanchot has described as follows: "[a] deviation in which the work disappears into the absence of the work, but in which the absence of the work always escapes the more it reduces itself to being nothing but the Work that has always disappeared already".[42]

Chris Rodley has remarked: "*eXistenZ* fuses all the components of cinema – storytelling, acting, production design, sound, images, music – to play with the viewer at the same time as representing the game to them".[43] This amounts to saying that Cronenberg has so organised *eXistenZ* that the game and the film representing the game are one. Given the truth of this, it would be reasonable to go on to suggest that *eXistenZ* is based on a self-reflexive procedure comparable to that evident in the way symbolist poetry is organised. (I argue elsewhere in this volume that an understanding of symbolist poetry is crucial for an understanding of Cronenberg's cinema.) Symbolist poetry exhibits, as Donald Davie has shown, an acute awareness of how to restructure the relation between the time of the events depicted or narrated in a given poem and the time taken by that poem to depict those events.[44] Mallarmé, for example, disrupts the standard order of tenses in his writing in order to disrupt the standard temporal order of narrative from within, and so discredit it. The surprising introduction of a present tense where a past tense would be expected compromises the sequences of tenses as a whole, leaving both past and present tenses suspect. The reader is left with only one order of time he or she can trust, which is the time that the poem takes in the telling. This is the time the poem takes to be spoken or read – or, applying the idea to *eXistenZ*, the time it takes the viewer to see the film. In most films, as in most poems or novels, the time of the depicted events and the time of the depiction itself differ from each other. For example, the events depicted in *The Searchers* (1956) last ten years; the film depicting them lasts a little under two hours. To take Cronenberg's procedure in *eXistenZ* as symbolist would, therefore, be to argue that he collapses the two times into one. And this, in fact, he does. The film begins securely enough, in the church hall. We see the events there, and we follow the escape of Allegra and Ted, in what seems a standard treatment of narrative action. However, as we discover subsequently, the events taking place prior to Allegra and Ted playing eXistenZ may have already been part of a game – either eXistenZ itself, or perhaps transCendenZ. What we see, therefore, is suspect. Are these actions real, or are they taking place elsewhere, in another, virtual reality? Since we cannot trust the veracity of the events in front of us, inasmuch as we are unsure of their status, all that we can trust is the process of their being presented to us. This sense of distrust is reinforced further by the fact that Cronenberg explicitly plays fast and loose with the film's depicted time. On the return of the players of eXistenZ to the church hall, one character says that the game has lasted for only twenty minutes. We are, however, at least 80 minutes into the film, and we have no clear idea of when eXistenZ began. Past and present are both called into question, and, as with the poetry of Eliot or Mallarmé, we are thrown back on the only thing we can be sure of, the fact of the film's self-presentation. This means that, unlike *The Searchers*, there is no other time, the time of what is depicted, to which we can refer the events we see on the screen. (Even the cuts and other transitions are part of the game, or so Allegra tells Ted – so that what we see is all there is to see.) In other words, by the end of the film, the time of the events depicted is shown to be simultaneous with the time taken by the film to depict those events. The two events themselves may, therefore, be thought of as identical, since we have no way of distinguishing between them. It seems clear, therefore, that Cronenberg's various strategies result in a merging of what is represented with the process of representing what is represented. Hence, the film in its totality may, or may not, be eXistenZ, just as eXistenZ itself may, or may not, be eXistenZ. In other words, the imaginative dynamic of *eXistenZ* is of a piece with that impulse in Cronenberg's cinema which – following Blanchot – I have characterised as an impulse towards impossibility. To say, as Rodley does, that film and game have the one virtual reality – that of eXistenZ – is to say that the film's existence is indistinguishable from that of the game. And since the game is subverted and questioned – undone, unworked, as it were – from within, so is the film.

A biographical note

David Cronenberg was born in Toronto, Ontario, on 15 March 1943.[45] His parents, Milton and Esther, already had a daughter, Denise. Their home was in an immigrant area – first Jewish, and then Italian. But when Cronenberg was beginning to grow up, most of the Jews moved out, as did the Cronenberg family in 1958. In the 1950s, Toronto was an essentially middle-class, respectable city. However, in the Cronenberg home, the artistic imaginations of the children were not repressed: they were actively encouraged. The parents were both deeply involved in literature, music and the world of books. Cronenberg's father Milton ran a bookshop, and wrote early Canadian comic books, as well as writing columns for Toronto newspapers. His mother Esther was an accompanist for choirs and a rehearsal pianist for the National Ballet of Canada. Denise became a dancer with the National Ballet, and later joined her brother's production team as chief costume designer. Cronenberg was educated at various local schools, and later, when the family moved to more affluent surroundings, he attended North Toronto Collegiate Institute. It was here that he met many of the people who would become part of his professional and personal life, including Carolyn Zeifman, from the wealthy suburb of Forest Hill, who would become his second wife.

As a boy, Cronenberg read comics, fantasy and science-fiction. At the same time, he developed an interest in science proper, and, as a result, fiction and science both became crucial to him. When he was sixteen, he submitted a short story to the *Magazine of Fantasy and Science Fiction*. The story was rejected, although the editors were encouraging. However, he did not return to story writing until he was at university, mainly because of a more pressing interest in biology. In 1963, he was enrolled (as an Ontario Scholar) in Toronto University to read biological sciences. However, it took only a few months to realise that he had made a mistake. He was excited by science, but not by the courses at the university, which he found stifling. So, in 1964, he transferred to the Honours programme in English language and literature. In this decision he was fully supported by his parents. He had a good first year in English, being the top student in the subject and winning a scholarship as a result. At this time, he had no thought of becoming a filmmaker. Strongly influenced by the work of William Burroughs, his ambition was to be a novelist.

In 1965, Cronenberg had become disillusioned with academic study; in this, he had much in common with other students of the time. Despite being first in his year at the university, he decided to drop out and travel to Europe. He still saw himself as a novelist, and thought that academic study was a hindrance to artistic expression. He left Toronto for Copenhagen, also spending time in London, Paris and Istanbul. According to his biographer, he enjoyed himself in these cities. When he returned to Toronto the following year, things had changed in a more liberated direction. A Toronto University fourth-year English student, David Secter, had completed a film, and there were regular screenings of American underground films (Brakhage, Anger, and so on) in the bohemian coffee-house at McMasters University. Many of these broke sexual taboos and ran up against the censor. Nevertheless, the work was screened, and it contributed to new thought about the cinema in the Canadian environment. Another young Canadian, John Hofsess, a friend of Ivan Reitman's (of *Ghost Busters* [1984] fame), completed an underground film, *Black Zero*, in 1967, in which Cronenberg appears briefly in a nude scene. Reitman was also to become a close friend of Cronenberg's. Cronenberg had returned to find new life in Toronto, and soon became part of it.

Cinema freed Cronenberg from the literary influences (especially Burroughs) that had inhibited his novel writing. He got to know people at the Canadian Motion Picture Equipment Company, a camera-rental service, and in particular the company head, Janet Good. She allowed Cronenberg to borrow equipment on deferred rental terms, sometimes forgoing rental altogether. Cronenberg began reading *American Cinematographer* and encyclopedias in order to find out about lenses, lighting, sound and editing. He wrote a script for two performers, and in January 1966 set about filming his first work, *Transfer*. The film is an underground work – Surrealist in quality and lasting seven minutes. In 16mm colour, it is about a psychiatrist and his patient, and is set in the middle of a field, for no explicable reason. The sound is by Margaret Hindson, who became Cronenberg's first wife in 1970.

In 1966 and 1967, there was great deal of activity on the independent and underground film front in Toronto. On 4 November

1966, there was a screening at Toronto University of student underground films from all the local universities, and Cronenberg and other filmmakers decided to set up the Canadian Film-Makers Co-operative, based on the one in New York. At the same time, a distribution company (non-profit-making) called Film Canada was established, with a cinema, Cinecity. In mid-June 1967, a three-day non-stop festival of underground and independent films was staged. All the main figures in the US underground cinema were there, and Cronenberg met many of them. His own film was screened, although it did not get a very favourable reception. In the summer of 1966, he made a second short film, *From the Drain*, which foreshadows *Shivers*. He also completed his BA in English at Toronto University. At this time, the federal Canadian government created the Canadian Film Development Corporation (later Telefilm Canada) to help finance the production of feature films; Cronenberg was later to make use of it. In 1969, he made his first long film, *Stereo*, in 35mm and black-and-white. It was partially funded by a Canada Council writing grant, and proved successful. Canadian and foreign critics at festivals were positive, and it was one of ten films selected to represent Canada's "new cinema" at a festival in Brussels.

In 1970-71, Cronenberg's career was at a critical point. The future of the underground cinema was unclear, and he no longer wanted to make films that were seen by only a handful of people. During this time he moved with his wife to a village in the south of France, where he spent a year. It was during this year that he made the decision to become a commercial film director. His wife was moving in an opposite direction, and getting involved in New Age religion. They were to split up some years after their return from France.

Cronenberg's first commercial film was *Shivers*. He began work on the script in 1972, at which time his father was dying. His father lost the ability to process calcium, so that his bones became brittle, and he died in 1973. Cronenberg was also having great difficulty getting finance, although eventually (after two years) the Canadian Film Development Corporation provided $75 000 of the overall budget of $180 000. Cinépix put up the remainder. Production began in Montreal in mid-August 1974. The release was set for October 1975 in Montreal, in both English and French versions. The English title was *The Parasite Murders*, the French title *Frissons* ("Shivers"), and the latter title stuck. It went on to gross US$5 million worldwide, and won a prize at the Spanish Festival of Fantasy Films. However, trouble was in store in Canada, from the critic Robert Fulford, editor of *Saturday Night* magazine.

Fulford also wrote film reviews under the name of Marshall Delaney. He had written an enthusiastic review of *Stereo*, but he hated

Shivers. His review was entitled "You Should Know How Bad This Film Is. After All, You Paid For It". It was published in September 1975 and conditioned the response to the film in Canada. Fulford used his attack as an opportunity to blast the Canadian Film Development Corporation. Fulford wanted "Canadian" films – films that were realistic, decent, and so on. Cronenberg had set his face against this kind of cinema, aiming at an imaginative and non-realist cinema that would explore themes and areas of experience which no Canadian had yet taken up. Canadian cinema was still under the influence of the documentarist John Grierson, who had run the National Film Board of Canada since leaving the GPO Film Unit in Britain at the end of the 1930s. All this made the Canadian Film Development Corporation apprehensive, and it refused support for his next film, *Rabid*. During this time, Cronenberg's private life was also in a state of turmoil as he was in the process of divorcing his first wife, Margaret. He was even evicted from his house, which he rented, by the landlady who thought he must be a pornographer, since Fulford, whom she knew, could not be wrong. I will leave the story of Cronenberg's life here, on this somewhat farcical note, occasioned by controversy of a kind that was to dog him throughout his career, especially in Britain and other Anglo-Saxon countries. He was now on his way as a filmmaker, and it would not be long before he came to be recognised – at least in Europe – as one of the contemporary cinema's major artists.

The essays

The aesthetic of later films such as *eXistenZ* and *Crash* is a developed version of the artistic presuppositions of much of Cronenberg's other work, and it is to the consideration of the earlier and the later work by the contributors to this volume that I now turn. Ian Conrich opens the collection with a fascinating account of the reception of Cronenberg's cinema by critics working for various British newspapers. Cronenberg began his career as one of a group of new horror film directors, including Romero, Hooper, Argento, Carpenter and De Palma, all of whom aimed at spectacular set-pieces of body horror. Cronenberg's early reputation as the "Baron of Blood" and the "King of Horror" was seized on by British critics, in what was to prove an all-too-typically English moralistic fit of revulsion. In interviews given during the 1970s and 1980s, Cronenberg himself emphasised the importance to his work of the body, conceiving of "a beauty contest for the inside of the human body",[46] and glorifying the beauty of diseased and ruptured flesh, in an attempt to change the aesthetic sensibilities of film-going audiences. The work resulting from this emphasis proved too much for certain sections of the British press. Arthur Thirkell, writing for *The Daily Mirror*, gave a typically excoriating opinion of the early films. Reviewing *Shivers* in 1976, he made a depressingly predictable call for tighter censorship, and described the film as "nauseous, trashy, revolting, and so sick-making that patrons would be advised to take a plastic bag along" (page 37). Dilys Powell found *Rabid* "degrading", while David Hughes declared himself "morally affronted" by *Scanners* (page 38). Conrich gives many further examples of the same kind of response, pointing out that the language of these critics, violent and visceral as it is, is dependent on the content of the films themselves for its graphic and outraged prurience. All this revulsion and puritanical stupidity culminated in the "video nasties" campaign of the early 1980s, and it was at the height of this so-called "moral" panic that *Videodrome* was released, occasioning attention from the police. I would note that the same disgraceful reaction of the British press to Cronenberg's work has been in evidence again more recently, in what was a profoundly distasteful campaign of moralistic virulence aimed at *Crash*. However, as Conrich indicates, Cronenberg's reputation was secured during the 1980s with the release of his films on video and the opening of a number of cinemas in London, such as the Phoenix, the Electric Cinema and, most famously, the Scala, dedicated to work of this kind. It was in this context that Cronenberg succeeded in reaching out to an audience more attuned to his sensibilities and aesthetic assumptions. It was for the taste of such an audience that horror fanzines such as *Fangoria* were to cater.

In a vigorous and witty essay, Jonathan Crane addresses the question of the extent to which we should see Cronenberg as a horror director. His field of enquiry covers the earlier films, from *Shivers* to *The Fly*, and he believes that Cronenberg differs from the other masters of contemporary horror, by virtue of his resurrection of the "mad scientist" figure, the figure of Dr Frankenstein. Dr Hobbes in *Shivers*, Dr Keloid in *Rabid*, and, of course, Dr Raglan in *The Brood* exemplify this trend, while in *Scanners* and *Videodrome* the sons of Frankenstein appear under the aegis of the corporation. As Crane has it, these two films "complicate the transposition of Dr Frankenstein to the present day by making the manufacture of new life and the pursuit of market share complementary exercises" (pages 55-56). *The Dead Zone* (1983) and *The Fly* continue to work through the image of the scientist. In the latter film, Brundle, like Frankenstein before him, must battle with his creation for control. However, the struggle takes place not in the Arctic or high in the Alps, but in Brundle's own flesh, and he "must decide whether to become something irrevocably new or remain all-too-human" (page 57). In drawing on a figure from the past, from the very beginning of horror literature, one might say that Cronenberg is using citation, a device typical of many directors contemporary with him. Cronenberg, however, is resolutely anti-ironic. One has only to contrast the sobriety, the dour seriousness, of Cronenberg's films with the knowing self-referentiality of Wes Craven's *Scream* (1996) to recognise the gulf that separates his work from the postmodern horror film. Crane goes on to argue that there is no point in trying to locate Cronenberg's cinema politically, as certain critics have tried to do. His cinema has its own concerns, and Cronenberg has resolutely pursued them. His work refuses assimilation to pre-established positions, and it offers the viewer nothing of transcendence or redemption. The essay sums up Cronenberg's achievement in a memorable assertion: "The real horror of Cronenberg's early work comes from having to oscillate between the degradations of everyday life and the damnation that the new flesh almost certainly holds" (page 66).

In a cogently argued essay, Murray Smith takes as his starting-point the view that horror arises from a particular type of curiosity or fascination about ourselves and the values we hold. This suggests two kinds of horror, the first based on sympathy with human values, so that if we sympathise with the monster, as we do with Karloff's monster in *Frankenstein* (1931), for example, this is due to the way in which the monster is conceived in terms of an anthropocentric moral scheme. The second mode is what interests Smith, inasmuch as it asks us to take the perspective of the inhuman. In the case of *Shivers*, this would be to take the perspective of the parasite. The film achieves this not by adopting the optical point of view of the parasite, but by dispelling our sympathy for the human victims of the parasite. As Smith notes, *Shivers* exhibits a far more intense interest in the rippling and undulating of human torsos as parasites stir beneath the skin than it does in the fear and alarm of those who remain uninfected. To adopt the perspective of the parasites is a matter of not having sympathy for their human victims, or – to go further – of not even regarding them as victims. *Crash* recapitulates this strategy, as it attempts to imagine an alternative human psychology in which the desire for pain, trauma and finally death is employed to overturn our conventional psychological assumptions. All this has to do with what is commonly called "body horror", exemplified in *The Fly* by the loss of bodily integrity. The loss of Seth's body parts is highlighted by the contrast between the hard edges of a computer keyboard and the teeth that dribble onto it. This contrast between the hard and the soft animates almost all of Cronenberg's work, especially those where the exposure of the viscera takes place in locations dominated by anonymous metal-and-glass buildings. Smith, however, draws attention to a second kind of horror, which he calls "moral horror". This is also exemplified in *The Fly*, in particular by Seth's refusal after his teleportation to treat Roni as a person. This reaches a climax in his attempt to "splice" Roni with himself, in the hope of recapturing his fast-disappearing humanity. In *The Fly*, moral and physical horror converge, as the fly bursts from the remains of the human body at the moment Seth thrusts Roni into the telepod. Here, Cronenberg's exploration of the inhuman reaches new levels of complexity and subtlety.

Smith ends his piece by calling into question the efficacy of psychoanalytic readings of Cronenberg's cinema. Barbara Creed proposes to undertake just such a reading. She draws on Freud's account of the Schreber case, since she considers that, of all Freud's case histories, this one offers the closest parallel to Cronenberg's cinema. Her primary concern is to disclose something of what she calls the "increasingly bleak, closed, homosexual universe" (page 84) of the later films, from *Dead Ringers* to *Crash*. They are films in which, as with Schreber, there is an oscillation between male and female, and a concomitant emphasis on the feminisation of the male. There are also elements of paranoia, bodily alteration, delusion and the desire for bliss or ecstasy. *Dead Ringers* exemplifies the nature of Creed's approach. She finds one compelling instance of how Cronenberg treats the homoerotic relationship in one of the final sequences, when Beverly cuts open Elliot's body. The meaning of this is ambiguous. It may be seen as an attempt to construct Elliot as a woman, or to reach into that part of the body where they were once joined. Furthermore, in undertaking the separation of himself from his brother, Beverly is himself assuming a feminine role, that of maternal castrator. This is a role he had assigned earlier to Claire, during the nightmare in which he dreamt that she was tearing him away from his brother. Creed sees this as a way of seeking total unification with his (br)other, a unity or symbiosis denied him in life, and it depends on the fact that both brothers come to occupy the feminine (maternal) position. *M. Butterfly* draws on themes central to *Dead Ringers*, themes of paranoia and self-delusion; the constraints of the body; the impossibility of same-sex love; and the desire for transcendence. Creed argues that Cronenberg represents the sexual relation between Gallimard and Song Liling as an ambiguity constructed around a deliberate confusion of anus and vagina. It is Gallimard's fetishisation of her body, his disavowal of his knowledge that her vagina is an anus, that allows him to take part in what is an amazing act of self-deception. This theme is taken further in the two later films, *Naked Lunch* and *Crash*. In both films, the anus is what signifies desire. In *Crash*, for example, after having sex with her husband James, Catherine arouses him by discussing Vaughan's anus: "Can you imagine what his anus looks like?...Would you like to sodomise him?

Would you like to put your penis right into his anus?...Tell me..." As Creed notes, while this conversation is going on, Catherine is lying with her back to James. As he becomes aroused by the thought of what he might do to Vaughan, James thrusts his penis into Catherine from behind. The woman thus acts as the go-between or conduit of male desire. The effect again depends on a profoundly unsettling oscillation between the masculine and feminine, male and female. Creed has written a powerful essay on the dynamic of the male psyche as represented in the later films, a dynamic which ultimately leaves the Cronenberg hero with nothing to confront except the "death and the loss of his male counterpart – whether twin, 'butterfly', boy or wounded road warrior" (page 100).

At one point in her essay, Creed refers to the way in which, in *Crash*, Cronenberg's fascination with bodily metamorphosis is realised in the wound. It bears witness to the transmutations and realignments of flesh and metal effected by the crash. A concern for the wound is central to Parveen Adams' essay on *Crash*. The overall purpose of this essay, the idiom of which is that of Lacanian psychoanalysis, is to extricate *Crash* from the field of the Other, the field of language and the symbolic. The argument begins from the recognition that the film is not a film dominated by desire. It is dominated rather by the death drive, a point that involves clarification of the status of the wound within the film. Adams refuses to subordinate the significance of the wound in the film to meanings derived from notions of castration, the point of entry into language, insisting that *Crash* is no more sadistic than it is masochistic. As she eloquently puts it: "The body retains its mortal frailty; the proximity of body and car, flesh and steel, skin and bone, dominates sexuality not at all as sadism, but as a world of the wound. Indeed, the film's sexuality is textured like a wound, gaping, open, unsutured" (page 104). What *Crash* is concerned to explore lies beyond the economy of the pleasure principle, of sadism and masochism, in what Lacan called "the unspeakable field of radical desire that is the field of absolute destruction".[47] This is the field of jouissance. *Crash* is located there. To make this point clearer, Adams distinguishes the meaning of the wound from the mark of the whip in masochism. The latter, she notes, is a little cut, and it means that someone else has put it there. It is the signature of the Other. (One might think here of the cuts on Nicki Brand's shoulder in *Videodrome*.) The wound, however, is not a writing *on* the body; it is rather an *un*writing *of* the body. It lies on the far side of representation. Wounds can get bigger or smaller, and they can close or open. Typically, they are sewn up (sutured), a work that reinscribes the wound as a scar, and so draws the body back into the social world of meaning and representation. The world of shared meaning and common interests, the world of the symbolic, the Other, is able to reassert its dominance, and subordinate the subject once again to its constraints. Adams' point is that, in *Crash*, this does not occur: scars do not heal the wound, they only alter it. The scar itself is a wound. As she notes, the characters revel in the exploration of their scars – "these crusts of a new and hybridised body" (page 104). Scars can be unpicked, and the wound reopened. The lived meaning of this fascination turns around the fact that the scar is the site at which libido is unbound, passing beyond representation. Beyond representation, unbound libido has nothing as its object, and is able, therefore, to break even the ultimate of boundaries, the line between life and death. *Crash*, in other words, is a striving to get beyond desire, to a place where it is possible to desire not to desire, "the place where Desire and Death bisect" (page 105). Adams' essay is complex and probing, with ramifications beyond those issues I have touched on, including the matter of the spatial organisation of the film, with respect to which she indicates what might be called "the *collapse* of [the] symbolic" (page 117). Cronenberg's handling of space, comparable in many ways to that of Bresson, develops an organisation of flatness appropriate to a hieroglyphic: his images say nothing, and yet they are redolent with a meaning from elsewhere. Cronenberg appears on this showing as a master of display, but display of a nothing, an empty place, a silence. He is seeking what Lacan calls the Real, that place where things exist in their material opacity and radiance, prior to their negation by the symbolic, leading his viewers to experience nothingness and emptiness in an almost material way – as a wound, opening and closing.

My own contribution also addresses one of the later films, *M. Butterfly*. It is a film that contains none of the characteristic instances of body horror that make so indelible an impression in much of the other work, and yet stylistically and thematically it touches on matters crucial to an overall sense of Cronenberg's achievement. I have begun from the idea that Cronenberg is a literary filmmaker. By this I mean that his aim is to confront us with a cinema that stands in a critical relation to what it presents, and that clarification of the nature of this undertaking is one that may be approached by way of literature. Bearing in mind Cronenberg's literary education, I have looked to the literature of the symbolists, a literature exemplified in poetry by writers such as Yeats, Pasternak, Eliot, Valéry and Stevens, as having a special pertinence here. Symbolism has been subjected to various approaches since the 1930s, from the historical emphasis of Edmund Wilson's *Axel's Castle* (1931) to the modernist perspective of Hugh Kenner's *The Pound Era* (1972). For this essay, I have drawn on the work of an equally distinguished critic, Donald Davie, whose work on the syntax of modern poetry (which first appeared during the 1950s) is especially sensitive to the relations between symbolism and music. The importance of this approach lies in Davie's alertness to what he has called the "eventfulness" – that is, the temporality of this kind of writing. Davie has described Eliot's poetry, for example, in terms that I believe are wholly appropriate to Cronenberg's later films: "whatever else symbolist poems may describe or adumbrate, one thing they always describe is themselves, their own way of coming into being, comporting themselves, and coming to an end".[48] My argument is that poetry understood in this way is trying to achieve a condition not unlike that of music, a point underlined by Eliot's characteristically symbolist title, *Four Quartets*. What Heidegger has called the "ecstases" of past, present and future are so shaped in symbolist poetry that we are made to live the elapsing of time, "its complex duration", as Davie has it, "with unusual attention to each present moment".[49] Eliot enacts precisely this "complex duration" in the opening of "Burnt Norton" (1935):

Time present and time past
Are both perhaps present in time future
And time future contained in time past.[50]

I want to suggest that, in Cronenberg's films, and particularly in *M. Butterfly*, past, present and future are so interwoven that they make of the present time something to be dwelt in and dwelt on, something lived. I have tried to locate what I see as the significance of this concern with time in terms of the way in which Cronenberg's style brings us to a confrontation with the "how" of our own lives. It seems to me that the value of Cronenberg's cinema, what it really amounts to for us, lies in the way it requires of us a first-person response. I would say, in the idiom of Heidegger, that, in so responding, we are thrown beyond or outside the boundaries of theoretical, impersonal or third-person understanding into a disclosing, to ourselves, of our ownmost possibility. We are forced to confront our own thrownness towards death. And it is by virtue of their so requiring self-reflection of us that it makes sense to compare these films with the work of the greatest of the modern poets.

Andrew Klevan's piece might seem, in this context, somewhat anomalous. I believe, however, that it raises important issues, and, since I am myself a target in the range of his often sharply worded indictments, I have felt justified in including it. He takes four discussions of *Dead Ringers*: an article in *Screen* by Barbara Creed; my book on the film; an account of the film by Steven Shaviro in *The Cinematic Body*; and an article by Florence Jacobowitz and Richard

Lippe published in *CineAction!*. Klevan is persuaded that there is a deplorable tendency in modern film scholarship to avoid the analysis of film style, a tendency exemplified by the four accounts of *Dead Ringers* to which he refers. As an example of the inadequacy he discerns in the work of the critics, and academic film writing more generally, I will refer to his discussion of my own account of how Howard Shore's music is used in the sequence depicting the Mantles' final separation. I suggest that the feeling of sadness which the music calls up implies the profundity of the loss which the twins are about to experience. I also suggest that the use of music here comes over to the viewer as "highly self-aware". Klevan takes this to be not only an inadequate characterisation of the music, but also an instance providing a clue as to why writers such as those he names are reluctant to make a closer scrutiny of the stylistic devices involved. He thinks that the fact that I do not discuss the music in more detail may mean that I am betraying an unacknowledged ambivalence about the music's quality. He does not specify what a closer discussion would amount to, but discussing the technical details of the score, or perhaps transcribing it, would presumably satisfy in some respects his requirements. This, I think, is central to his argument: film critics – academic ones, at any rate – evoke theoretical machinery or, as in my case, call upon the established classics of literature because they have no faith in the value of what they are studying – here Cronenberg's *Dead Ringers*. This idea emerges in a rather different form, when he says of Shaviro and myself that we both proclaim, in measured and no doubt overly pondered tones, that the viewer will experience a "loss of control", or will find the film "hard to master". Again, the point seems to be that these writers are (perhaps unawares?) searching for an alibi: no sooner have they elaborated an interpretation of the film than they at once absent themselves from the scene of the crime by claiming that the film must escape all such interpretation. The assertion of delirium disavows the evasions of exegesis. He would certainly wish us to read his own refusal to address the film directly as a manifestation of his reservations concerning it.

Related to this aspect of the indictment is Klevan's general characterisation of these writers and their habits of mind. He has the sense that *Dead Ringers* sets off trains of associations, as though it were giving off a pervasive aura of vague feelings and undefined ideas, to which the writers respond by sinking into an intoxicated reverie, borne along by their own word magic, and fearful of attending too closely to the film before them. The film induces a dream of thought, not thought itself. As an example of writing thus deplorably "light-headed", he turns to some remarks of Barbara Creed's on male hysteria in *Dead Ringers* and in Hollywood cinema more generally (certain films of Howard Hawks and Jerry Lewis, for example). (These are too long to quote here, and are accessible in the body of Klevan's text.) His objection is that the passage fails to "refine" our sense of hysteria in relation to these different films. However, it seems clear that this passage is in no way intended as an analysis of hysteria, but as a bringing together of different kinds of film in order that such an arrangement may induce the reader to see them under a new aspect. Thus, the movement from *Frankenstein* to *The Fly* suggests – and it does no more than suggest – that there might be something of value in seeing the male scientist as a maternal figure, inasmuch as he may be said to have created the monster out of his own "womb". It is a womb that is realised externally (and hence metaphorically) in *Frankenstein*, where the laboratory provides the birthplace of the creature, while its realisation in *The Fly* is internal, as Brundle gives birth to the man-fly out of his own flesh. He is himself, and he is not himself. It is in this sense – this is the thrust of Creed's argument – that a film of this sort has itself become a "hysterical" text. This means that, in a way similar to the symptom, the film exhibits a doubling that re-embodies the disruption of narrative meaning and psychological explanation that are consequent upon Brundle's condition in Brundle's own flesh – the flesh that produced the disruption in the first place. What is represented and the way in which that representation is effected may be said to constitute each other.

Insofar as the film presents Brundle in the process of constituting himself as the object of his experience, it also presents him as the self that is so ordering that object of experience. Given the kind of "object" Brundle is, this would seem to be a dialectic that, as Creed sees it, may plausibly be described as hysterical. Criticism can never be a matter of precisions given in advance, or of procedures that have a pertinence independent of their employment in an actual context of judgment. As F R Leavis has put it: "The business of the literary critic is to attain a peculiar completeness of response and to observe a peculiarly strict relevance in developing his response into commentary".[51] It may be that Creed's explanation of how hysteria stands to the films to which she refers is wrong, as the explanation of any critic may be wrong. The real question, however, is whether it effectively serves its purpose, which is the suggestive clarification of response, and while, for Klevan, at least on this occasion, Creed palpably does not achieve anything he regards as satisfactory, this specific failure does not of itself discredit her mode of writing or her kind of approach. Some remarks by Stanley Cavell are to the point here: "Describing one's experience of art is itself a form of art; the burden of describing it is like the burden of producing it. Art is often praised because it brings men together. But it also separates them".[52]

While I am by no means sure that Klevan's adverse characterisation of a certain kind of film criticism is not more pertinent to the theory-induced excesses of academic literary criticism, he means the points he is making to have a direct bearing on the essays collected in this volume. It is certainly true that the essays included here represent a wide range of approaches to Cronenberg's work, and all of them are, I would say, responsive in their different ways to its undoubted ambiguity. It is because of this that I referred earlier in my introduction to the work of Maurice Blanchot. Blanchot is a writer for whom literature is divided against itself. Treachery is its condition, and ambiguity its truth. Part of what I had in mind in referring to him was to invoke a writer whose response to this condition is to exhibit in the mode – the syntax, the paradoxes of statement, and so on – of his own prose the very condition he is attempting in that prose to explore. This, of course, is a symbolist procedure, and I have suggested that symbolist writing has a direct relevance to the study of Cronenberg. Klevan's approach seems to me to allow for none of this. He seems unwilling to countenance the kind of difficulty Wittgenstein has memorably addressed:

> The same strange illusion which we are under when we seem to seek the something which a face expresses whereas, in reality, we are giving ourselves up to the features before us – that same illusion possesses us even more strongly if repeating a tune to ourselves and letting it make its full impression on us, we say 'This tune says *something*', and it is as though I had to find *what* it says. And yet I know it doesn't say anything such that I might express in words or pictures what it says.[53]

In the elucidation of his own responses to music, Wittgenstein would seek for comparisons. Thus, he found certain themes of Brahms highly Kellerian – that is, a comparison with Keller helped him to illuminate the impression made on him by Brahms. Similarly, a piano piece by Schubert expressed for him the essence of pastness – "of the experience of long, long ago".[54] Aesthetic response is not only a matter of formal or stylistic analysis. The language-game differs from that of giving a report, or offering a description. The language of critical response is expressive, and there can be no guarantee of its success. What we are concerned with in aesthetic writing, of the kind gathered here, is the analysis of impressions, what an earlier age would have called "appreciation". Failure is never far distant, and, as for success – I will steal from Wittgenstein and say that assent is the only criterion.

Notes

1   Linda Ruth Williams, "The Inside-out of Masculinity: David Cronenberg's Visceral Pleasures", in Michele Aaron (ed), *The Body's Perilous Pleasures: Dangerous Desires and Contemporary Culture* (Edinburgh: Edinburgh University Press, 1999): 33.

2   Ibid: 34.

3   Philip Brophy, "Horrality – the Textuality of Contemporary Horror Films", *Screen* 27: 1 (January-February 1986): 8.

4   Williams: 34.

5   Ibid: 38.

6   Ludwig Wittgenstein, *Philosophical Investigations*, translated by G E M Anscombe (Oxford: Basil Blackwell, 1967): §109.

7   Ibid: §90. Emphasis in original.

8   Marie McGinn, *Wittgenstein and the* Philosophical Investigations (London; New York: Routledge, 1997): 14. Emphasis in original.

9   Ibid: 15.

10   Wittgenstein: §284. Emphases in original.

11   McGinn: 153.

12   Ibid. Emphasis in original.

13   Wittgenstein: §284.

14   Bernard Williams, "Wittgenstein and idealism", in *Moral Luck: Philosophical Papers 1973-1980* (Cambridge; London; New York; New Rochelle; Melbourne; Sydney: Cambridge University Press, 1981): 152.

15   Wittgenstein: §286. Emphasis in original.

16   McGinn: 156. Emphasis in original.

17   Wittgenstein: §286. Emphases in original.

18   McGinn: 156.

19   Williams (1981): 153. Emphasis in original.

20   Jonathan Lear, *Open Minded: Working Out the Logic of the Soul* (Cambridge, MA; London: Harvard University Press, 1998): 290.

21   Williams (1999): 42.

22   Maurice Blanchot, *The Gaze of Orpheus and other literary essays*, translated by Lydia Davis, edited by P Adams Sitney (New York: Station Hill,

1981): 41.

[23] Ibid: 42.

[24] Ibid: 43.

[25] *The Collected Poems of Wallace Stevens* (London; Boston: Faber and Faber, 1959): 241.

[26] Ibid: 242.

[27] Blanchot: 46.

[28] Emmanuel Levinas, *Existence and Existents*, translated by Alphonso Lingis (The Hague: Martinus Nijhoff, 1978): 58. Emphases in original.

[29] Simon Critchley, "*Il y a* – A Dying Stranger than Death (Blanchot with Levinas)", *The Oxford Literary Review* 15 (1993): 115.

[30] Levinas: 63.

[31] Critchley: 116.

[32] Tzvetan Todorov, *The Fantastic: A Structural Approach to a Literary Genre*, translated by Richard Howard (Ithaca, NY: Cornell University Press, 1975): 25.

[33] Ibid.

[34] Stephen King, "Nona", in *Skeleton Crew* (London; Sydney: Macdonald, 1985): 329-357.

[35] Todorov: 173.

[36] Ludwig Wittgenstein, *On Certainty*, edited by G E M Anscombe and G H von Wright, translated by Denis Paul and G E M Anscombe (Oxford: Basil Blackwell, 1969): §513. Emphasis in original.

[37] Todorov: 174.

[38] Ibid: 175.

[39] Maurice Blanchot, *The Space of Literature*, translated by Ann Smock (Lincoln; London: University of Nebraska Press, 1982): 144.

[40] Wittgenstein (1967): §201.

[41] Chris Rodley, "Game boy", *Sight and Sound* 9: 4 (April 1999): 10.

[42] Blanchot (1981): 147.

[43] Rodley: 9.

[44] Donald Davie, *The Poet in the Imaginary Museum: essays of two decades*, edited by Barry Alpert (Manchester: Carcanet, 1977): 93-103.

[45] For this account of Cronenberg's earlier career, I have summarised the relevant sections of Peter Morris' biography, *David Cronenberg: A Delicate Balance* (Toronto: ECW Press, 1994). I am deeply indebted to it.

[46] Quoted in Anne Billson, "Cronenberg on Cronenberg: a career in stereo", *Monthly Film Bulletin* 56: 660 (January 1989): 5.

[47] Jacques Lacan, *The Ethics of Psychoanalysis 1959-1960: The Seminar of Jacques Lacan, Book VII*, edited by Jacques-Alain Miller, translated by Dennis Porter (London: Tavistock/Routledge, 1992): 216.

[48] Davie: 98.

[49] Ibid: 103.

[50] T S Eliot, "Burnt Norton", *The Complete Poems and Plays of T. S. Eliot* (London: Faber and Faber, 1969): 171.

[51] F R Leavis, *The Common Pursuit* (London: Chatto & Windus, 1962): 213.

[52] Stanley Cavell, *Must we mean what we say?: A Book of Essays* (Cambridge; London; New York; Melbourne: Cambridge University Press, 1969): 193.

[53] Ludwig Wittgenstein, *The Blue and Brown Books* (Oxford: Basil Blackwell, 1972): 166. Emphases in original.

[54] These examples are cited by Frank Cioffi, *Wittgenstein on Freud and Frazer* (Cambridge: Cambridge University Press, 1998): 70.

An aesthetic sense: Cronenberg and neo-horror film culture

Ian Conrich

In August 1979, the first issue of *Fangoria* was launched. This American horror film fanzine aimed "to be the first classy, professional, pictorial news magazine covering the world of fantasy", and claimed that it was "much more than just another cheap monster magazine; each issue will include full-colour art, media news, techniques of special effects and makeup".[1] Driven by a photo-article content, for much of the 1980s *Fangoria* was the premier fan publication for the promotion, celebration and dissection of a new wave of horror films and filmmakers.

David Cronenberg belongs to a group of neo-horror directors who had emerged before the first *Fangoria*. As Philip Brophy writes, these filmmakers were producing horror which was distinctly different from its historical definition, and which was "involved in a violent awareness of itself as a saturated genre".[2] George Romero had filmed *Night of the Living Dead* (1968), *The Crazies* (1973), *Martin* (1979) and *Dawn of the Dead* (aka *Zombies*, 1979); Tobe Hooper had made *The Texas Chain Saw Massacre* (1974) and *Eaten Alive* (1976); Dario Argento had filmed *Deep Red* (1976) and *Suspiria* (1977); and there was also John Carpenter's *Halloween* (1978), Wes Craven's *The Hills Have Eyes* (1978), and Brian De Palma's *Carrie* (1976) and *The Fury* (1978). David Cronenberg had begun his feature film career making two underground and avant-garde, futuristic-biological thrillers, *Stereo* (1969) and *Crimes of the Future* (1970). *Shivers* (1976) was the first of his biological-horror films, and commercialised his provocative screen vision. *Rabid* (1977), *The Brood* (1979) and *Scanners* (1981) followed, with the later films being covered in the early issues of *Fangoria*; *The Brood* featured in issue 3 and the infamous *Scanners* head explosion was prominently displayed on the front cover of issue 10. These four films were Cronenberg's formative entries into the horror genre, and established him as a director of note. His films rapidly acquired a cult status, and by the early 1980s he had become recognised as one of the leading filmmakers of the horror New Wave – Carpenter once declared that Cronenberg was "better than the rest of us combined".[3] Cronenberg's early reputation was as the "Baron of Blood", the "King of Horror" and the "Master of Yuck", and this will be addressed with a focus on the British reception of his early exploitation horrors, and the horror fan culture in which his films were extolled.

Body horror

The horror New Wave demonstrated a desire for producing spectacular set-pieces designed to parade the fantastic anatomical creations of special effects technicians. Many of these body horror films were obsessed with the manufacture of the most convincing, visually explicit and fascinatingly original grotesques, and this led to filmmakers appearing dependent on the advances being made in special make-up effects technology. Cronenberg's interest in body horror – his perception of the anomalies and transformations that an infected, purulent and corrupted body may exhibit – presented considerable opportunities for experimentation with foam latex application and for the ever-innovative design of prosthetics. The special make-up effects on his horror films were the work of key industry figures – Joe Blasco (*Shivers* and *Rabid*), Chris Walas (*Scanners* and *The Fly* [1986]), Dick Smith (*Scanners*) and Rick Baker (*Videodrome* [1982]).

Rick Baker had worked with Dick Smith on the special make-up effects for *The Exorcist* (1973), a demon-possession horror film that shocked audiences with its disturbing transformation of a little girl-turned-body monstrous. The body horror subgenre effectively began with *The Exorcist*, and British reviewers of Cronenberg's films saw his early productions as establishing a similar attraction. David Robinson, reviewing *Shivers*, described the film as belonging to a "new (post-*Exorcist*) genre" and a response "to an apparent audience wish to be physically repelled".[4] He repeated the association in his review of *The Brood* four years later, when he described Cronenberg's creations as being distinctly "from the age of *The Exorcist*".[5]

There is a difference between *The Exorcist*'s body horror and Cronenberg's monstrous bodies. *The Exorcist*, made for Warner Bros, had a considerable production budget for a horror film, and, despite the opinion of some critics that its special effects – the little girl, Regan, vomiting copious amounts of green bile and her head dramatically rotating a full 360° – were crude and playful, the film does not quite equal the rawness of *Shivers* or *Rabid*. Cronenberg's early low-budget horrors are excessively corporeal, and, with their depictions of genetically engineered organisms and surgical and neurological abnormalities, are more identifiable as part of exploitation cinema. But, crucially, they are, as Nigel Andrews wrote, "a sans-pareil in low-budget 'exploitation'".[6] Dr Hobbes' experiments that lead to the creation of a phallic parasite that transforms its victims into sexual fiends in *Shivers* (working title: *Orgy of the Blood Parasites*), Dr Keloid's accidental development of a blood-hungry, armpit-residing, protruding organ in *Rabid*, and Dr Raglan's Psychoplasmics leading to a patient developing an external "womb" in *The Brood*, are what Tom Hutchinson describes as "of the penny-dreadful kind".[7]

The disparate parts of the body horror subgenre have too often been grouped together. Barbara Creed has attempted to classify the body monstrous into its multiple forms, and Cronenberg's monstrosities are an explicit combination of many of the categories and subdivisions of the grotesque body which she has identified – the metamorphosing or transforming body, the generative body, the invaded body, and the disintegrating or exploding body.[8] In an interview in 1978, Cronenberg stated that "the body is the centre of horror", and his films have continually focused on exploiting and manipulating weaknesses in the border separating the body external from the body internal.[9] He argues that the ruptured and visceral body should be glorified for its exquisiteness, and he conceives "a beauty contest for the inside of the human body where people would unzip themselves and show you the best spleen, [and] the best heart".[10] In another article, Cronenberg is quoted as saying:

> We've not devised an aesthetic for the inside of the body any more than we have developed an aesthetic of disease. Most people are disgusted...[b]ut if you develop an aesthetic for it, it ceases to be ugly. I'm trying to force the audience to change its aesthetic sense.[11]

It is this crucial question of aesthetic sense that separates the fans from the critics. Many reviewers and newspaper commentators have viewed Cronenberg's films as "sick"; in contrast, many fans of the neo-horror film have hailed Cronenberg as a genius.

Critics

Cronenberg's films have been subjected to considerable hostility from the British press. Arthur Thirkell, writing in *The Daily Mirror*, offered a most excoriating opinion of the early horrors. Reviewing *Shivers*, he wrote that "it is films like...[this] which make a case for tighter screen censorship. Its X certificate gives the public no real indication what to expect. I will tell them – it is nauseous, trashy, revolting and so sick-making that patrons would be advised to take a plastic bag along".[12] For *Rabid*, Thirkell wrote that the film was from the same "stable as that other lurid shocker, *Shivers*. It's about time the stable was mucked out".[13] Dilys Powell, critic for *The Sunday Times*, initially refused to review *Shivers*, as she found it so "degrading", and it was not until a week after the film's release that she offered a brief opinion.[14] David Hughes reviewed *Scanners* for *The Sunday Times*, but declared himself "morally affronted", objecting to Cronenberg's "bloodbath" in which "heads explode like ketchup bottles, veins bulge and burst with such telepathic effort that our laughter chokes on nausea".[15] Cronenberg's special effects set-pieces were often viewed as too repulsive, and reviewers warned their readership that they might be offended.[16]

The language employed by reviewers to describe the form and effect of Cronenberg's horrors draws on the physical and visceral content of the films. Anatomical references are scattered throughout reviews, perhaps in the belief that they assist with constructing an entertaining response. But their frequency suggests a lack of originality amongst writers, a particular overuse of news-speak that often works by puns and association for the expression of an opinion, and, finally, a one-dimensional approach to Cronenberg. A striking example is the head explosion in *Scanners*, which attracted the attention of many critics. Ian Christie's review for *The Daily Express* carried the headline "Bang! This could really blow your mind"; William Hall's *Weekender* review was titled "Head's you lose..."; and the header for *The Sunday Mirror* review screamed "OFF WITH HIS HEAD!"[17]. Critics often accused Cronenberg of revelling in gore and maximising the special effects moments. Yet, the critics' reviews could be accused of expressing a certain fascination in recounting and detailing the extent of the graphic nature of the films, and also exploiting certain violent episodes to sensationalise newspaper content.

For a number of critics, the films induced a feeling of revulsion and repugnance. The revolt of the body of the critic is apparent in Clive Hirschhorn's review for *The Sunday Express*, where he describes *Scanners* as "stomach-churning horror".[18] Molly Plowright's review of *The Brood* for the *Glasgow Herald* recognises that Cronenberg's films can be "hard to stomach", whilst others, such as Nicholas Wapshott writing in *The Times*, see them as "sickening".[19] A courageous Derek Malcolm only just managed to view *The Brood*, and afterwards wrote in *The Guardian*: "Goodness knows how I got through the movie without being sick".[20]

The opinion of critics that Cronenberg's films were grotesque was not the only reason why many British reviews were negative. The films were also charged with being too unbelievable, and weak in narrative and characterisation. In *The Sunday Times*, Alan Brien described *Rabid* as "scrappily produced...[and] full of loose ends"; David Castell wrote in his review of *The Brood* that "the monumental daftness of its plot defeats all possible suspension of disbelief"; for

Scanners, Alexander Walker wrote that "[t]he movie's story proves that Kronenberg [sic] can't tell one"; and Nigel Andrews in *The Financial Times* wrote that:

[T]he plot dodders on...Cronenberg should take leave-of-absence from his special-effects drawing-board – we can take the fissuring foreheads and exploding heads as read – and get back to devising compulsive plotlines and believable people.[21]

Andrews' response was a little surprising, as he had reviewed *The Brood* only the year before and praised the film for its "silky smooth and *continuo* plotline, with a regard for logic and motivation rare if not extinct in most of his [Cronenberg's] horror-dispensing rivals".[22] Such a positive response towards *The Brood* had been almost an exception.[23] Conversely, David Castell, one of the many reviewers who had been critical of the narrative structure of *The Brood*, was one of the very few writers to approve of the plot of *Scanners*, and acclaim Cronenberg as "a born storyteller".[24] Whilst Andrews had said that the plot of *Scanners* "doddered", Castell felt that Cronenberg "knows exactly the pace at which to take this fanciful science fiction".[25]

It would be incorrect to view films such as *The Brood* or *Scanners* as narratives constructed with a concern for the spectacular special effects moment. The special effects are certainly memorable and the films exhibit a distinct style, but there also remains a complex and developed plot. Cronenberg is a committed auteur, and his allegorical stories are inhabited by a variety of unlikeable characters and detailed with a cold pseudo-science. The underground films which Cronenberg had made earlier had moved "overground", and the experimental remained detectable in the exploitation horrors – most strikingly in *Videodrome* – which he was making for a mainstream and genre audience. There appeared, amongst critics, an unwillingness and an inability to understand a film that was unconventional, philosophical or disturbingly original as also being part of an exploitation cinema. Moreover, the majority of reviewers could not be forced to change their aesthetic sense.

Suppression

Shivers, *Rabid* and *The Brood* were suppressed mainly by erratic theatrical distribution in the United States and Europe. The distribution of *The Brood* was woeful in France, although better organised in Britain, and *Shivers* had a limited British release.[26] Cronenberg's first mainstream film was shown in London on a double bill with the forgotten Canadian horror film, *Cannibal Girls* (1973), directed by Ivan Reitman, at the small Classic cinemas at Piccadilly and Victoria.

Cronenberg's first three horror films had been commercially successful in their home country, Canada, but not without generating controversy with regard to their content and the government funding that *Shivers*, in particular, had received.[27] In Britain, there seemed to be minimal moral debate or panic surrounding the release of *Shivers*, *Rabid* and *The Brood*. The much-criticised Secretary of the British Board of Film Censors, Stephen Murphy, had resigned in 1975, and this seemed to appease local councils, and campaigning moral organisations and pressure groups. With Murphy's resignation, a significant amount of the furore which had surrounded the classification of a "New Savage Cinema" of works such as *The Devils* (1971), *Straw Dogs* (1970), *The Exorcist* and *Flesh for Frankenstein* (1974) had abated. There were episodes, however, such as the banning of *Shivers* in Cambridgeshire, "after a private viewing by the public protection committee. Complaints had been received from the public that some scenes were indecent".[28]

When *Scanners* was released in Britain over Easter 1981, John Du Pré, writing in *The Sunday People*, did his best to arouse the moral interests of religious organisations: "with a perverted sense of timing, [*Scanners*] has been launched on to the British cinema scene this Holy Week".[29] Four years later, when Britain was in a moral panic over supposed "video nasties", a videotape copy of *Scanners* was studied by police after a teenager had hanged himself; he had disappeared after leaving a friend's house where he had watched the film.[30] *Scanners* opened Cronenberg up to a wider audience, and much of this had been due to the considerable promotional support which the film had received. A well-organised advertising campaign in the many foreign markets and, most importantly, in the United States had exploited dramatic images of the special effects. In Britain, the commerciality of *Scanners* led to its re-release in late-1981 on a double bill with *The Hills Have Eyes*; at the same time, *The Brood* was re-released on a double bill with George Romero's *Dawn of the Dead*.

Exposure

The neo-horror double bill was a staple of many struggling British first-run cinemas in the late-1970s and early 1980s. With the dramatic decrease in cinema attendance and the decline in the quantity and general quality of new films being produced, cinemas turned to the horror package to attract a steady and dependable audience. For many years, horror films have had a dedicated following, and this particular resurgence in the genre, which was to peak in the mid-1980s, had enticed a significantly large group of new fans. In Britain, there had been few opportunities to view Cronenberg's early horrors on their first release, and this altered with the popular exposure that *Scanners* received. Moreover, there emerged two crucial markets in which the Cronenberg back catalogue was seen by a second audience: repertory cinema and video.

In London throughout the 1970s and 1980s, the cinéaste was presented with an enviable choice of repertory theatres at which to view a new cinema of violent and controversial films. There was the Phoenix in North London, the Electric Cinema in West London, and the Essential Cinema Club and the Scala in Central London. These theatres provided a cult cinema education, with their tantalisingly programmed double and triple bills and all-night retrospectives of neo-horror filmmakers. Mark Kermode, in his confessions of a horror fan, fondly remembers the experience:

> I started frequenting the Phoenix cinema in East Finchley which every Friday and Saturday night played late-night double bills of the sort of culty horror and fantasy films that I'd by now read so much about. From around the age of 15...it was possible to get into X-rated movies with ease, particularly late-nighters, and I began to spend every weekend either at the Phoenix or at the Scala.[31]

Packaged programmes of Cronenberg's horrors were an early feature of the Scala, the principal cult film repertory cinema. It had opened first at The Other Cinema in the late-1970s in the West End and then later moved, and reopened, in July 1981 in King's Cross, where it attracted a devoted audience to its daily changing programme of sexploitation, gay cinema, Euro-horror, erotica and Hong Kong action pictures.[32] The Scala also presented Saturday midnight movie programmes, and here an all-night Romero/Cronenberg (May 1982) or a complete Cronenberg retrospective (November 1983) would sit alongside other evenings of Russ Meyer, Andy Warhol or John Waters. Cronenberg's apocalyptic cinema of panic narratives and violently surreal images appealed to an audience of the post-punk generation. They also appealed to the connoisseurs of body horror who shared an aesthetic sense and were beginning to congregate at cinemas, forming unintended and irregular groups. As Mark Kermode writes, "an odd bond was formed by seeing the same faces at the same cinemas, watching the same movies, time after time".[33]

Repeat viewings and word of mouth are important for the cult status and extended cinema life of a film. Members of what is a limited audience demonstrate their devotion and desire for a specific cult film by ritualistically attending screenings. Cronenberg's cinema of explicit effects and intense stories were, for many viewers, too much, but for others this was the allure. The films may, on first release, have gained poor reviews and, in some countries, a weak reception, but these, too, remain factors for the emergence of a Cronenberg cult. As Danny Peary writes, "[c]ultists believe they are among the blessed few who have discovered something in particular films that the average moviegoer and critic have missed".[34]

The cult film experience of being at a screening with others who share the passion and awareness that a certain film is remarkable establishes a developed social space. In contrast, viewing the film at home on video removes this community. Films such as Cronenberg's horrors have been available on video in Britain, and initially this was not a threat to the repertories, but, as the video retail – as opposed to video rental – market grew in the late-1980s, there emerged a potent alternative to viewing cult film at the cinema, and this was a factor behind the closure of venues such as the Scala.

Videotape has been the most accessible way of viewing Cronenberg's early horrors. The penetration of the home video recorder into the British market was startling, and ownership rose significantly in the early 1980s – an explosion in acquisition of a new form of home communication technology that has been unmatched. Mark R Levy and Barrie Gunter state in their 1988 sociocultural study of British video ownership behaviour and use:

> Although the VCR had been around since the 1970s, it was not until 1980 that private ownership began to take off. Compared to 1979, when only negligible numbers of homes possessed a VCR, latest estimates [a 1988 Independent Broadcasting Authority report] reveal that more than half (55 per cent) of individuals...have acquired a VCR.[35]

The demand for home ownership of video recorders was matched by the rapid release of a vast range of pre-recorded film and programme titles on videotape. Video rental dominated the first wave of tape use, and in this "VCR rush" many new and small video rental businesses emerged. Cronenberg's early horrors were amongst the first of these rental releases in Britain. *Scanners* was released in 1982 by the major video label, Guild Home Video, whose catalogue also featured titles such as *Rebecca* (1940), *The Amityville Horror* (1979), *Dressed to Kill* (1980) and a fourteen-cassette collection of episodes of the television soap, *Dallas*. The smaller and more down-market video label, Intervision, had already released both *Shivers* and *Rabid*, in VHS and Beta formats, next to exploitation films such as *The*

Exorcist-imitation, *The Tempter* (1974), and the British sexploitation series of *Adventures of* films (1975-78).

The "VCR rush" attracted video companies hungry for quick profits, and many often obscure films of a violent and carnal nature were easily acquired for distribution, packaged with provocative covers, and exploited.[36] Horror was, in particular, an exploitable genre. In addition, the video renter was predominantly young; in Levy and Gunter's study, the most active rental age group was aged 16 to 24.[37] The neo-horror film had attracted a young audience and Cronenberg's early horrors were well-suited to video release.

Copies of *Shivers*, *Rabid*, *The Brood* or *Scanners* would have been available for rental from a wide variety of high street and local shops. In the early 1980s, there were less video shops in Britain than shops that contained a video area or carousel, and tapes could be rented from grocers, launderettes, newsagents and off-licences. Cronenberg's horrors had managed successfully to invade not only suburbia, but also the British home.

The boom in videotape retail was the second wave of tape use, and the third wave was video archiving. As both pre-recorded and blank videotapes became cheaper to purchase, in the late-1980s there was a growth in home video collections and video libraries. Copies of Cronenberg's films could be easily stored, and the eventual screening of Cronenberg's early horrors on terrestrial and satellite television allowed for off-air recordings.[38] Owning a copy of Cronenberg's horrors was now feasible, and it was also convenient and cheap. Similar to other home entertainment technology such as laserdisc and DVD, it became possible to skip or fast-forward to a selected part of a Cronenberg film, to view repeatedly, control and manipulate the image, rewind and replay a special effects moment and, where required, pause.

Fans

Cronenberg has said that he has sought to "show the unshowable".[39] His confrontational cinema has constructed a new visually violent experience, which his fans have found fascinating and aesthetically appealing. Establishing this cinema attraction, in which images of the body monstrous can appear as the body-beautiful, has required significant technical attention and expenditure on special effects.

In the Canadian press release for *Scanners*, co-executive producer Pierre David heralded the film as "the most spectacular...ever produced in Canada...we're using the services of six top special effects men from Canada and the U.S. and the results of their efforts will be extraordinary, thrilling action sequences". Such was the impact that

William Hall, in his review of the film, declared Dick Smith, the special make-up effects consultant, "the real maestro of this quite stunning shocker", and David Castell described Smith as a "wizard".[40] Clive Hirschhorn went further in his review, saying that *"Scanners* would be nothing without those remarkable special effects".[41]

To regard Cronenberg's vision as secondary to the ability of the skilled effects technicians is unfair. The special effects embellish the films, but they were conceived by Cronenberg. For instance, Cronenberg said of *Shivers* that "those images came right from my imagination", and that "[t]he parasite bugs came out of my childhood fascination with the microscopic, and with insects".[42] What Cronenberg had imagined for *Shivers* was then physically translated to the screen by the special effects artist Joe Blasco, who is described by Cronenberg as "[a]n unsung hero".[43]

Both Cronenberg and effects technicians such as Blasco are venerated in the American fanzine *Fangoria*, and recognised as important filmmakers of body horror. Cronenberg was one of the first of the neo-horror directors to be interviewed (issue 3); Joe Blasco was "discovered" and first featured in issue 20; whilst the special effects work of the technician Rick Baker was evaluated over issues 35 to 37. There were other fantasy-horror magazines that covered the horror New Wave and presented interviews with Cronenberg and features on his films – the British fanzines *Starburst*, *Fear* and *Shock Xpress*, the American fanzines *Cinefantastique* and *Gorezone*, and the French publication *Mad Movies*. None had an identity quite as explicit as the gore-filled *Fangoria*, which could be bought in Britain from selected shops. For Mark Kermode, *Fangoria* was the "new bible of hard-core horror fandom" and "the Sex Pistols of horror fanzines, loud, noisy, visually graphic and absolutely guaranteed to send your parents apoplectic with righteous indignation".[44] The content of *Fangoria* was, for Philip Brophy, reflected in its name: "[t]he title speaks volumes: gore, fantasy, phantasmagoria, fans".[45]

The earliest issues of the fanzine had lacked a stable identity, and contained residues of the science-fiction cinema which was featured in the sister fanzines *Starlog* and *Future Life*, from which *Fangoria* had emerged. The purple-coloured cover of *Fangoria* issue 3 featured a non-threatening Christopher Lee in the children's fantasy *An Arabian Adventure* (1979); Spock and *Star Trek: The Motion Picture* (1979) featured on the front of issue 4; and *The Empire Strikes Back* (1980) appeared on the orange-coloured cover of issue 6. By issues 8, 9 and 10 (1980), the fanzine's interest in the New Wave of horror was becoming clearer: issue 8 featured a close-up of a putrefying zombie's head from Lucio Fulci's *Zombi 2* (*Zombie Flesh-Eaters*, 1979); the blood-red-coloured cover of issue 9 displayed the bizarre image from

Motel Hell (1980), of a pig's head on a human's body, wielding a bloodied chainsaw; and the exploding *Scanners* head was on the front of issue 10. Issue 9 carried in its letters' page readers' thoughts on the science-fiction content of previous issues, and it was clear that it had to be removed. John P Kelley was just one of the readers to complain – "I now find it tasteless and boring to find a horror mag doing science-fiction and fantasy articles...There are TOO many magazines already doing science-fiction features...readers who want a horror-gore magazine will almost find it impossible to locate any".[46]

With issue 26, *Fangoria* introduced the first of its many "pull-out" posters – an A3 or A2 size, folded colour reproduction of a notable film image of the body monstrous. Number 9 in this "Scream Greats" series (issue 34) was a graphic enlargement of the horrific erupting body of Barry Convex (Les Carlson) in *Videodrome*, whilst poster number 11 (issue 36) was a scene from *The Brood*, in which Nola Carveth (Samantha Eggar) cradles in her hands a blood-covered newly born "child of rage". Of the latter, William Beard writes that it "is a scene that invariably makes audiences gag in disgust".[47] Here, it was being offered by *Fangoria* for readers to display on their walls in delight – a classic neo-horror film moment to be placed alongside the proud horror fan's growing gallery of gory images.

There is a resemblance between these posters of the body monstrous as body-beautiful and the fold-out posters of a naked "body of the month" featured in many pornographic magazines – most famously in *Playboy*. Both are glossy adorations of a flesh-fantastic which leaves little unshown. There is a perceived relationship between the opened bodies of pornography and splatter-obsessed hard core horror, for which Richard Gehr, in describing neo-horror, coined the term "carnography".[48]

In issue 11, reader Jim Mattes wrote to express of his frustration when buying *Fangoria* – "I'm in my twenties, and I find it rather embarrassing to hand a copy of your magazine, with one of its gruesome covers, to a nice old lady at a bookstore".[49] The first *Fangoria* readers' debate had been concerned with reducing the science-fiction content of the fanzine. The second readers' debate which occurred towards the end of the fanzine's second year, was now concerned with its excessively visceral content. The editorial for issue 12 (April 1981) stated "[w]e've had enough! In the past two months, over 50% of the letters we've received concerned one topic – the question of graphic violence, as depicted in films and as it appears in FANGORIA's coverage".[50] In that issue, a special page of letters was printed covering the debate, and, whilst readers supported *Fangoria*'s content – such as Richard Smith Jr.'s comments, "[a]re these namby-pamby, snot-nosed sissies ever going to shut up? Personally,

I like gory photos" – others such as Randy Turnbull advised the publishers that "it might be wise if you exercised restraint in your selection of photos. Printing page after page of sickening mayhem... tends to make FANGORIA look like an S&M rag".[51] Contrary to the popular impression that *Fangoria* had always been a fanzine obsessed with the publication of violent and gory film images, the early issues of the publication had exhibited an identity crisis.

An examination of the back pages of *Fangoria* produces another interesting matter. Commencing with issue 12, *Fangoria*'s first-time subscribers and readers who renewed their subscription were entitled to place, for free, a brief non-commercial advertisement in the classifieds. These messages provide a wealth of material for understanding the types of reader of the fanzine and their opinion of neo-horror films, and here it can be discerned that, although Cronenberg had his supporters, he was definitely not the most popular filmmaker. The names that are constantly cited and worshipped in readers' notes are the directors John Carpenter and George Romero, writer Stephen King and the special effects artists Tom Savini and Rick Baker. Cronenberg is mentioned in the occasional "penpals wanted" request – "Cronenberg, H G Lewis, Syd Barrett, Arthur Lee, Lovecraft, Romero and Velvet Underground fans write...".[52] Others include him in their "best of" list – "Don Henley is great, Bottin, Baker, Carpenter, Cronenberg & FANGORIA #1!", and "David Cronenberg, *Scanners*, Michael Ironside and Angus Scrimm are the greatest! Spielberg is an idiot!".[53] There are also the "Long Live" lists such as "Long Live Lovecraft, King, Cronenberg, Wirghtson [sic], Corben, Monty Python, Queen, A Flock of Seagulls".[54]

Certainly Cronenberg's films did not appeal to everyone, and the reaction of the British press is an example of this antipathy. A developed aesthetic sense for Cronenberg's biological-horrors could be found amongst fans of body horror films of the New Wave. An examination of messages placed by subscribers to the American fanzine *Fangoria* shows that Cronenberg was revered, but an estimation of fan's adoration of neo-horror "stars" indicates that Cronenberg was, surprisingly, not amongst the most honoured.

Notes

I would like to thank Paolo Tripodi for his helpful suggestions, and Julian Petley for allowing me to acquire his *Fangoria* collection.

[1] Kerry O'Quinn, "Welcome to the World of Fangoria!", *Fangoria* 1 (August 1979): 4.

[2] Philip Brophy, "Horrality – the Textuality of Contemporary Horror Films",

Screen 27: 1 (January-February 1986): 5.

3   Brian Case, "Schlock tactics", *Time Out* 12 April 1995: 155.

4   David Robinson, *The Times* 30 April 1976.

5   David Robinson, *The Times* 7 March 1980. See also Philip French, *The Observer* 9 March 1980.

6   Nigel Andrews, *The Financial Times* 7 March 1980.

7   Tom Hutchinson, *The Sunday Telegraph* 8 January 1978.

8   See Barbara Creed, "Horror and the Carnivalesque: The Body-monstrous", in Leslie Devereaux and Roger Hillman (eds), *Fields of Vision: Essays in Film Studies, Visual Anthropology, and Photography* (Berkeley; Los Angeles; London: University of California Press, 1995): 127-159.

9   Verina Glaessner, "The Terror Within", *Time Out* 6 January 1978: 12.

10   Anne Billson, "Cronenberg on Cronenberg: a career in stereo", *Monthly Film Bulletin* 56: 660 (January 1989): 5.

11   Alan Stanbrook, "Cronenberg's Creative Cancers", *Sight and Sound* 58: 1 (winter 1988/89): 56.

12   Arthur Thirkell, *The Daily Mirror* 30 April 1976.

13   Arthur Thirkell, *The Daily Mirror* 6 January 1978.

14   Dilys Powell, *The Sunday Times* 9 May 1976.

15   David Hughes, *The Sunday Times* 26 April 1981.

16   See, for instance, Felix Barker, *Evening News* 29 April 1976. Barker saw the parasitic "worm", in *Shivers*, as offensive and readers were warned. Russell Davies, *The Observer* 2 May 1976, described the parasites as "unimaginably vile" and as a cross between "sea-cucumbers and, to put it pointedly, turds".

17   Ian Christie, *The Daily Express* 18 April 1981; William Hall, *Weekender* 24 April 1981; Madeleine Harmsworth, *The Sunday Mirror* 26 April 1981.

18   Clive Hirschhorn, *Sunday Express* 26 April 1981.

19   Molly Plowright, *Glasgow Herald* 26 May 1980; Nicholas Wapshott, *The Times* 24 April 1981.

20   Derek Malcolm, *The Guardian* 6 March 1980.

21   Alan Brien, *The Sunday Times* 22 January 1978; David Castell, *The Sunday Telegraph* 9 March 1980; Alexander Walker, "Heads you wince...", *Evening Standard* 16 April 1981; Nigel Andrews, *The Financial Times* 24 April 1981.

[22] Nigel Andrews, *The Financial Times* 7 March 1980.

[23] Cronenberg remembers that *The Brood* "was generally not well-received here [in England] critically. There were two extremes; either considered brilliant or absolutely terrible". Eric Braun interview with Cronenberg, "The gentle art of mind boggling", *Films* 1: 7 (June 1981): 24.

[24] David Castell, *The Sunday Telegraph* 26 April 1981.

[25] Ibid.

[26] See Braun: 24, 89; Peter Morris, *David Cronenberg: A Delicate Balance* (Toronto: ECW Press, 1994): 76; Chris Rodley (ed), *Cronenberg on Cronenberg* (London; Boston: Faber and Faber, 1992): 52, 85.

[27] See Morris: 68-74.

[28] "Horror film banned", *The Times* 23 July 1976.

[29] John Du Pré, "Horrors for the Holiday", *The Sunday People* 19 April 1981.

[30] "Video-nasty boy found hanged", *The Daily Express* 11 October 1985: 26. Of Cronenberg's films, *Videodrome* attracted the most controversy as a result of the "video nasty" debate. The film was released theatrically in Britain, in 1983, at the peak of the panic and the BBC subsequently banned all reviews from its programmes.

[31] Mark Kermode, "I was a teenage horror fan. Or, 'How I learned to stop worrying and love Linda Blair'", in Martin Barker and Julian Petley (eds), *Ill Effects: The media/violence debate* (London; New York: Routledge, 1997): 59-60.

[32] See Jane Giles, "Scala!!!! Autopsy of a Cinema", in Stefan Jaworzyn (ed), *Shock Xpress* (London: Titan Books, 1994): 30-35.

[33] Kermode: 60.

[34] Danny Peary, *Cult Movies: The Classics, the Sleepers, the Weird, and the Wonderful* (New York: Dell Publishing, 1981): xiii.

[35] Mark R Levy and Barrie Gunter, *Home Video and the Changing Nature of the Television Audience* (London; Paris: John Libbey/IBA, 1988): 5.

[36] This led to a moral panic concerning video content, the lack of regulation over the age of the videotape renter and the control that the renter has over the video image. Films considered obscene and horrific were labelled "video nasties", by the British media. Officially, films were identified and banned and the 1984 Video Recordings Act stated that all videotapes had to be submitted to the British Board of Film Censors, for classification. None of Cronenberg's films was officially identified and banned.

[37] Levy and Gunter: 20.

[38] *Scanners* received its British terrestrial television première on Channel 4, 15 May 1992; *Rabid* soon followed, showing on a double bill with *Dead Ringers* (1988) on BBC-2, 31 May 1992; *Shivers* and *Videodrome* did not receive their premières until 19 January 1997, BBC-2.

[39] Rodley: 43.

[40] William Hall, "Heads you lose...".*, Weekender* 24 April 1981; David Castell, *The Sunday Telegraph* 26 April 1981.

[41] Clive Hirschhorn, *The Sunday Express* 26 April 1981.

[42] Rodley: 47.

[43] Ibid.

[44] Kermode: 59.

[45] Brophy: 3.

[46] "The Postal Zone", *Fangoria* 9 (November 1980): 5.

[47] William Beard, "The Visceral Mind: The Major Films of David Cronenberg", in Piers Handling (ed), *The Shape of Rage: The Films of David Cronenberg* (Toronto: General Publishing Co.; New York: New York Zoetrope; 1983): 35.

[48] Quoted in Isabel Cristina Pinedo, *Recreational Terror: Women and the Pleasures of Horror Film Viewing* (Albany: State University of New York Press, 1997): 61.

[49] "The Postal Zone", *Fangoria* 11 (February 1981): 7.

[50] Bob Martin, "Imagination Inc.", *Fangoria* 12 (April 1981): 4.

[51] "The Readers on Gore", *Fangoria* 12 (April 1981): 8.

[52] "Free subscriber ads", *Fangoria* 27 (May 1983): 65.

[53] "Free subscriber ads", *Fangoria* 28 (July 1983): 65; "Free subscriber ads", *Fangoria* 32 (January 1984): 66.

[54] "Free subscriber ads", *Fangoria* 33 (February 1984): 67.

A body apart: Cronenberg and genre

Jonathan Crane

At one time, David Cronenberg was a horror film director. His early films, home to venereal parasites, a rabid queen of porn and deadly telepathic insurgents, among others, deserve their generic designation. Yet, as Cronenberg's career has developed, his recent films cannot be so handily corralled. The grisly fancies and obvious hallmarks of the genre have been radically reconfigured, severely muted or abandoned. Cronenberg's later films – for example, his revisionist biography of beat writer William Burroughs, recast as a heterosexual literary outlaw, or *M. Butterfly* (1993), the story of a diffident attaché besotted with a Chinese opera singer who is really a man – cannot be easily or profitably read as horror films.[1]

In following this path and leaving behind the constraints of genre work, Cronenberg is charting a familiar career arc. Many filmmakers have made horror films with an eye to a better future. In this regard, genre films allow directors and actors, as well as those in technical and support positions, to make money and a name, and move on to larger budgets and more respectable imagery. In this light, Cronenberg's early films are utterly conventional. Each film, starting with his first commercial effort, *Shivers* (1976), builds on the success of the last,[2] until, by the end of his horror period, he is making Hollywood horror films with mogul Dino De Laurentiis, who produced *The Dead Zone* (1983), and Mel Brooks, whose production company bankrolled *The Fly* (1986).[3]

With *The Fly*, Cronenberg's best-reviewed and most economically successful genre film, he leaves off making horror films. Pre-1986, he is, to use an appellation common to the early period, "the Baron of Blood"; post-*The Fly*, he is "an internationally renowned director".[4] While there is a break in Cronenberg's work, the separation is neither clean nor complete. Cronenberg's early work was more than a careerist springboard. His grossest films, in both senses of the word, as vile and unformed, continue to exercise an influence over the more recent productions. While none of his latter films is a horror movie, none is absent of horrific moments. Reading the early imagery is crucial to a grasp of the more recent films. He may be tracking in a new direction, but Cronenberg's present course can only be plotted by determining his initial coordinates.

The assertion that Cronenberg's first work belongs to the horror genre is generally accepted without qualification. There may be some disputes about the purity of his genre efforts; a few critics will argue that the work also shares some important characteristics of the sci-fi genre. For instance, is not the cultivation of telepaths – by a pharmacological junta in *Scanners* (1981), and the attempt to re-engineer the body politic via television in *Videodrome* (1982) – more aptly defined as science-fiction? In the end, the balance generally tips towards horror, as, no matter how the threat is conceived, whether as part of an insidious corporate takeover or as the dangerous vision of a solitary, venomous imagination, the impact is always registered on the individual body; that is, while Cronenberg's films eschew the supernatural, and horrific threat comes not from the Devil, but from the basement lab or the R & D arm of a multinational, Cronenberg always registers the threat and examines its meaning at the level of the personal.

In a Cronenberg horror film, presenting threat at the level of the personal means that threat is literally embodied. All the films which compose the first period of Cronenberg's corpus feature menace fused with the flesh. The horrible, unlike the technologically wayward, is intimately personal. In this regard, Vivian Sobchack's distinction between the manifestation of fear in the SF film and the horror film is apposite:

> If the SF film expresses or elicits any fear, it is a fear which is far removed from the fear and terror of the horror film...It produces not the strong terror evoked by something already present and known in each of us, but the more diluted and less immediate fear of what we may yet become. The terrifying aspect of traditional horror films arises from a recognition that we are forever linked to the crudeness of our earthbound bodies.[5]

If Sobchack's line of demarcation stands, the origins of Cronenberg's menace need not become a point of genre confusion. With the emphasis placed not on origin, who created the threat, but on destination and function, where and how is the threat felt, we can avoid a border war. As long as the venereal parasites of *Shivers* crawl from, and into, the mouth and vagina, it does not really matter that they were originally intended as cheaper and more readily available substitutes for human organs in transplant surgery. In *The Brood* (1979), a radical therapy technique may have been intended to provide catharsis for the masses of psychically maimed (imagine primal scream therapy beyond the nth power), but, as long as the "creative cancers" caused by Psychoplasmics are individually delineated and personally embodied, the consequences of renegade therapy remain horrific.

While the mere presence of scientists is not sufficient cause to merit calling a text science-fiction, we still need to account for the omnipresence of the scientist in Cronenberg's horror films. Discounting any automatic link between scientists and sci-fi, what is to be made of the fact that scientists play a central, even dominant, role in every one of the early movies? The unexpected appearance of scientists significantly complicates the process of awarding a precise nomination for Cronenberg's work as the denizens of the laboratory have been long-absent from the horror film. Apart from a very few glaring exceptions, the man of science (a penis is almost always nestled beneath the lab coat) has departed from the scene. When scientists do appear, popping up like impertinent party-crashers, demanding an account for their presence, "What are *they* doing here?" is the only reasonable response in the face of such a provocative trespass.

This was not always the case. As Andrew Tudor writes in a marvellously thorough account of changes in the horror genre: "The belief that science is dangerous is as central to the horror movie as is a belief in the malevolent inclinations of ghosts, ghouls, vampires and zombies".[6] Once – Tudor is writing about the genre between the years 1930 and 1960 – the scientist was an equal among all the unearthly creatures and practitioners of the black arts who walked the night. Over a long period of decline, the scientist has gone missing. It is also worth noting that the precipitous decline of the scientist has been matched of late, although not to the point of extinction, by a waning in the supernatural as the well-spring of horror. Today, we more commonly expect the random serial killer or bestial clique, shorn of supernatural trappings, to create horror and havoc.

In revivifying an extinguished, retrograde element – the "mad scientist" – and dragging him back into the contemporary arena, Cronenberg erected a redoubt within the genre. In doing so, he made films with a dual allegiance. They belong to the genre but, at the same time, they are significantly removed from contemporaneous performances of the horrible. This departure has been insufficiently explored. It is far more common for Cronenberg's early work to be read for what it has in common with the films of other directors responsible for reinvigorating the genre in the 1970s than for what it does not. When considered as one of the many "nasty" directors of contemporary violent horror, in league with George Romero, Wes Craven, Lucio Fulci, Stuart Gordon, Sam Raimi, Steve Miner, Tobe

Hooper, John Carpenter *et al*, distinct and important departures from the genre are elided.

Simply highlighting the return of the AWOL scientist to the fold is insufficient. Faithfully detailing the type of scientist Cronenberg returns to life is crucial to understanding the nature of horror in the early films. Again, Tudor is helpful here.[7] He details four distinct varieties of scientific investigator. The founding father is Dr Frankenstein. At one time, the most influential of laboratory denizens, he is an indefatigable explorer who will not be kept from his appointment with destiny. Scientists of this ilk are singularly driven to uncover the mystery of all mysteries: the hallowed secret of life. In this campaign, they will give their all and discard most traditional values along the way, as successful completion of the quest holds infinite promise and reward for the single-minded pilgrim. While they may appear impossibly Machiavellian, with reason overrun by an insatiable will to power, it is important to remember that the quest was initiated with the best of intentions. The fault lies not in the pursuit of knowledge – good could have come from the research – but in giving too much rein to intellectual curiosity. They simply never know when to stop. The Doctor and his heirs are not intrinsically evil; rather, their failure lies in an inability accurately and ethically to compute the ratio between legitimate means and desirable ends.

The second wave of scientists arrive when the horror film engages the terror of nuclear annihilation. Scientists are no longer presented as lone, errant knights hunting a phantom, epistemological grail. Now the focus is on science as a community praxis. Individual identities and mad psyches are subsumed as the quest for knowledge becomes a corporate or, more generally, national enterprise. In decamping for the federal research institute, science sheds its connection with individual investigators. General Electric, not Thomas Edison, bring good things to light. In this shift, scientific progress no longer records the height of singular IQs. Neither does progress serve to register the moral depths to which ambitious, but ethically challenged, researchers will all-too-often plummet. Science is now a grand barometer for the development and progress of all humanity. Wary science is good for the whole; risky science puts the world in peril. As Tudor notes: "Science here neither corrupts nor commits blasphemy, but it is, by its very nature, a risky enterprise, and for that reason it can be dangerous".[8] As individual scientists become an army of faceless investigators, the couplet of science and sin is reconfigured as the pragmatic relation between cost and benefit. Frankenstein is now just an anonymous and often injudicious actuary.

By the mid to late-1960s, science has become incidental to the production of the horrible. Should science play a role in the genesis of onscreen horror, it does so without having any particular meaning – that is, in previous eras, science had a very precise articulation. By now, science carries no special significance beyond standing for one path among multiple options, for creating havoc. At this stage, it does not really matter whether the monstrous is created through necromancy or slipshod organic chemistry. Drawing distinctions between satanic wizards and nefarious physicists is genre trainspotting. Only the effects of horror are of interest as science fades from view.

As science continues to drift away from the foreground, it is subject to one last ignoble transformation. In most contemporary films, remembering that science is only infrequently heard from, it is now articulated into a general background of paranoia. In this context, science becomes one more thing that works against the protagonist. Instead of having no discernible valence and being of no particular interest, science must now bear the onus of a negative charge as just another instantiation of universal suspicion and dread.

This backdrop, in which the scientist tumbles from the lofty heights as God's one-time rival to another minor variation on monotonous threat, is the ground upon which Cronenberg's reappropriation of the scientist needs to be read. Why return such a disreputable figure, a vanquished player, back to centre-stage? This is a crucial question, given Cronenberg's status as a trailblazer in the genre. How is the vanguard reputation to be balanced with the antique players? This question is made even more pressing as a return to residual form is often read, in a period of corrosive irony, as a signature of nostalgic despair, a white flag raised in the face of semantic collapse and implosion.

At this juncture, it is important to remember that the residual need not be synonymous with insufferable nostalgia and semiotic irrelevance. In a far more positive vein, Raymond Williams writes that the residual is "older work kept available by certain groups as an extension of or alternative to dominant contemporary cultural production".[9] A return to residual form may not be a craven sign of cultural exhaustion. The past can, on occasion, serve as more than a warehouse for outmoded tropes and figures held in disrepute. Turning back may then be more than an act of cowardice on the part of those unable to face the dim prospect of the present. A return to residual form can be read as an act of renewal, a means whereby older forms are vigorously reclaimed and restored as figures of opposition.

Leaving aside, for the moment, a full exploration of how to read Cronenberg's resuscitation of the scientist (as a complete account will require a detailed look at how the scientist functions as an agent within Cronenberg's films as a whole), it is worth noting that the figure Cronenberg brings back to life is the most dated version of the horror film scientist. Cronenberg reaches as far back as the genre will allow, and returns Dr Frankenstein to the present. All Cronenberg's variations on the father are interested in restoring new life to the dead.

Cronenberg's first two commercial films, close companion-pieces telling very nearly the same tale, feature two scientists who bring forth new life from the lab. In *Shivers*, Dr Emil Hobbes, finding that life is too nasty and brutish, invents an aggressive, parasitic aphrodisiac to liberate the downtrodden. Life is intolerable, as modern men and women have been enslaved by excessive rationality. For Hobbes, we are the dead as long as there is no symmetry between pleasure and cogitation. The body must be restored to pleasure – if grey matter and flesh are to achieve the proper equilibrium. Plastic surgeon Dr Dan Keloid, the inventor of "neutral field tissue", is the Frankenstein figure in *Rabid* (1977). Here again, in order to restore proper function to the ruined body, the doctor has found a way to create human tissue that will grow wherever a damaged body needs it. Like Frankenstein before him, Dr Keloid defeats death by re-creating the flesh. The parallels between Dr Frankenstein, Hobbes and Keloid are clear. They all find life as we presently experience it to be flawed. Death takes life too easily, the vital force needs to put up a better fight, or life has become too much like death. In either case, these men intend to put life right.

The Brood features Dr Hal Raglan reprising the role of Frankenstein. Here Cronenberg reimagines Frankenstein as a psychologist or life counsellor. Raglan teaches his patients to survive the enervating blows of family trauma by converting feelings of anguish, inferiority and rage into the seeds of new life. Raglan radically supersedes his vaunted ancestor by hitting upon a method that makes all of Dr Frankenstein's cumbersome and expensive machinery unnecessary. With the right attitude and suitably empowered, desires themselves can create new life. Linking the exhortations of countless cheerleaders for the psyche with the experiments of Dr Frankenstein leads to the unexpected conclusion that the creator of the Monster is also the father of the contemporary human potential movement. Growing better every day in every way – magnanimously remaking the body from the inside out as an act of unblinkered self-love – is the home version of the great work done with chemical galvanism and electro-biology in Frankenstein's remote lab.

Moving off the couch and quitting analysis, the progeny of Frankenstein will next appear under the aegis of the corporation. *Scanners* and *Videodrome* complicate the transposition of Dr Frankenstein to the present day by making the manufacture of new life and the pursuit of market share complementary exercises; consequently, Frankenstein's work is distributed across rival films in direct competition with one another. And while each firm has a designated CEO, the creation of new life is now a systematic exercise parcelled across multiple departments. The introduction of Frankenstein to the free market strips the Doctor of his caste; corporations are meritocracies not aristocracies; and his singular mission, the life's work of one dedicated soul, is now a bureaucratic exercise delegated across a faceless sea of salaried rank and file.

In *Scanners*, Frankenstein's creations are externally normal but internally monstrous. They are telepaths. Mutations created by a tranquillizer intended to collect the frayed nerves of pregnant women, scanners are blessed and cursed by the ability to read minds, and psycho-kinetically remake and remodel their enemies. Riven by competing loyalties, as representatives of one firm or another, the scanners war for monopoly control. Unravelling the enigma of life now calls for entrepreneurial savvy, as well as anatomical genius. Once, the only threat to new life was an angry horde of frightened peasants ready to drive the misshapen stranger from their midst. In the post-industrial economy, unfettered market forces, the bane of protectionists everywhere, must be reckoned as creation's chief nemesis.

Videodrome details a war over broadcasting rights to the new flesh. Via television, two groups of antagonistic scientists aim to lead us, over the air, to the next step in evolution. As in *The Brood*, the machinery for making new men has been updated. Today, new life will be created by the pale fire of the cathode ray. Awash in the cool glow of the electronic hearth, the vast television audience will be reconstructed in the face of real, direct communication effects. Frankenstein, as a pivotal player in new technologies, will now succeed Rupert Murdoch and Ted Turner. Again, as with *Scanners*, the mechanism for realising Frankenstein's mission is, like the original Monster, an amalgamation.

Cronenberg's final horror films, *The Dead Zone* and *The Fly*, continue to run changes on the distant figure of the scientist. In *The Dead Zone*, while the parallels between scientific authority and the tale of Frankenstein are not as strong as in the other films, it is still the man of science who provides a powerful warrant for the possibility that being human entails more than might ever have been imagined. Life is not what we think it is. This ontological shift is, in great measure, the responsibility of Dr Sam Weizak, a doctor who has devoted his career to helping the victims of brain injury return to health. He is the degreed authority figure who first accepts the necessity to act boldly on information granted in psychic visions from beyond. Despite the Hippocratic oath, with its absolute injunction to do no harm, and, more importantly, a lifetime of fealty to the scientific method, Weizak affirms the morality of assassination upon hearing of convincing images from another plane. The possibility that life has a dimension beyond the empirical receives crucial support, and is underwritten by faith in the voice of science. The protagonist is free to accept his visions as a moral imperative to kill only after science certifies intangible spells as telling evidence of a realm separate but equal to this world. While Cronenberg's other films feature scientists playing a far more direct role in creating new life, Weizak's willingness to accept a greatly enlarged definition of what it means to be human leads to the embrace of a radical new way of being, a way of life that will entail drastic revisions in the natural or common law which defines moral behaviour.

Finally, for his last horror film in the early cycle, Cronenberg remakes the claustrophobic, classic 1958 chiller, *The Fly*. In this film, the most economical version of Cronenberg's Ur-tale, Frankenstein and his creation are one and the same. Lost in a jealous daze while downing too much drink, Dr Seth Brundle accidentally fuses his genes with those of a housefly. At first, Brundle delights in his new body. Something of a lab rat himself, Brundle's reconfigured flesh gives him a host of delightful freedoms. Eventually, with his body now too new, having moved too far from the human, the results of Brundle's drunken trial turn tragic. Brundle, like Frankenstein before him, most now battle his creation for control. This time, however, the battle does not take place across the icy Arctic or among the rugged scarps that surround Frankenstein's mountain aerie. This time, the battle takes shape in one flesh as Brundle must decide whether to become something irrevocably new or remain all-too-human.

Given the dialectical heart of the tale, where Monster and Creator define each other, it is to be expected that eventually maker and made would be ensnared as one. There may be no better way to address the unbearable ties that link Frankenstein and his scion than to sheathe the adversaries in the same skin. And while it may be ventured that Dr Brundle is a closer relation to Dr Jekyll, as the scientist once again becomes his own worst enemy, such an argument is unwarranted. Brundle-Fly is no *doppelgänger*. He is not a repressed version of the self, finally free to roam at will, while the Doctor's better half is remanded to the unconscious. Mistakes, such as opting for a criminal brain or operating scientific machinery under the influence, are not evidence of hidden desires. Sadly, horrible mishaps only confirm the vulnerability and malleability of the flesh.

Cronenberg's solitary reclamation project, the rejuvenation of the archaic Doctor in a variety of contexts, serves to split his films from the main body of the genre. This move, as noted above, is something more than the means whereby Cronenberg gives his work an indelible trade mark – it is also an oppositional gesture. Yet, a proclivity for quotation is not enough to define Cronenberg's practice as unique. Cronenberg is not alone in mining the horror genre's rich archives. Nearly all contemporary work in the genre quotes *ad nauseam* from the canon. If Cronenberg's films are somehow to be marked off from other work in the field, they cannot, in any way, be distinguished solely by virtue of the fact that they make explicit reference to earlier efforts in the genre. Instead, Cronenberg's work may be distinguished by the manner in which he refers to other horror films. Cronenberg's practice of citation, unlike the work of his confederates, is resolutely anti-ironic. In comparison to the typical postmodern horror film, Cronenberg's films are positively atavistic.

The postmodern predilection for self-referentiality can be duly satisfied only by lavishing extraordinary attention on the past. Such thorough examination, an impossibly unrelenting excavation, leads to the production of an endless parade of quotations which guarantee that the past remains readily available to the present.[10] This close attention, wherein the past is obsessively scanned, is not, however, especially beneficial for those images that have come before. The ironic gulf surrounding the contemporary representation of death ensures that the voice of the past can be heard only as the object of a jeering chorus.

Unlike most forms of recycling, which work to conserve resources while shepherding value from previous creations, unrestrained self-referentiality appropriates the past solely for the cavalier pleasures of the present. In addition, not only is the past treated in a dismissive manner, consumed in supercilious witticisms, but also it is used with great avidity. Given the absolute centrality of the ironic quote in the production of postmodern horror, the past is in extraordinary demand. No other filmic gesture better demonstrates a director's irrepressible black wit, celebrates audience savvy, and, most importantly, furthers the bombast of contemporary spectacle than the ironic quote. As the prime source for the ubiquitous pointed reference of today, the past may be nearing exhaustion.

Scream (1996), the recent and enormously popular tale of malevolent killers inspired by the work of previous monsters in the genre, provides a perfect point of departure for distinguishing between Cronenberg's style of reference and that which defines the genre's present orientation to the past.[11] In *Scream*, whenever reference is made to other horror films – as it is over and again, in dialogue, *mise en scène*, camera position, score, editing, camera movement, location, plot points, sound, and so on – the reference works not as a telling allusion, but as a visual or aural quip. Cinematic citation in the contemporary horror film almost always displays cultivated expertise as a form of masquerade mastery.

The questionable value of the past is made especially evident in the opening to *Scream*. The action commences when a short-lived protagonist is given a threat paired with a punishingly tricky question relating to the identity of the killer in the first *Friday the 13th* film (1980). When Drew Barrymore, a bit of casting that is also an inside reference, gives the wrong answer, she is viciously dispatched like a sorry quiz-show contestant. She should have known better, answered the question correctly, and lived. On this territory, in a genre defined by knowing pastiche, death is a matter of trivia and a trivial matter. Safe in their superior knowledge, securely distanced from the violence before them, the audience for such displays is free to revel in having known the right answer to the fatal riddle. Under the present regime, with countless victims beaten all the colours of the rainbow, the generic representation of gory death becomes a playful game for initiates only.

The trivialisation of death through the consistently arch reference to previous work in the genre, a monstrous version of cinematic homage, reaches an even more enfeebling point near the conclusion of the film. As the bloodshed draws to an end, the killers stalk their final victims through a well-appointed suburban home. Climactic scenes from *Halloween* (1978) play on the television as the casualties mount. Within the knowing constraints of the postmodern horror film, running clips from *Halloween* is at once the basis for a terrible wager and an appeal to the collective experience of the audience – horror aficionados who draw from the same well as the onscreen slashers. Only the most confident player, the most brazen killer, runs the competition's greatest hits in conjunction with their own dirty work. References made as part of a gruesome side-by-side comparison are now acts of calculating bravado.

Whatever has come before only exists to be topped. Thus, film feeds upon film as the genre embraces the acquisitive logic of cannibalism.[12] Consumption of the past is at once an act of triumph and, oddly, deference. The subsumed text, now bested, had to have traits that made it worthy of incorporation. In following this strategy, the genre has become wholly parasitical. Now, while genre films have always relied upon other works for sustenance – genre by definition requires a large measure of interdependence – the postmodern horror film is hyper-parasitical.

Ceaseless quotation is not, in and of itself, the only practice to define the contemporary horror film. With horror's past always on tap as an endless series of punch-lines, contemporary filmmakers also create films indentured to the spectacle. Just as comic routines build to the grand finale, with careful attention paid to punctuating the act with a series of big laughs along the way, so, too, is the present-day horror film constructed to provide entertaining blasts that culminate in an epic explosion of mayhem. In capturing the escalating rhythm of the horror spectacle, Wheeler Winston Dixon writes:

> As the level of graphic specificity continues to rise in the horror film, it is not so much the text of the film that matters, but rather the certainty of fleshly mutilation, torture, dismemberment, violent death, and cruelty. Suspense and mood have, for the most part, been dispensed with. It is the transgressions upon the flesh, upon the person(s) under torture that mesmerize the audience.[13]

Note Dixon's observation that suspense and mood have been, to great degree, exiled from the horror show. Liberated from the interminable anxiety of suspense, a fearfully uneasy state built on the slow, deliberate accretion of dreadful detail and the deferral of final confirmation, the audience is also loosed from the prison of narrative coherence.

In lieu of constructing intelligible sequences which have as their cumulative effect the production of horror, the contemporary horror film now comprises loose links of self-contained horrific moments. A grab bag of unintegrated bits and bursts of shock. The audience rockets from gruesome attack to attack in films that have been stripped of the connective tissue that makes intelligible narrative possible. Furthermore – and this point cannot be underscored too often – this acceleration is accomplished for the singular purpose of allowing the horror fan release from the niceties of narrative so as to luxuriate in the carving of the flesh. A concentration on cruel affect, wherein the text of the film is sacrificed together with the bleeding victim, leads to the double end of narrative and bodily integrity.

Contemporary narrative incoherence is then predicated and furthered by a close familiarity with previous productions. Through the production and recognition of winking quotation, audience and filmmakers alike certify their reciprocal fitness. In doing so, in ceaselessly talking back and forth across the fourth wall, narrative integrity is, at least for the duration, severely compromised. Not only are individual films corrupted, but the genre as a whole is sapped by doing duty as a handy, but shrinking, reservoir. Quotation also furthers the production of incoherent filmmaking by playing a crucial function in the success of spectacle. Spectacular death shots require a baseline against which to measure the calibre of the latest special effect. Without reference to the past, without pointing to that which has been surpassed, the grotesque depths of the spectacle cannot be apprehended. In a curious reversal, the better known the past, the more frequently it is dragged back onto the present stage, the more anaemic and depleted it becomes. The vampiric, intertextual feint, the sneering look back, is now a defining moment in the genre. When it comes to genre filmmaking, Santayana had it all wrong: those who know the past are condemned to repeat it.

At this point, given Cronenberg's celebrated status as one of the pioneers of the gore film, distinguishing his issue from other work in the genre appears to be turning into a matter of rocks and glasshouses. The honorific "Baron of Blood" was not, after all, awarded for singularly scrupulous delicacy in service to the narrative. When people recall *Scanners*, it is the film where the guy's head blows apart; *The Fly* remains alive in popular memory for housing the crowded medicine cabinet where the beleaguered Brundle-Fly stores his sloughed-off body parts: ears, fingernails and what certainly looks like a vestigial penis; *The Brood* remains memorable for Samantha Eggar's all-consuming dedication to the successful parturition of her offspring. These showpieces, and many more, are the equal of any other spectacular moment in the contemporary horror film. And, in fashioning gloriously repugnant spectacle, Cronenberg's most memorable sequences are of a piece with the gruesome tableaux created by his colleagues. All – and this is a defining characteristic for directors of postmodern horror films – prefer to show, rather than to tell.[14]

Similarly, if the previous discussion of Cronenberg's affection for the story of Frankenstein is at all justified, and he has told the same tale time after time, just how much can Cronenberg's work have strayed from the dominant practices in the genre? It is not as if his work, leaving aside the enormous inheritance from Shelley's original prototype, springs *sui generis* to the screen. *Shivers* makes regular and explicit reference to the zombie hordes celebrated in Romero's "living dead" films. Romero's influence is also easily detectable in *Rabid*. In *The Brood*, the key played by colour in the apperception of evil comes directly from Nicolas Roeg's classic *Don't Look Now* (1973). A crucial sequence in *Scanners*, involving a filling station and the imminent threat of explosion, bears more than a passing resemblance to a similar scene in Hitchcock's *The Birds* (1963) – and so on; the work does not exist without antecedent or referent.

The special effects for which Cronenberg's films are especially well-regarded by fans – the bladders that make the skin crawl (literally), to the grander appliances that turn bellies into gaping VCRs and men into flies – are not presented as if they have no connection with other work in the genre. Special effects in general, but particularly in horror, take to the screen as part of an arms race. Special effects not only play a role in the story, and in much contemporary horror special effects *are* the story, but also are the tools of brinkmanship. Like the winning wager in *Scream*, special effects are a challenge to others in the field. It would be an impossible mistake to imagine that, in this regard, as with the question of narrative sensitivity, early Cronenberg films are celebrated for their light touch and the director's Luddite indifference to the machinery of special effects.

Finally, if stunt-casting is to be questioned as a form of embodied sampling, what is to be made of the presence of Barbara Steele and Marilyn Chambers in Cronenberg's first two commercial features?[15] Steele, who reigned as the scream queen of horror for the generation between Janet Leigh and Jamie Lee, has a small role in *Shivers* as an amorous predator. An otherwise unremarkable part, too small to bear notice, becomes worth mentioning only because Steele plays the role. The part, only a brief cameo, works to reference Steele's contribution to the genre and set up a beneficial tension between *Shivers* and the films in Steele's curriculum vitae. After notable success in *Behind the Green Door* (1972) and other X-rated capers, Chambers' initial attempt to enter the mainstream, in *Rabid*, foregrounds horror's relatively recent move, at the time, towards greater sexual explicitness. Casting Chambers and giving her an armpit equipped with a limber sphincter, ringing a penis-like needle with which to attack her prey, was a signal Cronenberg triumph. What ordinary lamia could compete with a genuine adult film actress so armed?

These disclaimers, while supportable, are not sufficient reason to return Cronenberg's work to the fold. Firstly, the assertion that Cronenberg's work is not of a piece with the genre does not mean that he exists entirely apart from the genre. Genre work is, by definition, impure. The fact that Cronenberg's work is tagged with a genre designation guarantees that the films will carry traces of mutual influence. Cronenberg's work must, of necessity, overlap with other productions in the genre, but having some traits in common does not mean that the works have all traits in common. In short, genres are not subject to the law of the excluded middle: they are never either this or that. They are muddled, heterogenous creatures, and, as such, may be in and out of sync with any of the dominant codes in play at a particular moment. Sharing some common traits with other contemporary films is the minimum entrance requirement for establishing Cronenberg's group membership. Beyond that, his place is still at the margins.[16]

Of all the requisite gestures that Cronenberg makes in sympathy with mainstream practice, it is his reliance on elaborate special effects that is most in keeping with the principal conventions of the field. This fraternal trait, above all other community characteristics, makes it difficult to see where Cronenberg leaves off from dominant practice. Moving beyond the florid spectacle in Cronenberg's early films is not at all easy to do. His most flamboyant images remain shockingly memorable years after their original release, so that, in a genre presently dominated by the visual eruption of the body, it makes common sense to conflate Cronenberg's blistering images with all the defining moments of contemporary screen excess. Yet, while it is understandably easy to overlook what Cronenberg fails to share with the genre, as bodies splatter across the screen in endlessly inventive paroxysms of gore, it is crucial to recognise that Cronenberg's films, while bursting with clotted flesh, do not acquiesce to the genre's system-wide collapse into parody. The spectacle is yoked in service to something other than a parodic destruction of the body, the gutting of the genre's past and narrative incoherence.

Laying out the ground which Cronenberg covers, as well as marking the lines he does not cross, entails being sharply critical of the postmodern turn taken by the genre. This critique is engendered by a sense of loss. Following William Paul, who observes that, as the genre wolfs down its own tail, "with each new work daring to see how much more it may dare, then the mode itself must ultimately be self-consuming, reaching a point...in which its challenges are so excessive they become self-defeating",[17] the sense of loss comes with the diminishment of narrative possibility. There seem to be no new tales to tale and precious little that has not already been done to the twice- or thrice-told tale.

The compensation for this total write-off is that contemporary horror films, while they blaze through the past with ferocious relish, do so in a spirit of great, bumptious exuberance. Contemporary horror films can be extraordinarily fun, if you are in on the joke, as even the lowest of low-budget horror films taunts and vandalises its subject in high spirits. The sting of death, the cessation of the genre, is then tempered by an anarchic good humour that gives the potlatch a jubilant air of celebration. Unfortunately, Cronenberg's films – and this is true even of the later works – are not fun.

Cronenberg simply refuses to play. Where his work is most distinctly not of the genre, in tight combination with his refusal to parody elements of the genre's past, is in the near complete absence of humour in all his early films. There are very few, if any, moments of the slightest levity in these works. Cronenberg's films are resolutely sombre, even dour, in temperament; they are grim. Here, therefore, is the final line across which Cronenberg's horror films never stray.

Devoid of humour, acutely grave, Cronenberg's films stand well apart from the genre's standard issue. Disdaining more than a modicum of self-referentiality, refusing parody outright, and sober in the production of spectacle, Cronenberg's work represents a stolid inversion of all the dominant threads that define the genre to this date.

The latter half of this essay has argued an almost entirely negative definition of Cronenberg's work. His place in the genre is, however, framed by more than a series of resistant gestures. Instead of arguing what the work is not, what can be said for what the work does, as opposed to what it avoids doing? What else fills the space Cronenberg has cleared for the reclaimed scientist? Moreover, what diegematical duties is the scientist, the direct kin of Dr Frankenstein, expected to perform?

Firstly, while there is always a scientist in a Cronenberg horror show, he, solely in his capacity as a scientist, is never the predominant focus of the narrative. Instead, the scientist is the narrative catalyst. The scientist must be there to set the narrative off, but we are not singularly preoccupied with his actions as a matter of scientific investigation. Instead, the scientist acts as an alchemical agent responsible for breaking humans out of their current stasis. The effects of his work on either himself, the people around him, or both are then the dominant focus of the film. In this fashion, the narrative needs Dr Brundle to engineer the trauma, and Seth Brundle, the inadvertent victim of his own folly, to embody horror. Once the problem of how to re-engineer the body has been dispatched, often cursorily, the attention of the narrative fixes upon the incarnate horror of what Frankenstein's work has wrought. In short, what is bred in the lab holds no interest until it is out in the flesh. And, unlike much contemporary parody, where all that matters is how death looks, Cronenberg's spectacle is securely fastened to the ramifications of body trauma.

The Cronenberg scientist is always animated by the desire to overcome human inertia or stasis. Stasis, a term with a dual inflection – it signifies a balanced state, as well as a pathological blockage – vexes the scientist. We humans have, for any number of reasons, failed to develop with due alacrity. Stalled on the evolutionary ladder, bound to an outdated mode of being, humans need a leg up, and science intends to help. In each of the early films, horror erupts as an unintended consequence of the escape from stasis. Being released, the flesh which succeeds the old proves too much to bear, and chaos ensues.

For those not partial to Cronenberg, the oft-demonstrated link between any attempt to speed up human progress and cataclysmic failure offers more than enough evidence to indict him as a reactionary.[18] Through these eyes, Cronenberg argues that we must suffer the world as it is, or, should improvement be ventured, an already harsh world will become even more difficult to endure. An inordinately bleak future does not warrant trifling with the body and the world it is so well-shaped to fit. The solution to any act of rash hubris that would threaten the status quo, any reconformation of the flesh, seems to require casting a gimlet eye towards all that even hints of troubling social equilibrium.

Yet, while there is ample evidence to suggest that his critics are correct, as the films do end quite badly, a proviso is in order. As Judith Halberstam notes: "it is not always so simple to tell whether the presence of Gothic registers a conservative or a progressive move".[19] In making a mess of the body, the monstrous also makes a mess of signification, and drawing a stable conclusion from disturbed imagery is not an easy task. While Cronenberg's embodied horrors do, most often, seem to leave his protagonists in a much worse shape than when they started, as the new flesh shreds the old, it might not make good sense to dismiss Cronenberg's experiments with the flesh as vivid nightmares leaning towards the Right.

The problem with the position that points to Cronenberg as a guardian for homoeostasis is that his films are just as troubled by things as they are as by things as they could be. Stasis can be a pathological condition just as easily as it can be a refuge. In Cronenberg's horror films, the world as it is, the way things are, does not seem altogether worthy of preservation. In *Shivers*, the Starliner Towers, a yuppie-preserve stationed far apart from all the trials of modern life, while better appointed than most housing projects, is just as much in need of urban renewal. The families of *The Brood* are drunken enclaves incapable of offering anyone safe passage. In this world, and not the time of the new flesh, mothers and fathers devour their young. The cities of *Scanners* and *Videodrome* are run like pricey malls. Anyone not likely to be warmly welcomed at The Gap or Benetton is driven to the margins. In *The Dead Zone*, a coma has unbeatable advantages over the world of friends, family and the workplace. Maybe Cronenberg is a conservative at heart, but, if so, it would be hard to identify any latter-day conservative tougher on things as they are than the author of these films. There are no social structures in Cronenberg's films that would not benefit from more than a little social engineering. In sum, none of the films is absent of a strong critique of the contemporary organisation of social space and the slots we are allotted within it. Any level of the collective, whether it is family, social circle, corporation, Party or state, gets its pound of flesh. It may not collect with the spectacular style that the monstrous does, but the body pays before and after science.

Holding Cronenberg out as a progressive social critic, against those who reject the films in good conscience as politically offensive, is also inadvisable. Certainly the films offer a dim view of the institutions and groups who determine social roles and provide ersatz solace for the pain of living out our lot, but this must be measured against the unbelievable pain and blood that follow any attempt to rework the social fabric. Cronenberg's protagonists, champions of the new flesh, are, after all, not so confident. They commit suicide in *Rabid* and *Videodrome*; they beg to be euthanatised in *The Fly*; they are swallowed up by the horde in *Shivers*; or they are condemned, in *The Brood*, to carry the plague forward.[20]

The real horror of Cronenberg's early work comes from having to oscillate between the degradations of everyday life and the damnation that the new flesh almost certainly holds. His protagonists have no good choices. All they have is the courage to act. In most other contemporary horror films, characters are not presented with even these untenable options. They are there to die spectacular deaths alongside the expired conventions of the genre. When these parodies are expertly constructed, the lettered *cognoscente* can enjoy the thrill of fear. Cronenberg goes further: he gives us terror and sympathy in narratives that are all-too-coherent. Cronenberg has proven, against all the dominant practices of postmodern horror, that "tragic fear and pity may be aroused by the Spectacle".[21]

Notes

[1] I first saw *Dead Ringers* (1988), Cronenberg's initial move away from the genre, in a second-run cinema that typically runs horror movies and action pictures. The audience did not take to the story of brotherhood, gynaecology and madness. They expected work closer in tone and imagery to Cronenberg's earlier efforts, and were exceedingly vocal in their disappointment with the aberration cast before them.

[2] There is a fascinating tale for the political economist of film in Chris Rodley (ed), *Cronenberg on Cronenberg*, revised edition (London; Boston: Faber and Faber, 1997): 36-37, 69. Cronenberg's first two commercial films were financed by Canadian government grants and a French-Canadian soft porn film distributor. Later films were underwritten by a one-time tax shelter created by Canada to encourage a national film industry. Eventually, for his final horror films, Cronenberg secured financing in Hollywood.

[3] David Lynch did just the same. He broke in with a low-budget, arty gore film, *Eraserhead* (1977), and graduated to making films with both Dino De Laurentiis and Brooks: Laurentiis produced *Blue Velvet* (1986) and *Dune* (1984), and Mel Brooks' production company financed *The Elephant Man* (1980).

[4]   The "Baron of Blood" sobriquet comes from the jacket copy of an early career retrospective: Piers Handling (ed), *The Shape of Rage: The Films of David Cronenberg* (Toronto: General Publishing Co.; New York: New York Zoetrope; 1983). The more estimable description of Cronenberg as a filmmaker in global good repute comes from the back cover of a recent work, *Cronenberg on Cronenberg*, which encompasses both poles of his career.

[5]   Vivian Sobchack, *Screening Space: The American Science Fiction Film*, second edition (New York: Ungar, 1987): 38-39.

[6]   Andrew Tudor, *Monsters and Mad Scientists: A Cultural History of the Horror Movie* (Oxford: Basil Blackwell, 1989): 133.

[7]   Ibid: 133-158.

[8]   Ibid: 145.

[9]   Raymond Williams, *The Sociology of Culture* (New York: Schocken Books, 1982): 204. Here the term "oppositional" is not used with all the political force that Williams intends for it. "Oppositional" is used only to underline just how out of step Cronenberg's directorial choices are with those made in the genre as a whole. At this point, Cronenberg resists the pull of the genre and not the desires of the state. In addition, it would be inappropriate, without significantly more argument, to term Cronenberg's films "ideologically oppositional", as many critics and film scholars feel Cronenberg's early films are both reactionary and cruelly misogynistic.

[10]   An analogous cultural practice can be heard at work in rap and dance music. Here, through sampling, musical bits are gleamed from the past and reworked into contemporary hits. Generally, whatever their sound sense in previous incarnations, samples must now be heard in harness to the perfect beat. Deft textual references also serve as an index of the mixmaster's skills, and as a rigorous test of audience sophistication. The analogy collapses when we consider how each genre samples. Contemporary horror is anthropophagous – it samples only itself. Currently, pop music is open to anything.

[11]   *Scream* serves because it is of recent vintage. Almost any notable horror film made over the last few decades would also serve. See *The Evil Dead* (1983) and its sequels, the adventures of Freddy, Jason or Chucky; the later films in *The Night of the Living Dead* (1968) or *The Texas Chain Saw Massacre* (1974) series; Mario Bava's last works; and so on.

[12]   Once one starts substantiating the gluttonous postmodern appetite, there is no way to break the chain of endless cross-reference. The nod which *Scream* makes to the past engages a near-infinite train of allusions. In *Halloween*, the hapless doctor played by Donald Pleasence is named after John Gavin's character, Loomis, in *Psycho* (1960). To complicate matters further, Jamie Lee Curtis, the star of *Halloween*, is the daughter of Janet Leigh, who plays the ill-fated character in *Psycho*. In addition, all throughout *Halloween* the television plays scenes from *Forbidden Planet* (1956) and Howard Hawks' original version of *The Thing* (1951). The director of

Halloween, John Carpenter, would later remake *The Thing* in 1982. In 1998, to constrict a tight circle even closer, Jamie Lee Curtis and her mother appeared together in *Halloween H20: Twenty Years Later.*

[13] Wheeler Winston Dixon, *The Transparency of Spectacle: Meditations on the Moving Image* (Albany: State University of New York Press, 1998): 112.

[14] Isabel Cristina Pinedo, *Recreational Terror: Women and the Pleasures of Horror Film Viewing* (Albany: State University of New York Press, 1997): 18. Pinedo also provides a more detailed discussion of the formal features common to postmodern horror.

[15] The casting of new wave icon Deborah Harry in *Videodrome* could also be questioned. While Harry's offscreen image as *femme fatale* may have enhanced the credibility of her performance as a cool, sexual adventurer, it is unlikely, given the legion of bad performances turned in by moonlighting rock stars, that good faith in her thespian talents clinched the role.

[16] Cronenberg's early films were constrained not only by the genre, but also by very low budgets and the necessity to turn in a profit if subsequent projects were to be realised. Under these circumstances, capitulation to the market is not uncommon. If the films are tainted, if they have moments that are other-directed, little more has been established than the plain truth that they are products of a consumer culture.

[17] William Paul, *Laughing Screaming: Modern Hollywood Horror and Comedy* (New York: Columbia University Press, 1994): 429-430.

[18] Robin Wood, "Cronenberg: A Dissenting View", in Handling (ed): 115-135.

[19] Judith Halberstam, *Skin Shows: Gothic Horror and the Technology of Monsters* (Durham; London: Duke University Press, 1995): 23.

[20] *Scanners*, the lone hold-out, may offer hope. The promise of new world can, however, only be purchased after the protagonist commits an inverted – from the inside out – act of cannibalistic fratricide.

[21] Aristotle, *Poetics*, translated by Ingram Bywater (New York: The Modern Library, 1954): 239. To be true to Aristotle, while fear and pity may be aroused through Spectacle, he finds that doing so without appeal to Spectacle is the better aesthetic choice.

(A)moral monstrosity

Murray Smith

It's not disgust. It's fascination, but it's also a willingness to look at what is really there without flinching, and to say *this* is what we're made of, as strange and as disgusting as it might seem at times. I'm really saying that the inside of the body must have a completely different aesthctic...I could conceive of a beauty contest for the inside of the human body.[1]

If [audiences] try to apply the normal movie psychology to these characters, they're doomed to be confused, baffled and perhaps frustrated by *Crash*. Where are the sympathetic characters? Where is this recognizable domesticity that is then destroyed by Vaughan?[2]

Sympathy for black slime

Bites: And who might you be, sir?
Treves: Just one of the curious. I'd like to scc it.
        (*The Elephant Man* [1980])

From *Shivers* (1976) to *Crash* (1996), the intersection of sex and horror is a subject to which David Cronenberg has returned again and again – although not without variation, as I hope to demonstrate in the course of this essay. *Shivers*, Cronenberg's first full-length feature film, tells the story of an ultra-modern apartment complex whose inhabitants become infected with a parasite which acts, in the words of the scientist who manufactures it, like a combination of a venereal disease and an aphrodisiac, precipitating all manner of familiar and unfamiliar forms of sex. Reactions to the film have fallen broadly into two groups. The first – and very critical – view of the film was voiced by the Canadian critic Robert Fulford, who railed against this "perverse, disgusting" film before it was even released.[3] A fuller expression of such a view was provided by Robin Wood in his seminal work on the contemporary horror film:

Shivers...is a film single-mindedly about sexual liberation, a prospect it views with unmitigated horror. The entire film is premised on and motivated by sexual disgust...At the same time, the film shows absolutely no feeling for traditional relationships (or for human beings, for that matter): with its unremitting ugliness and crudity, it is very rare in its achievement of *total* negation.[4]

For Wood, the film is essentially a conservative reaction to the changes wrought by the permissive society, insofar as it expresses – in his view – an unalloyed fear and hatred of the human body and human sexuality (especially unconventional sexuality). Wood justifies his reaction to the film by recourse to a general interpretive principle which he establishes for the horror film, in which he states that the "reactionary" tendency in the horror film is marked by the "presentation of the monster as totally non-human. The 'progressiveness' of the horror film depends partly on the monster's capacity to arouse sympathy; one can feel little for a mass of viscous black slime."[5]

Other critics, however, see the film very differently. According to this contrasting view, far from being simply appalled by the effects of the parasite, the film evinces a certain delight in the disruption of the pristine apartment complex and its pampered inhabitants by an uncontrollable epidemic of sexual hysteria. Cronenberg himself has noted that certain French critics "saw *Shivers* as being an attack on the bourgeois life, and bourgeois ideas of morality and sexuality. They sensed the glee with which we were tearing them apart."[6] According to this view, the film is a post-Freudian allegory concerning the way in which our libido is channelled and constrained by social and moral conventions – a view-point which certainly echoes the motivations of Dr Emil Hobbes, the inventor of the parasite, who creates it in order to liberate us from an excess of rationality ("man is an animal that thinks too much, an over-rational animal that's lost touch with its body and its instincts"). To the extent that this is true, Hobbes must be seen as the hero of the film, albeit one whose presence is almost wholly delegated to his parasitic progeny. (Hobbes himself only appears in one quite brief scene close to the beginning of the film.)

While both of these views of the film tap into aspects of its aesthetic, neither of them captures the ambivalence and complexity of *Shivers*. Robert C Soloman offers an alternative to Wood's postulate regarding the horror film, one which is useful in developing a subtler view of Cronenberg's work:

The revolting and disgusting is attractive in its own right... because it reminds us of something essential about ourselves. We live in a sanitized society, in which even criminal executions have been whittled down to a clinical, private injection...[horror reminds] us of our most basic vulnerabilities.[7]

In effect, Soloman proposes that horror arises from a particular type of *curiosity* or *fascination* about what we are and what we value.[8] From this starting-point, I would suggest that horror can be created in (at least) two basic ways. Firstly, horror can be created by counterposing what (we think) we are and what we value about being human (our capacity for emotion or complexity, for example) with its opposite, and by firmly rooting our sympathies *with* the human. Horror texts which depend on this kind of dynamic must, in various ways, be anthropocentric, unambiguously establishing the human as the centre of dramatic, moral and emotional interest. That is, our sympathies, antipathies and emotional responses are shaped by moral schemes which are unabashedly anthropocentric, according most value to whatever the particular moral scheme defines as human. The species of horror favoured by Wood is a particular version of this, where the truly valuable human qualities are found to be embodied by what *seems* – as a result of social prejudice, according to Wood's formula – to be threatening, monstrous and inhuman.

More unusually, horror can be created not only by juxtaposing the human with the "inhuman" or the "ahuman", and by shoring up our sympathetic attachment to the human, but also by asking us to adopt in some sense the *perspective* of the inhuman – the parasite's perspective, to take the case of *Shivers*. Cronenberg has described his intentions along these lines in the following way:

> With *Shivers* I'm a venereal disease having the greatest time of my life, and encouraging everybody to get into it. To take a venereal disease's point of view might be considered demonic, depending on who you are. In a way, Robert Fulford's attack on me at the time is...understandable; he was a good bourgeois, responding with horror to everything I did. He would not take the disease's point of view, not even for ninety minutes.[9]

But to what extent can this taking of the disease's "point of view" be achieved? What exactly would it mean to take the perspective of a parasite? Can the parasites see or think at all in our sense? What, after all, is it like to be a parasite? I will argue that such pathogen-perspective-taking does occur in the film, but not in the usual senses of adopting the epistemic or optical point of view of the parasite, nor by attracting our sympathy or empathy in a direct sense. Instead of pursuing these "positive" strategies, our "interest focus" is shifted towards the parasites and away from the human characters by dampening our sympathy for the human victims of the parasite.[10]

The parasites in *Shivers* are the vehicle of dehumanisation, stripping the infected characters of any kind of complexity –

emotional, rational, moral – so that they become mere sex zombies, dominated by sheer carnal appetite, like the parasites within them. Cronenberg maximises the horror here by depicting the dehumanisation of the most vulnerable and sentimentalised groups – the very young and the very old – as well as by making the spread of the parasite indiscriminate, afflicting the morally deserving and undeserving alike. But, if this were all there is to it, the film would exemplify the first of my two types of horror, building up our sympathies with the figures of humanity only then to show these figures consumed by the inhuman. *Shivers*, however, goes beyond this by flattening the contrast between the human and the inhuman in the first place. Although the film features a nominally sympathetic protagonist, it invests little energy in bringing the protagonist and his last-ditch stand against the inhuman parasites to life. The film is much more interested in the rippling and undulating of human torsos as parasites stir beneath the skin (see illustrations), and the perverse, driven behaviour of the infected, than in expressing the alarm and horror of those who remain uninfected. Adopting the "perspective" of the parasites, therefore, is less a matter of having an active sympathy for them – Wood is right about this – than of not sympathising with the human victims of the parasites, or even regarding them *as victims.*

Crash, in a sense, provides a recapitulation of this strategy. The film is not, of course, a horror or science-fiction film in a conventional sense, using imagined future technologies (like the parasites in *Shivers*) to pose new (or, for that matter, old) moral and social dilemmas. It is a film, however, which uses an alternative social backdrop (more a distillation of our own society than a futuristic one) to imagine an alternative human psychology, one which is dominated by a desire for transcendence through pain, excoriation, trauma and ultimately death – all of it mediated by the technology and materials of the car (metal, glass, rubber, foam, leather, plastic, and so on). The extent to which the film attempts to overturn our conventional psychological assumptions is revealed most clearly in the film's closing sequence, which revolves around a kind of automotive *pas de deux*, in which Ballard (James Spader) batters his wife Catherine's (Deborah Kara Unger) vehicle from behind, eventually forcing it down a freeway embankment. Rushing to her as she lays thrown from the vehicle, the following anxious exchange occurs:

Ballard: Catherine, are you alright?
Catherine: James... I don't know...
Ballard: Are you hurt?
Catherine: I think I'm alright... I think I'm alright.
Ballard: Maybe the next one, darling... Maybe the next one.

In any film operating along conventional psychological lines – which is to say, almost any other film – these lines would act as an expression of relief that Catherine has survived the crash, as if the car chase and ramming were high-risk recreational activities, such as mountain climbing, free-fall parachuting, or indeed consensual sadomasochism. But the stakes in *Crash* are much higher. Catherine's utterances express *disappointment* in the fact that she has not died in the contrived accident. Transcendence has been denied, or at least deferred. Whether we construe her statement in this way, however, is the measure of the degree to which the film has managed to take us inside this alternative psychology – to make us understand another kind of "inhuman" perspective, in which "techno-sex" enacts "a calculated refusal to see the crash partner as a human being",[11] just as the parasite reduces all humans to the status of things to-be-fucked.

Physical and moral horror

Treves: Am I a good man, or am I a bad man?
(*The Elephant Man*)

Midway between *Shivers* and *Crash*, Cronenberg made *The Fly* (1986), his most commercially successful film. It shares with *Shivers* a narrative concerning (apparent) sexual liberation through disease: in this case, a scientist accidentally triggers a mutation of his genes into those of a fly, in the course of developing a teleportation device. In the early stages of this transformation, Seth Brundle (the scientist, played by Jeff Goldblum) is filled with energy, especially sexual energy. He denounces society's "fear of the flesh" and, riding the crest of his transmogrification, declares: "I've become free, I've been released". At this point in its narrative, however, *The Fly* departs from the mix of amoral fascination and heady intoxication with the idea of a complete surrender to (or transformation of) the libido that we find in *Shivers*. In *The Fly*, the human costs of the "emancipatory" disease are dwelt upon and realised in a way that is only hinted at in *Shivers*. In this way, the film creates horror by the first of the two methods discussed earlier – by rooting our sympathies in the anthropocentric, and, above all, by engaging us *morally* – where *Shivers* cleaves to a purer fascination with its horrific subject-matter, and diminishes our sympathy for the human.

These costs are spelt out in terms of both *physical* and *moral* horror. Cronenberg is widely known as an exponent of – indeed, a virtuoso of – "body horror", and this what I have in mind in talking of physical horror, which arises out of the reduction of the human (and all its associated attributes and values) to the merely material, the merely physical. In *The Fly*, such physicality is, moreover, characterised additionally as deformed, dysfunctional or mutant, most extravagantly in the scene in which the heroine gives birth to a maggot the size of a newborn human (a fantasy, it turns out, but one which is visualised, and only retroactively revealed as a fantasy). Other examples of physical horror abound in the film: an early and striking instance is the "inverted baboon" – the baboon whose physical being is turned inside out as a result of a defective prototype of Brundle's teleportation process (see illustration). The baboon is not only reduced to a mess of bloody flesh, however, but also transformed according to the logical complement of Darwin's principle of evolution – the rapid demise of the unfittest[12] – for the baboon is utterly unsuited to survival in its new form (just as Seth will become, in his final incarnation as "Brundletelefly", crawling pitifully from the teleporter in the final scene of the film). The evocation of horror through a focus on the merely material is also adumbrated by a food motif, in which the base and potentially revolting quality of food – especially processed foods, such as a fast food cheeseburger, or a steak transported by Seth's telepods – is stressed. This motif culminates in the extraordinary scene in which Seth, now substantially transformed into "Brundlefly", demonstrates and records on video – in the manner of an educational show for children – the way in which he now, like a fly, consumes his food by vomiting an acid onto it which reduces any food to a liquid pulp. And, in an earlier scene, as Brundle and journalist-girlfriend Roni (Veronica) Quaife (Geena Davis) drive to his lab, Seth complains of motion sickness – a subtler intimation of that combination of pure materiality (in the form of vomit) and dysfunctionality (insofar as motion sickness arises from a malfunction in our sense of balance) which becomes a central motif in the film.

The physical horror of deformed and dysfunctional materiality is related to another bodily fear upon which Cronenberg consistently plays in *The Fly* and elsewhere: the loss of bodily integrity (wholeness, oneness, unity). The baboon cannot survive for long because its skin is now *inside* its raw, open flesh. Later in the film, human flesh is torn apart to expose the interior tissues of the body, first when an arm wrestler's arm is broken, a shard of bone protruding through the skin (see illustration), and later when Brundlefly vomits acid over the hand and foot of Stathis Borans (John Getz), Roni's boss, during the film's climax (see illustrations). But this loss of bodily integrity is played up above all in Brundle's disintegration, as his teeth, fingernails and external organs start to fall off, his entire body oozing pus and exuding slime. (Later in the film, Seth gathers together these discarded body parts, dubbing them the "Brundle Museum of Natural History".) The dissolution of his body into this organic "goop" is highlighted by its contrast with the hard, clean edges of machine technology – as, for example, when a handful of teeth and a mouthful of blood dribble from Brundle's mouth onto his computer keyboard.

This contrast between "hard" and "soft" animates almost all of Cronenberg's work. His devotion to revealing the soft, pulsating innards of humans is obvious, whether this takes the rudimentary form of guts spilling out (*Videodrome* [1982]) and heads exploding (*Scanners* [1981]), or the more elaborate opportunities provided by the appearance of new orifices on the stomach (*Videodrome*) or prehensile organs in the armpit (*Rabid* [1977]). What is less obvious is the consistently "hard" backdrop to these exposures of the inner body, manifested in locations dominated by anonymous metal-and-glass buildings (*Crimes of the Future* [1970], *Shivers*, *Crash*) and metallic inventions (*The Fly*), all of this illuminated by an even, cool lighting which usually eschews pronounced chiaroscuro effects. The credit sequence of *The Fly* provides another variation on this theme: a seething but indefinable mass, which seems to have a queasily organic quality – like a microscopic close-up of some larvae or parasite – turns out to be nothing more than an electronically-treated view of the participants of a scientific convention milling around in another of Cronenberg's antiseptic, corporate buildings. *Crash* might be seen as the apotheosis of this interplay, as it focuses on the collision of flesh with the unyielding materials of car culture. This culture is given expression through not only the setting, props and lighting in the film, but also the instrumentation of the score, pervaded by the steely timbre of the electric guitar). The collision of the hard and the soft is manifested in the film not only through the car crashes, but also, for example, through the steering wheel tattoo on Vaughan's (Elias Koteas) chest, and Gabrielle's (Rosanna Arquette) leg braces, pinching flesh and leather. It is no coincidence that the title of William Burroughs' second novel – *The Soft Machine* (1961) – comes to mind in relation to Cronenberg's iconography, although the conjunction of "softness" and "machinery" in Cronenberg differs somewhat from its combination in Burroughs. For Burroughs, the organic can be perceived as a kind of mechanism or machine, while for Cronenberg the convergence of machine technology and the human body only seems to highlight the differences between the two.

There is, however, another form of horror present in the film, just as disturbing and at least as significant, but perhaps less readily identified than physical horror. I have in mind what I will call *moral horror*, which the film imbricates and "interdefines" with the physical horror discussed so far. Initially, this moral horror is dramatised around the figure of Stathis Borans. Stathis is not only Roni's boss – the editor of the science journal, *Particle*, for which she writes – but also an ex-lover. From the moment that Roni becomes involved with Seth, Stathis adopts a proprietorial and possessive attitude towards her, even as he appeals to the rhetoric of "free love". He tells her when and where she is "allowed" to see Seth; he lets himself into Roni's apartment without her knowledge, using a set of keys he has retained from their days as lovers; and he takes a shower in her apartment, as if marking his territory. When Stathis realises that the relationship between Seth and Roni has blossomed into a full-blown romance, he flies into an aggressive, jealous rage. For the most part, however, there is nothing *physically* threatening or horrific about his behaviour towards Roni. Instead, he taunts and cajoles her with remarks such as: "Do I have permission to claim your body when this is all over?" and "What about sex? I'm not saying love or affection. Just stress-releasing sex, you and me?".

This latter question earns the rejoinder "You're disgusting" from Roni. It is no coincidence that Roni appeals here to the language of horror (which is routinely discussed in terms of revulsion, disgust and loathing), for Stathis' behaviour towards her represents a parallel moral threat to those we have examined in the physical sphere. He acts as if she had no desires, feelings or thoughts of her own, as if she had no autonomy. In short, Stathis acts as if Roni were *just a body* – once again, a merely physical thing – rather than a *person* possessed of all the dispositional attributes and moral rights we ascribe to persons.[13]

As the film develops, the locus of this moral monstrosity shifts from Stathis to Seth (the connection between the two characters is underlined by their shared initials, SB). As Seth's physical transformation into the fly progresses, so *his* status as a person is gradually eroded. This first becomes apparent in his attitude towards sex. Believing himself to have been "cleansed" and renewed by the experience of teleportation, Seth finds that he has hitherto unknown levels of strength, stamina and libido. Here the sex motif and the aforementioned food motif intersect as kindred manifestations of obsessive carnal appetite. Seth's diet becomes comprised mostly of sugar and other energy-boosting foods. Picking up on and mimicking Seth's new cast of mind, Roni playfully bites him while making love, saying: "I just want to eat you up...it's the flesh, it just makes you crazy". Ironically, in saying this she adumbrates the way in which Seth will quickly come to see her as little more than matter, as grist for both his lust and his teleporter. Frustrated by Roni's sexual and physical exhaustion, Seth urges her to undergo the teleportation process, on the assumption that this will "rejuvenate" Roni as it has supercharged Seth. (This gesture is repeated in the final scene of the film, in which Brundlefly tries to teleport Roni against her will.) Sensing, however, that Seth has been damaged rather than improved by the teleportation, she recoils at the suggestion that she, too, should subject herself to the process. Seth's behaviour now starts to resemble Stathis': angered by Roni's refusal to comply with his wishes, he throws her out of his lab, and picks up a woman from a bar. In addition to sating his sexual mania, Seth plans to use her as his next experimental subject for teleportation.

Once Seth realises what is happening to him, his morally monstrous behaviour subsides – but only for so long. As the mutation takes an ever-tighter grip on his body, he begins to *embrace* his new, fly-like being; he talks of the disease as "a disease with a purpose... maybe not such a bad disease after all". He sums up the new attitudes which go with his new condition in a speech on "insect politics": insects, he tells us, are "brutal" and lack all "compassion". Brundlefly demonstrates just this point as he abducts Roni from hospital, disregarding her desire for an abortion, so that he can save his child-to-be. And, in the climactic scene, Brundlefly attempts to "splice" Roni with himself in the hope – paradoxically – of restoring his rapidly disappearing humanity. Thus, Brundlefly exhibits the same disregard for Roni's personhood as does Stathis – although Brundlefly's morally monstrous actions are writ large and conjoined with the physical horror of his metamorphosis. Physical and moral horror compound one another as Seth's loss of control over his body (as a result of disease) is echoed by Roni's loss of control over her body (as a result of Seth's denial of her autonomy).

Seth's characterisation of the "disease" as "purposeful" captures not only the telos of his mutation, but points to an idea that informs almost the whole of Cronenberg's œuvre: the notion that disease, far from being a threat to organic processes (sex, ageing, digestion), is the *model* of them. The notion is handled, however, quite differently in *The Fly* and *Shivers*. When *Shivers* reaches the point in its narrative when the changes effected by the purposeful disease start to raise moral questions, the film plays down the moral dimension for the sake of an amoral fascination with the process of physical transformation and dehumanisation, and an absurdist mockery of bourgeois order and sexual propriety. In the case of *The Fly*, by contrast, physical and moral horror are accentuated and made to converge. This process reaches its apogee in the final scene of the film, as the fly's anatomy bursts out from within Seth's human frame at the very moment that he forces Roni into the telepod.

The contrast between the two films can be seen most clearly in their respective placing of humour and of romance, and in their very different endings. The romance in *Shivers*, between the doctor and a nurse, is hardly developed at all. In contrast, the first third of *The Fly* gives much of its attention to the developing romance between Roni and Seth, compellingly embodied in the performances of (and chemistry between) Geena Davis and Jeff Goldblum (real-life lovers at the time). The romance between Seth and Roni and the humour of the film are closely related, insofar as their relationship is characterised by playfulness and wit. The very first scene of the film, where the two of them meet at a science convention, shows them verbally sparring with one another in a manner redolent of the screwball couple. Upon first taking Roni back to his loft-apartment-laboratory, Seth teases her by vamping a mock-horror motif on a piano, self-consciously playing up the stereotype of the mad scientist, the isolated, eccentric geek with evil designs on her.[14] This kind of humour becomes more poignant as the film and the disease progress, setting into relief both Seth's physical degeneration and the catastrophic impact of his transformation on the romance. In one quite wrenching scene, Roni returns to Seth four weeks after leaving him, only to discover an ageing, stooped, whispering cripple in place of the physically robust and exuberant man with whom she had fallen in love. At the end of this scene, as Seth describes the progress of the disease, he vomits on a doughnut – in the manner of a fly breaking down food into a pulp – and quips in embarrassment, "Oh, that's disgusting" (see illustration). A similar event occurs later when Seth – Brundlefly – jokes about the "Brundle Museum of Natural History" to Roni. Grotesquely humorous as these moments are, they are more than merely comic. Seth's droll remarks are evidence of the *persistence* of his character in spite of his ravaged, superating body – evidence of his remaining humanity, even as the fly's physiognomy overwhelms his human form. The emotional tenor of the doughnut incident is also complicated by a reaction shot of Roni, exhibiting both physical revulsion *and* an appalled, tragic recognition of the fate that has overtaken both Seth and the life-affirming relationship they once had. This kind of exchange and, in particular, reaction shots of a distressed Roni, caught between a realisation of what Seth has become and the memory of what he so recently was, recur throughout the second half of the film. Moreover, the film draws here on the associations of the Beauty and the Beast myth, of an unbridgeable gap between lover and loved, and of an excruciating discrepancy between outer, physical ugliness and inner "beauty of feeling".[15]

The loss and destruction of this romance play an important role in the horrific climax of the film. Both the sense of loss and the sense of horror are made palpable for us by the emotionally saturated quality of the final scene, and, in particular, through the empathic cues within the scene – most obviously Davis' grief-stricken facial and vocal expressions, and perhaps even the doleful eyes of what has now become "Brundletelefly", the last vestige of human form "it" possesses (insofar as the eyes are still *expressive*).[16] And Brundletelefly's final gesture – lifting Roni's gun to its head in order to communicate a desire to be put out of its deformed and dysfunctional existence – is a morally redemptive gesture which confirms a shred of humanity and *selflessness* still left within it: a shred of Seth, as it were. In all these ways, *The Fly* emphasises the anthropomorphic, the emotional and the moral, in contrast to the suppression of these elements in *Shivers*. Indeed, one measure of the film's commitment to these traditional sources of dramatic interest is its kinship with Aristotelian tragedy – for what is the film if not the depiction of a fundamentally good man, undermined by the fatal flaw of scientific hubris, whose downfall evokes in us not only horror and revulsion, but also pity and fear?[17]

Fly fucking

The reader may have noticed that I have managed to discuss Cronenberg's films without reference to castration anxiety or abjection, in spite of the fact that they are not only horror films, but also *about* sex to a considerable degree. I do not wish to rule out the possibility that such psychoanalytic notions can make, or indeed have made, a contribution to our understanding of horror.[18] I do challenge, however, the assumption that psychoanalysis *must* form the basis of an account of horror, as has been argued on many occasions. In my remarks above, I discussed certain fears and fascinations which horror – or many horror films – trade upon: loss of bodily integrity, for example. To this one might add the fears of loss of vision and loss of motor control.[19] I am well aware that some of these phenomena crop up in psychoanalytic accounts of horror, but I see no compelling reason to see them as necessarily, or solely, rooted in infantile traumas. And I would add that one cannot simply adduce the pervasiveness of Freudian imagery in horror films as evidence of the accuracy of Freudian and other psychoanalytic theories. This argument is entirely circular, and no more persuasive than arguing that the pervasive presence of Christian imagery in horror films is evidence of the existence of God or Satan.

One of the major alternatives to psychoanalytic approaches to horror in recent years has been Noël Carroll's ambitious and thought-provoking *The Philosophy of Horror*. Carroll's account of horror, like my discussion of horror and, in particular, my analysis of *Shivers*, depends crucially on the notions of curiosity and fascination. At the risk of indulging in what the Danes oddly enough call "fly fucking",[20] I want to underline the difference between Carroll's use of these terms and my own. Carroll's account of horror is twofold, incorporating both a "universal" and a more modest, but still very broad, "general" hypothesis. The "universal" thesis – universal because Carroll claims that it applies to all manifestations of "art-horror"[21] – maintains that we find monsters and the monstrous at once disgusting and fascinating, both emotions arising from the fact that monstrosity (for Carroll) is rooted in categorical confusions. The "general" thesis, meanwhile, argues that many (if not all) horror fictions are structured by a "drama of disclosure", in which the enigma posed by the impossible entity – the monster – is gradually revealed, investigated and resolved. This is Carroll's most radical proposal, insofar as it explains the "paradox of horror" – the fact that consumers of horror gain pleasure from that which horrifies and disgusts them – by locating the explanation in the narrative structure in which the horror arises, rather than in the horror *per se*. Carroll quotes a particularly felicitous passage from the 18th-century aestheticians J and A L Aikin in support of the "general" thesis: "We rather chuse to suffer the smart pang of a violent emotion than the uneasy craving of an unsatisfied desire".[22] In other words, horror is the "price to be paid"[23] in the horror genre for the fulfilment of narrative curiosity.

Some critics, including Soloman, have noted that this seems to sidestep the specificity of horror.[24] However, Carroll goes to some lengths to anticipate and neutralise this objection. It is important to recognise how his two theses – universal and general – are skilfully interlinked in Carroll's argument: the (universal) fascination with, and curiosity in, the horrific "receive[s] especial amplification" in the widespread ("general") "narratives of disclosure and discovery".[25] It is fair to say, however, that pride of place in Carroll's account goes to the general, rather than the universal, thesis – in spite of the fact that, by definition, the universal is the more comprehensive thesis. The sense that the general thesis is favoured by Carroll arises from the fact that it is introduced first and as the major plank in his solution to the paradox of horror, and from the fact that he seems a little disdainful of "art-horror" which seems to depend little on narrative disclosure and greatly on sheer horrified fascination.[26] The real key to the disagreement between Carroll and Soloman lies in this area, and, in particular, hinges on the question of how the fascination and disgust provoked by the horrific relate to one another. Carroll canvases two possibilities: the two emotions are either "coexistent" or "integrated". In the first case, the categorical confusions and violations at the heart of horror evoke two distinct emotions, with the positive emotion (fascination) sufficiently outweighing the negative emotion (disgust) such that our interest is maintained. In the second case, it is the *disgust itself* which gives rise to pleasurable fascination: diminish the disgust and our curiosity is curtailed. It is in this sense that the two states are integrated. For Carroll, the two emotions are coexistent; that is why he can say that horror is the "price to be paid" for curiosity – a negative cost, rather than a positive, enabling condition. In my view – as in Soloman's and, I would argue, Cronenberg's – the two emotions are integrated. While Carroll is adamant that we do not "crave disgust", we may recall that, for Soloman, the "revolting and disgusting is attractive in its own right".[27] In the account I have adumbrated here, the horrific phenomenon is the principal object of our interest and attention. This redefines Carroll's universal thesis along integrationist lines, and significantly shifts the balance of explanatory weight away from the general and towards the universal principle. The curiosity at stake here is, precisely, what is often called "morbid curiosity" – although one need not accept the implication in this phrase that such curiosity is necessarily pathological. Curiosity in the disgusting and the monstrous is the underlying well-spring of "art-horror", no matter how that curiosity is then shaped by narrative and moral currents which, as my discussions of *Shivers* and *The Fly* demonstrate, may flow in very diverse directions.

Notes

[1]   David Cronenberg, quoted in Anne Billson, "Cronenberg on Cronenberg: a career in stereo", *Monthly Film Bulletin* 56: 660 (January 1989): 5.

[2]   David Cronenberg, quoted in Chris Rodley (ed), *Cronenberg on Cronenberg*, revised edition (London; Boston: Faber and Faber, 1997): 194.

[3]   For Cronenberg's account of how Fulford came to see the film and his reaction to it, see Rodley: 51.

[4]   Robin Wood, "An Introduction to the American Horror Film", in Bill Nichols (ed), *Movies and Methods volume II: An Anthology* (Berkeley; Los Angeles; London: University of California Press, 1985): 216-217. Emphasis in original.

[5]   Wood: 216.

[6]   Cronenberg, quoted in Rodley: 50.

[7]   Robert C Soloman, review of Noël Carroll, *The Philosophy of Horror*, in *Philosophy and Literature* 16 (1992): 173.

[8]   I regard "curiosity" and "fascination" as closely related attitudes which typically accompany one another – when we are fascinated by something, we are usually curious about it.

[9]   Cronenberg, quoted in Rodley: 151.

[10]   A more detailed discussion of sympathy, empathy and point of view can be found in Murray Smith, *Engaging Characters: Fiction, Emotion, and the Cinema* (Oxford: Clarendon Press, 1995). A preliminary discussion of the

adoption of the "parasite's perspective" in *Shivers*, set within a broader discussion of various kinds of "perversity", can be found in my essay, "Gangsters, Cannibals, Aesthetes: or, Apparently Perverse Allegiance", in Carl Plantinga and Greg Smith (eds), *Passionate Views: Film, Cognition and Emotion* (Baltimore: Johns Hopkins University Press, 1999): 217-238. The notion of a narrative focus of "interest" – in the sense of a narrative favouring the "good" and benefit of particular figures in the narrative over others – is posited by Seymour Chatman in "Characters and Narrators: Filter, Center, Slant, and Interest-Focus", *Poetics Today* 7: 2 (1986): 189-204, reprinted in Seymour Chatman, *Coming to Terms: The Rhetoric of Narrative in Fiction and Film* (Ithaca; London: Cornell University Press, 1990): chapter 9.

[11]   Roy Grundmann, "Plight of the Crash Fest Mummies: David Cronenberg's *Crash*", *Cineaste* 22: 4 (March 1997): 27. Grundmann also notes that anal sex seems to perform a similar "dehumanising" function in the film.

[12]   Actually, "survival of the fittest" is not Darwin's phrase, but Herbert Spencer's summary description of Darwin's theory of evolution.

[13]   For more on the notion of personhood, see Smith: chapters 1 and 4.

[14]   This is the first of several nods to – or at least striking parallels with – those staples of melodramatic horror, *The Hunchback of Notre Dame* (1923) and *The Phantom of the Opera* (1925). Seth's vamping on the piano recalls the famous scene in the latter in which the Phantom tries to seduce the heroine by playing the organ. More generally, both *The Phantom of the Opera* and *The Fly* involve the seduction-abduction of a female love object by a disfigured male. In both films, the male figure tries to seduce the woman by offering her the chance to further her career (as an opera singer and a journalist, respectively). With respect to *The Hunchback of Notre Dame*, Brundlefly's visage bears more than a passing resemblance to the gnarled face of Quasimodo as played by Lon Chaney; and Brundlefly's use of the roof as a vantage point and refuge in *The Fly* surely alludes to Quasimodo's station on the battlements of the cathedral of Notre Dame. All three films allude to the myth of Beauty and the Beast – a point to which I return. Indeed, one might think of *The Fly* as an attempt to reinvent this myth for the gore-loving, post-classical, "body horror" generation.

[15]   On the notion of "inner beauty" or "beauty of soul", see Colin McGinn, *Ethics, Evil, and Fiction* (Oxford: Clarendon Press, 1997). Like David Lynch's *The Elephant Man*, *The Fly* was produced by Mel Brooks. In both cases, the support of a more mainstream production context seems to have affected the way in which each director dealt with their characteristic thematic and stylistic interests. In both cases, these interests were channelled into more traditional narrative forms and evoked more commonplace dramatic emotions. Both films evoke the pathos associated with the Beauty and the Beast myth, in which a hideously deformed character struggles to achieve or maintain a dignity that their physical being denies them (Brundle describes himself as "an insect who dreamt he was a man"). This is not to suggest that in either case the "authentic" director was somehow corrupted by a more mainstream context – the two films are among the two directors' most successful projects – but to recognise the impact that such a context is likely

to have on the characteristic style of such idiosyncratic directors.

[16]   On the significance of facial expression and empathy in film in general, see Carl Plantinga, "The Scene of Empathy and the Human Face on Film", in Plantinga and Smith (eds): 239-255; and Smith: 98-102, 159-160, 173-175.

[17]   Cynthia A Freeland has also noted the connections between the film and Aristotelian tragic form, likening Roni's role – in guiding viewer perception – to the Greek chorus. She suggests that this is symptomatic of an underlying sexism in the film, which appears to depict a strong, professional female counterpart to the male hero, but in fact makes her role entirely subordinate to the tragedy of the male figure. While I think Freeland is right on this point, she overlooks the other ways in which male sexism – in the form of both Stathis' and Seth's morally monstrous denial of her autonomy – is an explicit object of criticism in the film. See Cynthia A Freeland, "Feminist Frameworks for Horror Films", in David Bordwell and Noël Carroll (eds), *Post-Theory: Reconstructing Film Studies* (Madison; London: The University of Wisconsin Press, 1996): 211-212.

[18]   Although, with *The Fly*, as Freeland (211) argues, "[i]t is difficult to force a reading of the monstrousness [in *The Fly*] as a feminization of" the male body. Locating the source of horror in archaic male fears of feminisation is particularly associated with Barbara Creed, *The Monstrous-Feminine: Film, feminism, psychoanalysis* (London; New York: Routledge, 1993).

[19]   On the loss of control of particular bodily functions and an overall sense of integration, and the connection between such experiences and the horror film, see Torben Grodal, *Moving Pictures: A New Theory of Film Genres, Feelings, and Cognition* (Oxford: Clarendon Press, 1997): 110-111.

[20]   "Flueknepperi" ("fly fucking") translates as something like "splitting hairs".

[21]   "Art-horror" designates the emotion arising from *fictional representations* of horrific entities and events, as distinct from the horror which is a response to an actual event. See Noël Carroll, *The Philosophy of Horror: or Paradoxes of the Heart* (New York; London: Routledge, 1990): 27.

[22]   Ibid: 181, quoted from J and A L Aikin, "Of the Pleasure Derived From Objects of Terror; with Sir Bertrand, a Fragment", *Miscellaneous Pieces, in Prose* (London: [printed for J Johnson], 1773): 123.

[23]   Ibid: 184.

[24]   See Soloman: 172-173; and Daniel Shaw, "A Humean Definition of Horror: Carroll's *The Philosophy of Horror; or, Paradoxes of the Heart*", http://www.mailbase.ac.uk/lists/film-philosophy, 26 August 1997.

[25]   Carroll: 190.

[26]   Ibid: 193.

[27]   Ibid: 185; Soloman: 173.

The naked crunch: Cronenberg's homoerotic bodies

Barbara Creed

Homoerotic, homophobic, misogynist, melancholic – Cronenberg's films of the 1990s are profoundly contradictory. To some degree, they all seem to embrace the ideal of love/desire between men, yet each text can be read in Freudian terms as a "defense against a homosexual wish".[1] Much has been written on the horrific, disgusting, metamorphosing flesh of the Cronenberg world, but very little, if anything, on the homoerotic body of his increasingly bleak, closed, homosexual universe. Of all Freud's case histories, it is Schreber's story[2] that offers a number of interesting parallels with the Cronenberg narrative. In both texts we find an oscillation between male and female, an emphasis on the feminisation of the male, the prominence of surrogate figures, bodily alterations, paranoia, self-delusion, and a desire for bliss or *jouissance*.

A major difference between the two texts is the specific nature of Schreber's fantasies[3] (his belief that he could live without his vital organs – stomach, lungs, bladder, and so on), and his conviction that, if he were to save the world and "restore it to its lost state of bliss", he must be "transformed from a man into a woman".[4] While Cronenberg's characters similarly live in bizarre – sometimes paranoid – fantasy worlds, their desire to experience states of symbiotic union, bliss or transcendence is not part of a larger plan to save the world. Rather, the journey of these solitary figures is an intensely personal one – although the transformation they seek similarly involves a degree of bodily alteration and feminisation. Another major difference between the two is the emphasis on the anus in Cronenberg's texts. Anality figures at the expense of the vaginal; this trajectory is accompanied by a barely disguised, but ambivalent, wish to eliminate the (uterine) woman – although the female characters are themselves strong fascinating figures.

Seth Brundle, the human/insect from Cronenberg's cult 1986 film, *The Fly*, expresses a central desire of Cronenberg's characters – to free themselves from the "sick grey fear of the flesh". Critics point to the image of the body in Cronenberg's films in relation to the fluid nature of bodily boundaries with emphasis on the fragile limit between inside and outside, between the proper and improper body.[5] His films have explored the transformation of ordinary individuals into sex-starved zombies (*Shivers* [1976], *Rabid* [1977]), sado-masochistic addicts (*Videodrome* [1982]), libidinous insects (*The Fly*) and animalistic wombs (*The Brood* [1979]). If a dominant theme connects all these representations of Cronenberg's 1970s and 1980s films it is that of the ambiguous nature of the body in states of transformation or metamorphosis. Cronenberg's bodies are always the site of both horror and pleasure. His representation of the body in the context of abjection – that is, a body without stable boundaries – challenges phallocentric myths of the body which seek to confirm the body as a classical, discrete, harmonious form – the outer sign of our inner perfection as human beings. Cronenberg fans – myself included – take pleasure in the way in which his films deconstruct prevailing conceptions of what it means to be human. There is something delicious in viewing the disgusting images that stem from Cronenberg's in-your-face attitude towards the humanist body.[6]

In his more recent films, there is a new and compelling emphasis on the relationship between abjection, bodily borders and homoeroticism. Although these texts dwell less on images drawn from sci-fi horror – in some instances adopting an elegiac, classical mood – Cronenberg's interest in the body, transformation and abjection is still very evident. Cronenberg explores the connection between the body and homoeroticism via the permeable – rather than fixed – nature of the boundary. Eschewing the essentialist approach of gay identity politics,[7] Cronenberg is not interested in representing his queer male characters in terms of "laudatory", "positive" images. This, in itself, is a good thing. All four texts, however, are simultaneously homoerotic and homophobic. A further emblematic quality is the presence of – in Eve Kosofsky Sedgwick's terms – the workings of a "homosocial" dynamic.[8] This operates in Cronenberg's films between the male characters in situations in which male/female relationships are used to consolidate male/male relationships.

The first clear evidence of this change of direction for Cronenberg can be seen in *Dead Ringers* (1988), based on Bari Wood and Jack Geasland's book, *Twins* (1977), which drew its material from an actual event – the suicide/death of two Manhattan gynaecologists (the Marcus twins) who were identical twins, and who, like Cronenberg's male protagonists, were found dead in their apartment. Apart from a nightmare dream sequence and the murder/suicide at the end, Cronenberg's usual emphasis on horrific images of bodily transformation is largely absent from this film. In an interview he stated: "*Dead Ringers*, to me, is as close to a classical tragedy as I've come, in that it's inevitable right from the opening what the twins' destiny will be".[9]

Beverly and Elliot Mantle (both played by Jeremy Irons) are male gynaecologists who share a medical practice and their female patients. Arrogant and worldly-wise, Elliot instructs his brilliant but socially awkward twin, Beverly, in the ways of the world. When a famous actress, Claire Niveau (Geneviève Bujold), comes to the brothers' fertility clinic in the hope of finding a cure for her infertility, Beverly discovers that she is "trifurcate" – she possesses three identical entrances to the uterus. Obsessed by their own doubleness (they live as "one"), the twins are enthralled by her unique triple-headed cervix.

After having sex with Claire, Elliot passes her on to Beverly (Claire is at first unaware of the switch), who falls deeply in love with her. Beverly is fascinated by Claire's freakish reproductive system, which he describes as "fabulously rare". In a sense, the "doubled" masculine and the "triple" feminine both signify monstrous terms. Although an elegant, beautiful woman, Claire Niveau is essentially one of Cronenberg's womb monsters,[10] but her monstrous malformation is hidden from view. Cronenberg invented the idea of a trifurcate cervix to signify Claire's "fabulous" difference from other women, and to explain the source of her fascination for the twins who, until now, have remained immune to love. She signifies what Pam Cook has described as "a maternal fantasy figure"[11] – mother, lover, monster.

Unable to control his obsession with Claire and the guilt he feels at betraying Elliot, Beverly gradually descends into madness. In the final sequence, Elliot, having joined his twin in a drug-induced slide into psychosis, lies on the examination bench. Beverly cuts open his brother's stomach with a set of medieval instruments which he has had specially designed for operating on "mutant women". Lying across the mutilated body of his brother, Beverly later commits suicide. The final shot reveals the dead couple, swathed in sheets, immobile and frozen in death like an ancient classical sculpture.

On its release, *Dead Ringers* received critical acclaim, as well as a number of prestigious film awards. Viewers responded positively to its cool elegance, classical style, distanced camera, chilling narrative and seamless acting by Jeremy Irons in the two main roles. It was praised for its serious examination of a number of political and social issues such as the power of the medical profession over the female body, abuse of technology, the impossibility of relationships, and the body as a site of horror in the late-20th century. The depiction of the relationship between the Mantle twins, which explores themes of unity and wholeness, and the psychosis brought about by a fear of difference and the threat of separation, endows the horrific medical narrative with a serious classical mood. Strangely, very little critical comment has been made of the film's exploration of homoeroticism and its barely concealed confusion about the limits of representability in relation to the depiction of homosexual desire.

In Plato's *Symposium*,[12] the comic poet Aristophanes argues that men and women once enjoyed masculine and feminine natures. He draws on the notion of twins, and their separation, to offer an explanation for the origin of all forms of sexual desire: heterosexual, bisexual and homosexual. Francette Pacteau[13] draws upon Aristophanes' myth to explore the nature of androgyny. According to the myth, human beings were originally spherical creatures with two faces, four legs and four arms. Some were half-woman and half-man; some half-man and half-man; and a third was half-woman and half-woman. One day, the creatures upset Zeus who, as a punishment, split the spheres in half, causing each to wander the earth searching for its other half. Hence each of us longs for our "other half" without whom we feel incomplete.

Elliot and Beverly resemble Plato's split creatures.[14] Separated during the act of birth, the twins cling together like lovers fearful of separation. They live as if one organism – working, sleeping, thinking in unison. In *Dead Ringers*, Cronenberg's depiction of this relationship is designed to arouse our full understanding and elicit strong identification, but his dominant representation of the brothers' love for each other as conventionally perverse undermines the film's radical potential. In the film's opening sequence, the twins – as nine-year-old boys – discuss their anxiety about girls and sex. One claims to have "discovered why sex is" – that is, why humans have to engage in heterosexual mating in the first place. "It's because humans don't live underwater". Mystified, his brother asks him to explain. "Well, fish don't use sex because they just lay the eggs and fertilise them in the water. Humans can't do that because they don't live in the water. They have to internalise the water. Therefore we have sex." He concludes that, if humans propagated the species in the same way as fish, they would have "a kind of sex...where you wouldn't have to touch each other". "I like that idea", says the other twin who, in the next breath, asks his brother if he has heard of scuba diving. "Self-contained underwater breathing apparatus", comes the rapid reply – his expression conveying pleasure at the possibility of a perfectly separate, self-generating existence.

When the twins suddenly set eyes on a neighbourhood girl, they ask her to have sex with them in their "bath-tub" as an "experiment". As the camera suddenly switches to reveal the twins (identical clothes, bifocals and intent expressions) from her point of view, we cannot help concur when she yells, "Fuck off, you freaks...I know for a fact you don't even know what fuck is!". The boys conclude: "They're so different from us, and all because we don't live underwater". The next sequence cuts to the twins who are operating on a female doll, its skin peeled back and its uterus on display. "What's the diagnosis?", says one. "Inter-ovular surgery", replies the other, offering a macabre solution to their fear of sexual difference. Like Schreber, the twins yearn to achieve a state of bliss (in their case, union) through bodily transformation; in the end, they realise their aim, but only by embracing feminisation and death.

As adult men, the twins appear to have organised their lives as if "living underwater". Sealed off from the outside world in their steel and glass apartment, which is carefully lit with a bluish light in order to create a rippling watery effect, they move around like deep-sea divers swimming in unison. Their shared anxiety over the feminine is reflected in their chosen careers – as gynaecologists, they can examine, codify and control the female reproductive system which, when Beverly later descends into madness, he describes as "mutant".

Drawing on stereotypes about homosexuality, Cronenberg carefully constructs the twins' personalities in terms of a male/female opposition which he later deconstructs: Elliot is worldly, self-assured, detached; Beverly is timid, emotional, shy. The stereotyping of homosexual lovers in terms of a male/female dichotomy is based on the phallocentric premise that the original authentic and natural model of all relationships is that of sexual opposition – of a union between the masculine and feminine. The "truth" of the twins' sexual identities is inscribed in their personalities and actions. When Claire realises the depth of the brother's attachment to each other, she questions Beverly about the nature of their relationship, suggesting that it may be homosexual. She asks Beverly why his mother gave him a girl's name. "What are you trying to suggest?", he asks in an agitated manner. "That I'm gay or something? That my mother wanted girls?".

The association of homosexuality with effeminacy, and the pairing of a feminine homosexual with a masculine partner draw upon the traditional association of homosexuality with sodomy ("proper" sex must involve penetration) – an act which, prior to the 18th century, was not viewed as necessarily excluding vaginal sex with women.[15] Compared to *Naked Lunch* (1991) and *Crash* (1996), *Dead Ringers* does not reveal an obvious interest in – even celebration of – anal sex. There is one sequence, however, when the subject is raised by inference. Having completely lost control of his sanity, Beverly, while examining a female patient, says: "What exactly did you have intercourse with?...I was once asked to treat a woman who had had intercourse with a Labrador retriever." Bev's reference to bestiality points to an underlying suggestion of anal sexuality, of sex in the "doggy" position. Unable to continue with the examination, he breaks down, screaming to Elly: "There's nothing the matter with the instrument. It's the body. The woman's body was all wrong."

Presumably, the woman's body, with its vaginal and uterine cavities, is "all wrong" because it is not a male body like his own. Even worse, the female body is capable of mating with animals, of crossing the boundary between human and animal, a possibility that seems both to repel and to attract Beverly as he sinks further into psychosis. It is almost immediately after this episode that he orders a set of silver instruments "for working on mutant women". A kindred spirit, the silversmith, who is also a famous artist, comments: "Mutant women. That's a great theme for a show".

When Claire discovers that the brothers are identical twins who cannot operate independently of each other, she turns on them: "Do you live together? Do you sleep in the same bed?...What is it with you, chum? You can't get it up unless your brother is watching?". The twins themselves reinforce their narcissistic identification in numerous ways. They affectionately refer to each other as "Elly" and "Bev" as if they were twin girls. When Beverly first dates Claire, Elliot says: "Don't worry, you'll be alright. Just do me!". When Elliot tries to drag information out of Beverly about his evening with Claire, he states: "You haven't had any experience until I've had it, too". Beverly tells Claire that he and Elliot have always "shared everything". "I'm not a thing!", she replies angrily. When Elliot hires twin prostitutes for the evening, he tells one to call him "Elly" and the other to call him "Bev". Even in the operating room their identities merge; in one scene, we see the brothers both dressed in identical red gowns, going through the same motions, transforming surgery into an act of mimicry.

The fact that the brothers are identical twins, both played by the same actor, is central to the film's representation of homoeroticism. Our first sight of Beverly and Elliot Mantle clearly establishes their "single" identity; they are not only "dead ringers" for each other, they also share identical ideas, passions, desires and dislikes. Their very different personalities do not create a sense of difference; rather, they present the twins as if "two sides of the same coin". More importantly, the film's sophisticated use of special effects, which permit Jeremy Irons to give two utterly convincing performances as Beverly and Elliot, clearly establishes what Lee Edelman describes as an instance of "homographesis" – that is, "the cultural mechanism by which writing is brought into relation to the question of sexual difference in order to conceive the gay body as text". In other words, the homosexual, unlike the heterosexual subject, is represented in an overdetermined way in relation to his body "that always demands to be read, a body on which his 'sexuality' is always already inscribed".[16]

This effect is most clearly achieved in *Dead Ringers* through the film's intense specularisation of the twins-as-twins. The viewer's attention is focused constantly on Jeremy Irons and his amazing double performance. The Mantle twins are created through special effects and tricks of perception. Like Plato's separated spherical beings, the Mantle twins exist before our eyes as identical parts of the same whole. We read their desire for each other through the cinematic process by which their doubleness is already, and repeatedly, inscribed in relation to the body.

Cronenberg's obsession with the flesh and with the way in which the transgression of boundaries can be represented on the body assumes a specific significance in his films about desire between men. Their transgression is doubly marked: firstly, in relation to Cronenberg's interests as a director in abjection and the body; and secondly, in relation to the way in which cinema has conventionally represented the "gay body as text". The convergence of the two discourses about the body (authorial and cinematic) in *Dead Ringers* has resulted in a text in which the homosexual body is symbolically and literally doubled.

To some extent, the uncanny effect of the twins' doubleness is diffused by the representation of woman as even more monstrous; but the fact that her difference, the trifurcate cervix, is hidden from sight is a crucial one – the ultimate effect is to downplay her difference in contrast to the twins' monstrous doubleness which constructs their love for each other as both terrifying and tragic. Towards the end, when Beverly's delusions have engulfed him completely, he takes the gynaecological instruments he designed for operating on mutant women to Claire's apartment. When she asks him what "these tools" are for, he replies: "They're for separating Siamese twins". In his mind, mutant women and the male couple have become one and the same.

In the final sequence, Beverly, tormented by grotesque bodily fantasies, places his twin on the gynaecological couch and cuts open his brother's body as if he were a woman. The meaning of this bloody act is ambiguous: it can be read as a sexual attempt to construct Elly as a woman, or as an attempt to open up that part of the body where once they were joined. In separating himself from his brother, Beverly also assumes the feminine role – that of maternal castrator – assigned to Claire in his nightmare in which he dreamed that she was tearing him apart from his brother. In this way, he seeks total unification with his (br)other – a symbiosis denied him in life.

Cronenberg has stated that the classical form of *Dead Ringers* is crucial to its meaning: "And as with any classical tragedy, there's something magnificent, or elegiacally beautiful, or somehow comforting, despite the fact that it's very sad".[17] Like the climax of a classical opera, play or novel, the lovers are doomed. Despite the film's misogyny and overdetermined images of stereotyped notions of homosexuality, there is something profoundly moving about the

ending *Dead Ringers* is a deeply contradictory text whose problematic representations haunt us long after the final scene. Unable to accept the depth of their love for each other, the Mantle twins, tormented by an embryonic desire for reunion and erotic bliss, a desire they have cloaked (as the name "Mantle" suggests) throughout their lives, die naked and folded into each other's bloodied bodies.

M. Butterfly (1993) has been seen by some critics[18] as atypical of Cronenberg's interests because of its focus on race and imperialism, rather than on thematics central to horror and science-fiction. Nevertheless, it is completely understandable that Cronenberg would be attracted to this tale. Its central theme of doomed love between men indicates that it has much in common with his most recent work. In particular, it draws on themes central to *Dead Ringers* – paranoia and self-delusion, the constraints of the body, the fragile boundary between masculine and feminine, the impossibility of same-sex love, and a desire for transcendence. Based on a story reported in the French press, *M. Butterfly* tells the story of René Gallimard (another role for Jeremy Irons), a French diplomat stationed in China. One night, Gallimard attends a Beijing opera performance of Puccini's *Madama Butterfly* (*Madam Butterfly*, 1904), and is strangely moved by one of the sopranos, Song Liling, who sings the opera's famous aria, "Un bel dì, vedremo...". Afterwards, he meets Song Liling (John Lone) and tells her: "You made me see the beauty of the story, of her death. It's pure sacrifice." Despite, or perhaps because of, Song Liling's biting reply ("Because it's an Oriental who kills herself for a Westerner, you find her beautiful"), Gallimard is fascinated.

Unaware that Song Liling is a female impersonator (I shall use the pronoun "she" to refer to Song Liling), Gallimard falls in love with the actor whom he comes to call his "Butterfly". Convincing Gallimard that she follows the "ancient Oriental ways of love" and is exceedingly modest, Song Liling never once, in their twenty-year relationship, appears naked before Gallimard. Song Liling, who is also an undercover agent for Chinese intelligence, pretends to Gallimard that she is pregnant. On returning from a long stay in the countryside, she even produces a baby son (on loan from the government) whom Gallimard believes he has fathered. After providing his own government with a number of poor intelligence predictions, Gallimard is ordered back to France. Prior to this, Gallimard's wife has faded from the scene. With assistance from her government, Song Liling moves to Paris. Eventually, Gallimard and Song Liling are charged with treason. The court is amazed to learn that Gallimard did not know that Song Liling was a man. In the final scene, Gallimard, now in prison, dresses up as Madam Butterfly, whose part he is to play in a prison drama. During the performance before his fellow prisoners, Gallimard cuts his throat and dies.

Like *Dead Ringers, M. Butterfly* relies upon special effects for its representation of the male body caught up in a homoerotic relationship. Although we, the audience, recognise that Song Liling is a man living as a woman, Gallimard remains oblivious to the truth. Despite the fact that some critics claim that Cronenberg "makes no attempt to convince the audience of John Lone's femininity",[19] I would argue that, on the contrary, Cronenberg carefully constructs Song Liling's sexual identity as ambiguous. Furthermore, it is clear that Gallimard, who is represented as a kind of sleepwalker in relation to politics, did not know about Song Liling's true identity because he wanted to remain ignorant. Butterfly represented the ideal woman of his dreams, and he did not want that dream shattered. Like the Mantle twins, Gallimard lives in a closed, private world of his own making.

It is also possible to see why Gallimard is taken in by Song Liling's masquerade, particularly in those moments when the couple have sex. Cronenberg represents Song Liling's ambiguous sexuality around a deliberately constructed confusion between vagina and anus – a construction explored more fully in *Naked Lunch*. Not only does Gallimard have sex with Song Liling, but also he even thinks he has fathered their child, while all the time "believing" she is anatomically female. She/he gives birth to a baby for/by him from her anus/vagina. Gallimard's fantasy of feminisation is complete. Woman provides the "face" of the relationship in which the actual partner is a man. Gallimard's fetishisation of her body ("I know, but..."), by which he imagines that her anus is a vagina, permits him to take part in this amazing act of self-deception. A self-consciously abject figure, Song Liling lives in a borderland between the opposite ends of masculinity and femininity. Although her metamorphosis from caterpillar to butterfly appears to be complete, traces of the transition are always visible. Her life as a "butterfly" is a performance enacted for an audience of one. Butterfly's difference – her queerness – is written onto her body in a striking illustration of Edelman's notion of cinematic homographesis.

When Song Liling asks a Party member why women's roles in the Beijing Opera are played by men, the answer she receives is that this is "most probably a remnant of the reactionary and patriarchal social structure". "No", Song Liling replies. "It's because only a man knows how a woman is supposed to act". During the trial, we learn exactly what this means. When the prosecutor asks if Gallimard was aware that Song Liling was a man, the latter replies: "He never saw me completely naked, ever...In all our years together, René never explored my body...He was very responsive to my ancient Oriental ways of love out of which I invented myself just for him." Gallimard fell in love with a woman who never revealed her body, who offered her anus as a vagina, and who never asked for sexual pleasure. The implications of Song Liling's statement – that men make better "women" than women – points to the masquerade that informs and constructs phallocentric notions of desire that deny women sexual pleasure. Gallimard's tragedy is that he prefers the masquerade to reality. When Gallimard escorts a woman home from a diplomatic party, he says to her, after she has undressed, "You look exactly as I imagined you would under your clothes". His tone is one of disappointment – not pleasure.

After the trial, when the lovers are left briefly alone in the police wagon, Song Liling forces Gallimard to recognise his true identity. Undressing, he falls to his knees, imploring Gallimard to declare his love. Instead, Gallimard refuses. "What I loved was the lie. The perfect lie. It's been destroyed...I'm a man who loved a woman created by a man. Anything else simply falls short." Later in prison, when Gallimard realises that he has lost his Butterfly forever, he takes on her persona. In a stage performance before the prisoners, Gallimard transforms his body (kimono, wig) and face (lipstick, make-up) into that of the Oriental woman – Madam Butterfly – who is prepared to die for love. "The man I loved was not worthy", he says to the audience. "He didn't deserve even a second glance. Instead, I gave him my love, all my love." As Gallimard cuts her throat, she utters her final words signifying the complete transformation of male into female, a metamorphosis rendered absolute by the act of death. "My name is René Gallimard. Also known as Madam Butterfly." It is important to note that Cronenberg cuts between Gallimard's performance as Madam Butterfly and images of Song Liling, dressed a man, returning to China by plane. Gallimard has taken Song Liling's place as the Oriental transvestite: Song Liling has taken Gallimard's place as the European man. If the boundaries of race and gender are mutable, perhaps those between the sexes can also be crossed.[20] As Gallimard/Butterfly dies, the blood spurting from the wound in her neck covers her body, kimono, face and wig, making it impossible to identify her as either male or female. Her bodily transformation transports her into a world where gender boundaries are meaningless.

Gallimard's death scene reminds us of his first meeting with Song Liling and his description of Madam Butterfly's death as "pure sacrifice". Through suicide, feminisation and self-mutilation, Gallimard re-creates the "perfect lie" – "a woman created by a man". During his performance in prison, Gallimard also tells his prison audience that: "There is a vision of the Orient that I have. Slender women in cheongsams and kimonos who die for the love of unworthy foreign devils. Who are born and raised to be perfect women, and who take whatever punishment we give them and spring back. Strengthened by love, unconditionally. It was a vision that has become my life." Like Schreber, Gallimard believes he has "a mission to redeem the world and restore it to a state of lost bliss". He could only achieve this if he "first transformed from man into a woman".[21]

Steven Shaviro has described Cronenberg as "a literalist of the body".[22] Nowhere is this more evident than in *Naked Lunch*, in which Cronenberg takes his interest in states of paranoia, homoeroticism and transcendence to new heights. Inspired by William Burroughs' famous cult novel of the same name, Cronenberg's film is an attempt to capture the spirit of what has been described as an "unfilmable" work.[23] The themes of *Naked Lunch* are evident in Cronenberg's other films discussed here: bodily abnormality and transformation, homosexuality, feminisation, homosociality, misogyny, sex and death. Of all these motifs, the film's interest in homosexuality is the strongest. *Naked Lunch* also returns to the more familiar Cronenberg terrain of sci-fi schlock. Burroughs' novel, of course, was subject to an obscenity trial on its publication in 1959, because of its references to homosexuality which at the time were seen to be pornographic. According to Cronenberg, the "sex in *Naked Lunch* is beyond gay. It's sci-fi sex; it has metaphorical meaning every way."[24] While the sex is certainly sci-fi and metaphorical, it is not, in my view, "beyond gay"; the sex is clearly and disturbingly gay.

Naked Lunch is set in New York City in 1953. William Lee (Peter Weller) is a writer who earns a living as a pest exterminator; his wife Joan (Judy Davis) has become addicted to the bug powder he uses to exterminate cockroaches. Bill begins to hallucinate, and at one point imagines that his typewriter is metamorphosing into a giant cockroach whose wings spread open to reveal a talking arsehole. The creature tells him that his wife is not "really a woman", that she is actually an "agent of Interzone", and that he must kill her. One evening, after visiting a drug dealer, Dr Benway, who prescribes a narcotic made from Brazilian centipedes, Bill returns to their apartment to find Joan having sex with a friend. Appearing completely unfazed by the situation, he invites Joan to play their usual game of William Tell. She obliges by placing a glass on her head; he takes aim but – supposedly controlled by the bug – he fires the bullet into her brain, killing her instantly.[25]

Distraught, Bill takes to the streets, seeking solace in the world of drugs. Enmeshed in a paranoid hallucinatory state, he enters a nightmare world of his own making called Interzone. Populated by junkies, homosexuals, writers, witches, talking arseholes (a conceit from the Burroughs' novel) and monsters who go by the name of "mugwamps", Interzone is a place where "anything goes". Strangely,

Bill is liberated by this surreal world where he meets an odd assortment of characters: gay Arab boys; Tom Frost, a writer; Joan Frost (who is a double of Joan Lee); Yves Cloquet, a decadent homosexual; Kiki, a young boy who becomes his lover; and the transsexual Dr Benway, who, in his female disguise as the witch Fadela, is having a lesbian relationship with Joan. Safely ensconced in Interzone, Bill, on orders from his bug/typewriter, begins writing a report which will become Bill's/Burroughs' infamous novel.

It has been argued that Cronenberg's film departs from the theme of homosexuality and eroticism that is central to Burroughs' *Naked Lunch*.[26] It does, however, explore homosexual desire from its own distinctly bizarre perspective. The central duo in *Naked Lunch* are Bill and the talking typewriter/arsehole. It is not by accident that Cronenberg has chosen the anus – a stereotypical signifier of male homosexual pleasure – as Bill's *alter ego* or *doppelgänger*. The talking anus gives voice to a series of transgressive desires that Bill almost always carries out: it orders him to kill his wife; to use homosexuality as a cover-up for his espionage activities; to seduce Joan Frost; and to accept the truth of his instinctive knowledge that women are not human, but are a different species from men. In the scene in which the typewriter tells Bill that "homosexuality is the best all-around cover an agent ever had", he orders him not to type like a "pansy", but to be "forceful". As Bill does as he is told, the typewriter metamorphoses into an anus in the throes of orgasm. The bug tells Bill his superiors are delighted that he is prepared to become a homosexual in the interest of the cause. The metamorphosing typewriter/bug/anus brings together in a perverse metaphor the combination of anus, writing and same-sex desire; it provides another bizarre instance of homographesis.

Created out of his own drug-induced states, Interzone becomes Bill's personal haven, a place that offers an endless supply of drugs and sex, and where he can fantasise about his fear of women and desire for men. Bill's anxieties about women permeate the narrative, which commences and ends with Joan's death – in order to enter and leave Interzone (the space of fantasy, creativity and homoeroticism), he must first shoot his wife. His fear of woman is expressed most vividly in a surreal scene in which the writer imagines that his typewriter/anus is locked in a deadly battle with Tom Frost's vaginal typewriter; the two erogenous zones engage in a gory duel, with the anus winning the contest. What is represented as slippage between anus and vagina in *M. Butterfly* becomes a clear-cut contest between hostile zones in *Naked Lunch*. Although Cronenberg creates situations in which Bill appears to express heterosexual desire (mainly for his wife Joan and Joan Frost – both played by Judy Davis), the narrative outcome of these situations almost always leads to a homosexual or lesbian experience. It seems as if all roads in Interzone lead only to a homosexual destination which is always represented in bizarre or surreal sci-fi contexts.

It is no accident that Bill's gay bug metamorphoses into an anus with a male voice. A metaphorical monster, it functions as Bill's *alter ego*, giving expression to paranoid, misogynist thoughts which serve to explain/justify his growing, but repressed, desire for men: "Your wife is not really your wife. She is an agent of Interzone...an élite corps centipede." When Bill meets Kiki in a gay bar, he tells the boy that he is a faggot, not by nature but by circumstance. Later, he tells the Frosts that he did not come to Interzone for the boys. Tom Frost does not believe him. In a strange – but key – scene, he tells Bill that desire is not necessarily "intentional" or "conscious". "If you look carefully at my lips, you'll realise I'm actually saying something else". Cronenberg has Tom utter these words at the very moment that his lips go out of sync with the sound. "I'm not actually telling you about the several ways I'm gradually murdering Joan", he continues as he communicates "telepathically" with Bill. The episode makes it clear that we should not necessarily believe Bill when he says he does not desire other men.

Other signs support Tom's view that desire is not conscious, and that Bill is homosexual – whether he recognises it or not. Bill takes a boy lover. Yves Cloquet talks about Bill's entrance at a party with "those three Interzone boys", and Bill himself becomes a master of the art of telling outrageous anus stories that leave the sophisticated Cloquet lost for words. Even the scene of heterosexual lovemaking between Bill and Joan Frost turns suddenly into one of lesbian desire. As they make love across the desk, Joan's hand (not Bill's) enters a vaginal hole in the typewriter, and she caresses its raw, fleshy, pulsating interior. Joan is aroused by her own sex. Just as another part of the typewriter sprouts a penis-like protuberance, suggesting Bill's arousal, the camera pans to a fetishistic image of a menacing woman wearing jodhpurs, long black boots and sporting a whip. This is Fadela, the lesbian housekeeper to whom – Tom says – Joan rushes whenever "she feels attracted to a man".

Cronenberg clearly has no interest in representing same-sex desire in the context of "positive" gay images. Rather, his interest is in the surreal and offbeat. Although Bill is something of a classic stereotype (homosexual/writer/spy), his fantasy world, Interzone, is completely bizarre. One of the most horrific moments occurs when Bill trades his lover Kiki for information from Yves Cloquet. Bill fantasises that Yves, transformed into a giant reptilian insect, rapes the boy in a cage. This is the only representation of homosexual sex in the film – it is horrific and sadistic. In the concluding sequences, we discover that Padela is actually a man, the powerful Dr Benway who controls the drug factories of Interzone. Dr Benway rips apart his outer female (latex) body, while the camera holds the image of one sex emerging from another just long enough to emphasise that the dominant generating fantasy of Interzone is one of paranoia, mutation, feminisation and same-sex desire. Once again, the representation of homosexuality is written indelibly onto the body – a body on which sexuality "is always already inscribed". We are not very far at all from the world of *Dead Ringers* and *M. Butterfly*.

With the completion of *Crash*, it is clear that a case can be made for interpreting Cronenberg's recent films in the context of homosexuality, anality, feminisation, sacrifice and death. As with Cronenberg's other films on homoeroticism, *Crash* is an adaptation, this time from the 1973 novel of the same name by J G Ballard. Once again, Cronenberg isolates his characters in a sealed-off, fantastic world of his own making. Bleak and detached, *Crash* is similar in mood to Cronenberg's other films but, in contrast to these, it offers us a male protagonist, Vaughan (Elias Koteas), whose homosexual desires are combined with an aggressively macho demeanour.

The central male character, James Ballard (James Spader), is involved in a car crash in which he suffers a series of wounds. During his recovery, he meets the other survivor of the crash, Dr Helen Remington (Holly Hunter), whose husband was killed, and a strange man, Vaughan, who is excited by the sight of James' wounds. Helen, James and his wife Catherine become involved in a bizarre cult of crash survivors who, led by Vaughan and his friends Gabrielle (Rosanna Arquette) and Peter, re-enact the car crashes of dead celebrities such as James Dean and Jayne Mansfield. All the group members are obsessed with the erotic potential of car crashes and the mutilated victims who survive.

In *Crash*, Cronenberg's fascination with bodily metamorphosis is vividly realised in relation to the wound. His accident survivors all bear the imprint of metal on flesh; those whose bodies are held together by prosthetic devices signify this union in a confronting manner. Cronenberg represents the erotic potential of the crash in a series of shattering sequences. In one, James, Helen and Vaughan become sexually aroused by the sight of the wounded victims of a freeway crash; the mass accident has been caused by Colin who, dressed in drag as Jayne Mansfield, has successfully reconstructed the star's fatal accident. Like Gallimard, Colin has attained a state of bliss by staging his death as a woman. In another, James, finding himself aroused by the wound in Gabrielle's leg, fucks it with his penis. Like the Interzone of *Naked Lunch*, *Crash*'s Accident-zone creates a space in which characters are free to push sexual desire to its limits – in both films, this limit is defined in terms of same-sex desire. Whereas this desire was primarily expressed in *Naked Lunch* in metaphoric terms, around conversations between Bill and the talking anus, in *Crash* metaphoric language is replaced by confronting images of copulation. The crash zone creates a world where sex and death are intimately related, conferring on the (male) characters a sense of absolute freedom to explore the relationship between sex and death. For Vaughan, this represents the future. He tells James that the car crash is "a liberation of sexual energy". His strongest desire is "to experience that...To live that...". Such a liberation, however, is not an ordinary one. It involves homoerotic desire. Vaughan and James embrace, touching each other's bodies, tattoo scars and wounds. Afterwards, Vaughan attempts to run down James in his car, but Vaughan's own car careers off the highway and crashes into a bus, killing him instantly. Like Schreber, Vaughan also achieves his state of bliss through transformation – a moment of liberating sexual energy attained through the intersection of homoerotic desire, sex and death. At the same time, Helen and Gabrielle make love in another car.

As I have argued elsewhere,[27] the scene of lesbian sex in *Crash* is like an afterthought, a token gesture to female desire. While Cronenberg's female protagonists are almost always strong, enigmatic figures, their stories are secondary to those of the male characters. Joan Frost's lesbian desires in *Naked Lunch* are similarly represented in a perfunctory manner. Understandably, perhaps, Cronenberg is interested in the psyche of his own sex, and this is explored more powerfully in *Crash* than in any of his other films. As with *Naked Lunch*, the anus is a central signifier of desire. While having sex with her husband James, Catherine arouses him by discussing Vaughan's anus: "Can you imagine what his anus looks like?...Would you like to sodomise him? Would you like to put your penis right into his anus?... Tell me...". Throughout this scene of erotic talk, Catherine is lying with her back to James. As he becomes aroused by the thought of what he might do with Vaughan, James thrusts his penis into Catherine from behind. The woman thus acts as the go-between, or conduit, of male desire; she verbalises, gives voice and body to their – as yet – unspoken, unrealised desires. When asked why he portrayed the majority of sexual encounters in the film as "rear-entry or anal", Cronenberg replied that "it felt right, getting both of the actors looking towards the camera and not at each other. It helped the sort of 'disconnected' thing."[28] Cronenberg's reference to sex as a "disconnected thing" points either to a desire to avoid intimacy, and/or to a desire to avoid intimacy in a heterosexual context. When Vaughan and James embrace, they face each other.

Another key motif of the Cronenberg universe is that of homosociality; we can see its importance in relation to Cronenberg's choice of actress. In relation to the Joan Lee/Frost character of *Naked Lunch*, Cronenberg has said that it was "very important that she be able to hold her own against the homosexual maleness of the movie". He wanted an actor who was "strong, powerful, magnetic and charismatic".[29] Played by Judy Davis, Joan Frost is an enigmatic, strong woman who seems more at home in Interzone than any of the male characters. Cronenberg's description also fits his other female leads, particularly Geneviève Bujold in *Dead Ringers*, and his two female leads, Holly Hunter and Deborah Kara Unger, in *Crash*. The "homosexual maleness" of *Naked Lunch* could also be described as a form of homosociality which, in his recent films, is ultimately expressed as a form of same-sex desire between men which works to exclude women. The male relationships in *Crash* are based on a homosocial bond saturated in violence, injury and death. In the Cronenberg world, homosociality signifies the complete exclusion/ rejection of women who are seen by the male characters either as monstrous (*Dead Ringers*), inadequate (*M. Butterfly*) or threatening to creativity (*Naked Lunch*), or as anal and alienated surrogate figures (*Crash*).

Critics of Cronenberg's earlier films (*Scanners* [1981], *Videodrome, The Fly*) emphasise the central themes of bodily invasion and transformation, corporeality and "the monstrous intersection of physiology and technology".[30] Spectators respond with a mixture of horror and disgust marked by perverse pleasure. According to Shaviro, "[t]here is no vision of transcendence in the claustrophobic world of these films...Passion is anchored in and expressed by the brute facticity of bodily transmutations".[31] In her discussion of *Dead Ringers*, Pam Cook describes Cronenberg as "one of the great melancholics of modern cinema", his heroes unable "in the end to reconcile themselves with the real world" or, in particular, with women.[32] Cronenberg's later films (*M. Butterfly, Naked Lunch, Crash*) incorporate these, as well as new themes of homoeroticism, feminisation, *jouissance* and death. The Cronenberg hero of the 1990s seeks bliss in the arms of another man, but finds that his desire to transcend the flesh remains anchored in the body. The heroes of *Dead Ringers* and *M. Butterfly* retreat from women into the arms of other men who – as both Song Liling and René Gallimard state – know how "a woman is supposed to act". The failure of love, combined with the refusal of the films to represent the act of love between men as a liberating desire, gives rise to a profound sense of loss which the narrative is unable/unwilling to resolve. In search of transformation, metamorphosis and bliss, the Cronenberg hero is confronted, in the final analysis, with death and the loss of his male counterpart – whether twin, "butterfly", boy or wounded road warrior.

Notes

1   Sigmund Freud, *Case Histories II (The Pelican Freud Library, volume 9)*, edited by Angela Richards and translated by James Strachey (Harmondsworth: Penguin Books, 1979): 198.

2   Ibid: 131-223.

3   See Gilles Deleuze and Félix Guattari, "The Body without Organs", in *Anti-Oedipus Capitalism and Schizophrenia*, translated by Robert Hurley, Mark Seem and Helen R Lane (London: The Athlone Press, 1984): 9-16.

4   Freud: 146.

5   Steven Shaviro, "Bodies of Fear: David Cronenberg", in *The Cinematic Body* (Minneapolis; London: University of Minnesota Press, 1993): 127-158; Mary B Campbell, "Biological Alchemy and the Films of David Cronenberg", in Barry Keith Grant (ed), *Planks of Reason: Essays on the Horror Film* (Metuchen, NJ; London: The Scarecrow Press, 1984): 307-320.

6   Shaviro.

7   Diana Fuss, "Lesbian and Gay Theory: The Question of Identity Politics", in *Essentially Speaking: Feminism, Nature & Difference* (New York; London: Routledge, 1989): 97-112.

8   Eve Kosofsky Sedgwick, *Between Men: English Literature and Male Homosocial Desire* (New York: Columbia University Press, 1985).

9   Cronenberg interviewed by Anne Billson, "Cronenberg on Cronenberg: a career in stereo", *Monthly Film Bulletin* 56: 660 (January 1989): 6.

10   Barbara Creed, "Phallic panic: male hysteria and *Dead Ringers*", *Screen* 31: 2 (summer 1990): 125-146.

11   Pam Cook, "Dead Ringers", *Monthly Film Bulletin* 56: 660 (January 1989): 4.

12   Plato, "The Symposium", in *The Portable Plato* (Harmondsworth: Penguin Books, 1982).

13   Francette Pacteau, "The Impossible Referent: representations of the androgyne", in Victor Burgin, James Donald and Cora Kaplan (eds), *Formations of Fantasy* (London; New York: Methuen, 1986): 62-84.

14   Shelley Kay, "Double or Nothing", *Cinema Papers* 74 (July 1989): 32-35. Kay draws on Aristophanes to explore the representation of twins in *Dead Ringers* and *A Zed & Two Noughts* (1985).

[15] Lee Edelman, *Homographesis: essays in gay literary and cultural theory* (New York; London. Routledge, 1994). 11.

[16] Ibid: 10.

[17] Billson: 6.

[18] Asuman Suner, "Postmodern Double Cross: Reading David Cronenberg's *M. Butterfly* as a Horror Story", *Cinema Journal* 37: 2 (winter 1998): 49-64.

[19] John Harkness, "M. Butterfly", *Sight and Sound* 4: 5 (May 1994): 45.

[20] Suner presents an excellent discussion of these themes in the film.

[21] Freud: 146.

[22] Shaviro: 129.

[23] Evan Williams, "Cronenberg Feasts on Monsters of the Mind", *The Australian Weekend Review* 2-3 May 1992: 12; "*Naked Lunch* Dressed for Screen Test", *The Weekend Australian* 29 February-1 March 1992: 3.

[24] Amy Taubin, "The wrong body", *Sight and Sound* 1: 11 (March 1992): 8.

[25] Burroughs himself accidentally shot his wife Joan while playing a game of "William Tell". He later claimed that he would not have written a word if he had not killed his wife: "I am forced to the appalling conclusion that I would never have become a writer but for Joan's death". Quoted in Lynn Snowdon, "Which is the Fly and Which is the Human?", *Esquire* February 1992: 112-116.

[26] Taubin.

[27] Barbara Creed, "Anal wounds, metallic kisses", *Screen* 39: 2 (summer 1998): 175-179.

[28] Chris Rodley, "Crash" [interview with David Cronenberg], *Sight and Sound* 6: 6 (June 1996): 7-11.

[29] *The Naked Lunch* press kit, 1992.

[30] Shaviro: 129.

[31] Ibid.

[32] Cook: 3.

Death drive

Parveen Adams

Since this is a book about film, we will start with the question of the
voyeur. The voyeur as voyeur completes a space. Just think of the
conventional image of the voyeur at the keyhole. Think of the rustle
that disturbs his gaze. The eye is withdrawn from the keyhole and the
space that had included the voyeur now has a hole in it. In this sense,
had the voyeur's gaze completed space.

Obviously. not all looking is voyeuristic. So what is the difference
between the eye at the keyhole, which peeps at the scene, and the
eye in front of a painting, viewing a perspectival scene? In each case,
you perceive a three-dimensional space, and in each case there is a
certain completion of a space. But, in psychoanalytic terms, two
different psychical spaces are at stake. The difference in Lacanian
terms is that, in the case of the peeping Tom, the eye is placed within
a perverse structure; in the case of the gallery spectator, the eye is
placed within a neurotic structure. In one case, you complete the
space as object; in the other, as subject.[1]

My point is threefold: (1) that we can talk of psychical space; (2)
that it is not a monolithic space; (3) that this psychical space is usually
thought of as being three-dimensional.

This essay is about Cronenberg's film, *Crash* (1996), and my thesis
is that it puts you at the very limit of three-dimensional space. This is
also to say that it puts you at the limit of psychical space as such. At
the edge of three-dimensional space, *Crash* substitutes what I will call
"flatness". To give you some idea of what I mean I suggest that you
think not in terms of the depth of a three-dimensional space, but in
terms of a thick surface. What would it be like if what we saw was the
world depositing itself in layers on a surface instead of as lines
converging to a point?

Of course, there are many other features of the film that contribute
to the flatness, but the idea of a thick surface suffices to raise the
question as to the kind of psychical space *Crash* produces. Both
neurosis and perversion have shown in different ways how there is a
completion of space, so that space itself binds us one way or another.
But, where space swallows up the voyeur, *Crash* swallows up space,
producing the effect of flatness. If this is true, *Crash* cannot

accommodate a space of voyeuristic desire. Indeed, *Crash* is far from any desiring state; *Crash* is not dominated by desire. It will be my argument that it is rather dominated by the death drive.

The three-dimensional psychical organisation of space I have been speaking about is a space correlated with the field of the Other.[2] In Lacanian theory, all inter-subjective relations are mediated by the Other. Inter-subjective relations are automatically articulated to the illusionistic space of centrally organised perspective. *Crash*, for reasons that will become clearer in this essay, tries to reverse this effect of verisimilitude. At the level of formal appearance, it does this through its flatness.

This involves an argument about the status of the *wound* within the film which opposes the idea of the wound as having the unequivocal signification of castration. Conversely, I shall argue that the wound is a refusal of the Other, and therefore that the image no longer opens up to the field of the Other.

Wounds

I want to show that the film concerns neither neurotic nor perverse desire. Nor is it about phallic *jouissance*, or about the Other *jouissance*, or about perverse *jouissance*. Lacan shows that phallic *jouissance* is like a kind of masturbatory *jouissance* insofar as its object is only peripherally related to another person, the underlying fantasies concerning something else. Both men and women partake of phallic *jouissance* where desire never goes beyond the "No" of the father's prohibition on the incestuous wish. But the woman is not subject in the same way to these limits as is the man. As Bruce Fink says: "not all of a woman comes under the law of the signifier".[3] She also comes elsewhere. This elsewhere, which has moved beyond the place of phallic *jouissance*, is what Lacan calls the Other *jouissance*, where sexuality has been sublimated from the phallic. It is this Other *jouissance* that Lacan alleges is shared by mystics. But neither phallic nor the Other *jouissance* seems appropriate to *Crash*.

What about perverse *jouissance*? Firstly, something needs to be said about masochism and sadism. Let me indicate the kind of argument that could be developed about sadism. Consider this quotation from de Sade: "lend me the part of your body that will give me a moment of satisfaction and, if you care to, use for own pleasure that part of my body which appeals to you".[4] It could easily seem that this aspect of sadism is relevant in *Crash*, where also the body is always breaking into pieces. But Lacan's idea of sadism is really quite different from that in *Crash*. Sadism always acts upon a whole and would-be perfect body. It may intend to inflict damage and pain, but it must start and (as a form of repetition) start again from this body. Hence those miraculous cures in de Sade – at the end of an encounter, victims are cut, bruised and bloodied if not worse, yet, by the application of some precious unguent, everyone is restored. In effect, the victim is indestructible. Lacan links this figure of indestructibility to the eternal suffering in de Sade's fundamental fantasm. Certainly, *Crash* has no equivalent of this indestructible victim. On the contrary, the characters seem always on the verge of injury, moving inexorably towards the fatal encounter of that thing which augments another logic – the "inevitable accident" which somehow describes a register that is no longer that of phallic *jouissance*, or the Other *jouissance*, or even perverse *jouissance* but describes the space in which Death begins to appear as the object of a new desire, the desire not to desire. I will elaborate on this below.

At this stage in the argument, we must clarify this differentiation between sadism and the desire which unfolds in *Crash*. Far from the indestructible victim, far from the magical unguents that make possible the repetition of the sadistic scene, what is at stake in *Crash* is quite different. The body retains its mortal frailty; the proximity of body and car, flesh and steel, skin and bone, dominates sexuality not at all as sadism, but as a world of the wound. Indeed, the film's sexuality is textured like a wound, gaping, open, unsutured.

This also suggests that *Crash* is no more masochistic than it is sadistic. Masochism is commonly thought of as involving pleasure in pain, and certainly the economy of masochism falls under the sway of the pleasure principle. But there is a beyond of the pleasure principle that allows Lacan to write of "the unspeakable field of radical desire that is the field of absolute destruction".[5] What is at stake here is not pleasure, but *jouissance*; pleasure is the barrier to *jouissance*. No one who has seen *Crash* will doubt that it sets out to break that barrier.[6]

Let us also distinguish the meaning of the wound from the mark of the whip in masochism. The latter is a little castration, represented by the cut, by the cut *as* representation, as differentiation, as the Other's signature. The world of the wound is quite different; it is not a writing on the body so much as an unwriting of the body. It is already the other side of representation. A wound can get larger or smaller, close up or open. It is not so much the navel of meaning; here it becomes the birth canal of death. Normally, the closing of the wound, the work of suture, creates the reinscription of the scar and draws the body back towards representation. But, in *Crash*, the wound is not healed but merely transformed by scars. The scar is also a wound. The characters in *Crash* revel in the exploration of scars, these transformations of skin and tissue, these crusts of a new and hybridised body. Although the wound is healed, the scar remains its memorial and an invocation to a continuous reopening of the wound. A scar is not fixed.

The sexuality of *Crash* proliferates through the scar and the wound. Two thirds of the way through the novel J G Ballard writes: "The world was beginning to flower into wounds".[7] Indeed, in the novel, the wounds of Vaughan's body begin to reopen shortly before his own sought-for, fatal crash:

> Vaughan picked repeatedly at the scabs running across his knuckles. The scars on his knees, healed now for more than a year, were beginning to re-open. The points of blood seeped through the worn fabric of his jeans. Red flecks appeared on the lower curvature of the dashboard locker...Blood mingled with the dried semen on the seats, marking my own hands with dark points.[8]

The film does not represent the literal reopening of wounds, but finds its own way to portray its logic of the wound. The scar involves a fascination and an excitement about the moment when libido passes beyond representation. Libido unbound. But what could that mean? It is far from any idea of freedom, for it is unbound in the sense of having no object, or rather having nothing as its object. Now to be finally unbound, libido must break down all barriers, or it would remain constrained. It must even break down the last barrier, that which marks the boundary between life and death. This is the last scar that is to be opened. Viewed from the point of view of desire, a desire without an object must be a wish not to wish, the place where Desire and Death bisect each other.

Death drive

I should now justify the sketch of the film that I have presented to you. Stéphane Bouquet, writing in *Cahiers du Cinéma*, a lyrical and appreciative review of *Crash*, under the title "Sweet movie":

> A man, a woman, a car, and there we have a very good film, a powerful experience of cinema...an immersion in a radical and new universe. A man, a woman, a car, it does not matter which of them provided that there is a triangle. Sometimes the man changes, or the woman; sometimes, there are two men together, or two women. What is important is neither sex nor identity, but the moment when beings meet, bump each other, run into each other.[9]

Stéphane Bouquet treats that first time in the film in which human beings "run into each other", that is, the accident in which Ballard kills Helen Remington's husband – a scene which includes a moment of disruptive sexuality – as the *primal scene* of *Crash*, a primal scene in Freud's sense, a scene played out over and over again, albeit in different combinations:

> *Crash* is thus a film constructed on repetition, but a repetition that is a-dramatic, non-progressive, serial...There is no acceleration, no urgency, no stake to be suddenly revealed. There is the same rhythm always, this same slowness, frankly welcome in a film which could have easily allowed itself to be intoxicated with speed. Quite simply, people make love, and love again, amidst more or less damaged cars.[10]

Bouquet gives the film this erotic dimension, and also the dimension of the hybridisation of automobile and human. He reads this aspect in terms of Cronenberg's concern with the effect that the car can have on the imaginary. He speaks of the scene in which Vaughan orchestrates a real replay of James Dean's fatal accident:

> Vaughan...works to derealise the car, to project it into the space of fantasy, to circle it with a heroic aura, by reconstituting celebrated accidents in open air clandestine theatres. In a long, detailed and splendid sequence (bleu nuit), one sees him replay James Dean's accident in reality, presenting the cars and the protagonists of the drama, reproducing the crash, and emerging from it, as if the force of the automobile had been to install an imaginary space where desire could never encounter the reality principle.[11]

Bouquet's review contains vivid accounts of the traumatising medical imagery and of the cold objective way in which the film is shot, its pure exteriority. I do not quite disagree with any of this. And yet, I find that it is not enough. I certainly hope to show that this is no "sweet movie".

It is not just a question of disagreeing with other critics. For it will also be part of my argument that one of the difficulties in analysing the film is that the effect of the film on the spectator is to conceal something about the film. Certainly Bouquet's review gives a perfectly adequate account of one's reactions to the film. But his commentary on the triangle, the question of repetition, and the imaginary space of domination over reality need to be reformulated.

A man, a woman and an automobile. But what is the identity designated by the term "automobile"? It is not the automobile qua inanimate machine. Nor will any old automobile do. It is not just sheet metal, but crumpled sheet metal that might do. A battered automobile. Or a bruised, bloodied and battered human. Indeed, the third term is not necessarily on the side of the automobile; it can perfectly well be human. Actually, it is not the one or the other as such that is needed. What is necessary is the wound that will connect them both. The film overflows with wounds. Partly through what Bouquet calls the "[most] traumatising medical imagery: the neck braces, the pins, the prostheses, the apparatuses to hold in place the wounds which cannot close".[12] Indeed, the film is dominated by the wound. So it is not necessarily a question of a man, a woman and a car. It is the wound that is primary. Therefore, why bother to speak of a triangle so redolent of the Freudian Oedipal triangle? Of course, one usually thinks of a wound in terms of castration in many narratives, but in *Crash* a wound is just a wound. Indeed, the remarkable thing about *Crash* is that it does not refer to the Oedipal or to castration. The wound in *Crash* is less related to the sexual organ, male or female (although we might think of it as both the origin and the residue of the organ), and more to do with the Freudian drive for Life.

Secondly, consider the idea of the imaginary space of desire that Bouquet talks of – Vaughan, he says, works to project the car into the space of fantasy. But does the film really work at the level of the imaginary domination of reality? It seems to me that *Crash* is much more ferocious than this; it seems to me that it bears closely on the Real and on the quite terrible *jouissance* in which all subjectivity is submerged.

Lastly, consider how repetition actually works in the film. There is no one register of repetition in general; how we understand it depends on what repetition bears upon – in Lacanian terms, whether the repetition was at the level of the Imaginary, the Symbolic or the Real. Now the characters copulate over and over again in more or less damaged cars. But how are we to interpret this repetition? If it were at the level of the Symbolic, it would go on repeating itself as if it were repressed material within analysis, as speech which continues to insist, even while facing resistance. But this is not the level at which the repetition of *Crash* works. I want to suggest that in fact the repetition exists at the level of the Real, and that this puts the spectator of the film at the edge of the symbolic and its ordering of reality.

Surely Bouquet is right to make the first crash in the film a primal scene, the point from which all other crashes are repetitions. The primal scene is always accompanied for the child with elements of violence and excitement for which the child has no model of assimilation. According to orthodox definitions of trauma, that which is traumatic involves a violent shock and implies a wound. Yet, *Crash* does not picture scenes of trauma, nor does it traumatise us, its viewers. Somehow *Crash* depicts trauma that does not traumatise. We will see what this might mean later on.

What kind of thing is the repetition of trauma? It is founded on a return of *jouissance*, yet paradoxically this *jouissance* is not available to the subject. For repetition itself produces the loss of *jouissance*. This is the domain of the death drive, where the trauma repeats and something is lost over and over again. In *Crash*, on the other hand, with each repetition a little more is gained.

Usually this something that insists and insists again has a life of its own, quite outside the pleasure principle. What is different with *Crash* is that the film seeks the repetition, and submits to the ever-repeating loss of repetition. Moreover, we do not inhabit the space of the nightmare. How can this be? It is possible because the film alters the psychical situation of the viewer by depriving us of all the usual parameters of depth. Many viewers have commented on the way in which we are made to attend to the surface of the film. I call this effect "flatness", and I will show later how the film achieves it at the expense of psychical depth. The flatness of this filmic world puts the viewer at the very edge of the psychical situations known to psychoanalysis, including all the psychopathologies it traditionally describes. This is what enables the reading of the film in terms of a wound that does not succumb to the interpretation of castration.

Spectators will deal with the film in their own ways, but its logic remains unequivocal: repetition follows repetition in order that the wound is kept open. The wound is both the boundary between life and death, but refuses to be the boundary, and allows life and death to communicate in an alarming space. The wound marks the spot where death nearly realised itself in an accident. But the wound is not just a premature memorial; it also and ferociously aims at pure libido and immortality – to be achieved through the intensification of sexual energy released by car accidents, into the unbound beyond. The sexuality of this death requires the death of the sexed subject as its price, just as it offers the immortality of the Real to its victim. This is a description from the outside; the characters of the film and its spectators live from within the experience, which is that the end of one's subjection to desire is almost reached and that eternity will soon start after just one more accident...

Let us consider more closely how what I am calling the wound relates to life, death and sexuality. This wound connects the life and death drives in the film. My thesis is that fundamentally it plays the part of Lacan's *lamella*, the libido as indestructible life. This is Lacan's account of the *lamella* in *Les quatre concepts fondamentaux de la psychanalyse* (*The Four Fundamental Concepts of Psychoanalysis*, 1973):

> The lamella is something extra-flat, which moves like the amoeba. It is just a little more complicated. But it goes everywhere. And as it is something...that is related to what the sexed being loses in sexuality, it is, like the amoeba in relation to sexed beings, immortal – because it survives any division, any scissiparous intervention. And it can run around.[13]

The *lamella* is certainly running around in *Crash*. You see it arising in all the scenes of death. If the crash produces the wound, the wound is the very token of palpitating life. You can see how the attempt at the experience of sexuality in the Real relies upon the wound. To make up for the insufficiency of the partial drive, there is the wound, the lost part of sexuality, indestructible life. Death is set aside; immortality is secured in the legend of the mortal who perishes by death-by-accident.

Death has a function in *Crash*, paradoxical as it may seem, to ensure life. What is at stake here is pure life, the *lamella*. While the crash secures a death, something creeps and crawls out of it. Death nurtures life. This is the significance of the wound. The crash creates the wound and residue of indestructible life that survives death. This wound is to be found on the body of the car, as well as on the human body. We can now understand the way in which *Crash* relates automobile and human. On both of them, the wound figures their bodywork. It reminds me of Vaughan's desire to drive an automobile that had actually been in a fatal crash – he would do it up just enough to get it going. The wreck is ideal for Vaughan's whole project that involves the death that would fuel a legend. A human dies in a car accident; the wrecked body of the car secretes the sexual energy released at death; another human harnesses this energy in the entrails of the car by "merging" with it in the sexual act; this human, in turn, dies in a car accident and achieves the indestructible life of a legend. Vaughan seeks to overcome death and attain indestructible life by becoming a legend. He continuously seeks *jouissance* in after-the-crash encounters; but it is his final crash that will make the *lamella* go spinning off. Vaughan had spoken of the incredible sexual energy released only by crash deaths. He waits his turn. This far exceeds the limits of the imaginary realm of domination over reality.

We can now ask how the endless scenes of sex work to keep the wound open. Sex, cars and scars. It could not be more explicit than in the scene between Ballard and Gabrielle, a young woman with the most pronounced gait, encased in metal callipers, showing a deep cleavage, a substitute female genital, in one of her legs, a giant cleft leftover from some accident. This wound is what holds Ballard's attention, and finally it is the wound that he penetrates.

This takes place in a car. The scene materialises the analogy between body and machine. Gabrielle's body is like a second car awkwardly encased within the first. Her limbs, half-artificial, half-natural, threaten at the joints, creak and resist and scream, as Ballard lifts and bends parts of her body in his rapture at its awkward hybridity. Gabrielle herself experiences all this with awful enjoyment. It is *enjoyment of the wound* at its purest.

Certainly Gabrielle is scarred, but then scars are everywhere – on the bodies of cars and humans both as the effects and the signs of crashes. This is graphically portrayed in the centre spread of the film, a double and related *tour de force* – a scene of carnage, the multiple car crash, the background against which, in the car wash scene that follows, Vaughan and Catherine's bodies copulate strangely in the throes of a struggle for life. Wandering through the scene of the multiple crashes, we see smoking wrecks, we look through windows at trapped bodies staring vacantly in shock, and at the injuries of freed and living passengers and the injuries of dead ones. Here a disbelieving Vaughan discovers himself outstripped in satisfaction as he finds the stuntman Seagrave's scalped and dismembered body, breasts and long-haired scalp torn off and scattered in various directions. Seagrave had gone ahead with the Jayne Mansfield crash after all – and so successfully! Success not only at the level of verisimilitude – the "big tits" which he had wanted so that the crowd could see them "get all cut up and crushed on the dashboard"; the head embedded in the windscreen; the little dead chihuahuas parked on the back seat – but a success measured by the exact repetition of Jayne Mansfield's crash. In fact, Seagrave had perfected the Mansfield crash, since the crucial ingredient, his own death, was included. The film is indeed about the re-emergent failure to integrate some impossible kernel of the Real – until you succeed with your death in being born a legend. Seagrave was the first to star on the opening night after his rehearsals for death, and thus enjoy the ultimate copulation of fragmented body and metal.

Crashes excite, and Vaughan is clearly excited. But Catherine has also been wandering around the scene of disaster with a growing sensitivity and excitement about cars. She sits on a bench next to a dazed and bloodied woman with bubbles of blood on her face. She allows Vaughan to place her first against the bonnet of a wrecked car, and then inside it, to photograph her inclusion in the scene. This moment marks her inclusion in Vaughan's world of accident.

Where is the wound in this sequence of crashes and car wash? The answer is that it is both multiple and dispersed. There are many wounds, but the whole scene is a wound, and my sentence earlier about that which creeps and crawls out of the crash materialises here. The wound is the opening of the gap of the Real. Life ebbs and flows through the wound. Catherine has remained unscarred so far, but she emerges from the car wash covered in bruises. The copulation with Vaughan transmits the wound. This scene is the image of hybridisation. The open car quite literally closes around them before it moves forward to be battered with water and embraced by bristling brushes. What is being done to the car is repeated inside the car. We hear and see the battery and assault. Is this violence? This is the New World Passion on the back seat of a 1950s Lincoln. The cross and the scourge are not the instruments of this Passion. It is a Passion that marks the body, but it concerns the refashioning of the human body in the likeness of colliding machines.

The scene with Catherine is extended in time and in intensity. It is shot in a way that conveys the unmistakable inseparability of bodies and cars in desire. Here we have the wear and tear of the leathered driving seat, erupting just behind Ballard's right ear. Bodies crash with the same rhythm as the violent swirls of the water-storms hurled at the battered Lincoln. Out of the unholy marriage of cars and bodies in the accident sequence is born a back-seat Passion. This unholy marriage has death as its witness. It is the proximity of the death-by-car-accident (that which will make the legend and defeat death) that releases the life force and intensifies *jouissance*.

After the Passion, the body of Catherine laid out on her bed, a body now bruised, mottled and marked, and Ballard's tender exploration of these. The scene feels religious, as if she had undergone an initiation rite by a wound. But the wound does not signify castration here, but rather the very life substance that is usually subjected to castration. And so it is men who have to outfit themselves with wounds before they can enjoy together. There *is* a progression in the film in the sense that the fundamental relations are clarified, and the extraneous features gradually drop away. Gender, object choice, sexual aim – all these fundamental marks of identity begin to fade into the background. The relation to the wound is what insists. After the penetration of Gabrielle's wound by Ballard, the wound detaches itself as the very condition of *jouissance*. Hence the power of the men's tattoos in that most difficult scene between Ballard and Vaughan.

Perhaps you can now agree that the sex scenes maintain the openness of the wound. Despite the primal scene and the repetitions of the events in the film, we are not dealing with trauma as we know it. What the film creates is trauma that is not traumatising. In fact, it shows us what a world where trauma failed to operate would be like. That is to say, it lays bare trauma as a condition of our psychical and social life.

Emptying the depths

To return to the question of the cinematic effects of *Crash* on the viewer's psychical situation. A strong effect of the film, and one that is often commented upon, is a certain *flatness* of the film. To what, precisely, is this effect due? And what does it mean? I want to suggest that this is a cinematic effect that corresponds to a psychical situation. That situation, in turn, is related to the depth of space (or to its lack) which is the register – indeed, almost the index – of the subject's relation to the Other. This is clarified by some remarks Lacan makes about the subject, the Other, and space in his unpublished Seminar, *Crucial Problems of Psychoanalysis*.[14] Obviously these remarks are based on the Lacanian assumption that the subject is always and only defined in relation to the Other, and that therefore space is not a pre-given container of that relation, but is rather an effect of that relation. The idea that subjects react to each other within a neutral ground of geometrical space is quite alien to Lacan. For him, the subject is firstly a subject of the signifier, a subject that is an effect of language. This well-known proposition defines two dimensions of the subject, provides, as it were, the surface of the subject. But what gives depth to the subject, what is the three-dimensional space of the subject, lies in the subject's relation to the Other. Indeed, the depth of space is precisely the field of the Other.

Here we see a fundamental relation between spatiality and the mechanism of identification. In psychoanalysis, the term identification refers to the process whereby the subject takes up an attribute of the Other and comes to be determined by it. While most accounts of identification are concerned with the content of identification, I am concerned with the way in which identification comes about. Lacan modifies his reference to the three-dimensional space of the field of the Other by adding "except that it is not space, it is time". That is to say, before the subject can enter into three-dimensional *space*, there is a series of things it has to do in *time*. For it is this element of time that allows the subject to appear in the field of the Other in the first place.

In the 1940s, Lacan had developed a theory of what he called "logical time".[15] It was based on the logic of the game of prisoners, where each of three prisoners has either a black or a white disk on his back and the first one to work out the colour of the disk on his own back is to win his freedom. For Lacan, the time of the game is not merely chronological, but is differentiated by three moments – the moment of seeing, the time of comprehending, and the moment of

112

concluding. Much later, Lacan went on to use these moments to map the movement of analysis. In the Seminar on *Crucial Problems of Psychoanalysis*, he uses the three moments to map the movement of identification, claiming that the culmination of these three moments is to be found in any identification.

This is the identification that *Crash* denies the spectator, by using techniques that thwart comprehension and scatter its elements to the four winds. And thus the spectator is thrown back again and again on the moment of seeing. Without the identification with the Other, there can be no access to the three-dimensional space of the Other. There is barely the subject as surface, and this makes for the flatness of *Crash*.

There is a type of shooting that Cronenberg employs that is closely connected to this flatness. It involves a limited, narrow direction of view where you remain in the same place even though you are moving, and where what you see does not vary – you see one side of the car body and an unvarying strip of open road. Is not space flattened when you move and nothing changes? It is clear from his interview with Chris Rodley that the scenes I am talking about are also important for Cronenberg:

> [S]ometimes the simplest things are the most difficult to do. The way I put the camera on the cars, for instance. The framing is not quite normal...I *do* want to suggest people wrapped up in their cars: their relationship to their cars. So the framing is unusual, but in a very simple way.
>
> It's really a matter of exactly where you put the camera. Not that simple. Each day, after choreographing the first scene to be shot, that would be the first thing I would do. I put it more *outboard* of the car body so that the windshield pillar was halfway through the frame, and the other half is looking right down the car body. That meant building rigs. You don't see that much because it takes a lot of time and it's hard to do. Shooting on a platform means you can dolly while the cars are moving. We had six Lincolns; one of them cut in half, one of them made into a pick-up truck so that I could dolly and put lights on from behind.[16]

No secret beyond the door

I have introduced the idea of flatness in *Crash* in the form of a thick surface. This is achieved in at least two ways: firstly, a layering so that the world appears somewhat compressed; secondly, the way in which the protagonists are "wrapped up in their cars" (Cronenberg's description in the interview) which leads to a shrinking of three-dimensional space. In one way or another, space is deprived of its depth. This has its correlate at the psychical level – the withdrawal from the space of the Other. So this is a means whereby the drive is released. For, in *Crash*, we come close to the death drive.

Something about the way in which the flatness was produced escaped me until I read Dana Polan's review of Hubert Damisch's book on perspective in *Camera Obscura*.[17] The argument is that perspective "demonstrate[s] its own activity as interpellation of a subject".[18] Polan quotes Damisch:

> [C]ostruzione legittima proposes in its very arrangement a formal apparatus that, between point of view, vanishing point, and 'distance point,' and organized as it is around the position of the 'subject' taken as origin of the perspective construction and as index of a *here* as of a *there*, represents the equivalent of the network of adverbs of place, if not of personal pronouns: in other words, what linguists call an apparatus of enunciation.[19]

Polan is interested in this argument, but suggests that, as far as *film* is concerned, it is the work of Christian Metz which pinpoints the conditions that set up a field of enunciation:

> In particular, Christian Metz's most recent work looks at frames within frames, windows within windows, doors within doors, and so on, all within the cinematic frame, as a way of pinpointing the work of enunciation in film.[20]

It struck me that these elements were singularly missing from *Crash*, but I could not easily elaborate the argument. I needed a comparison, and the multiplicity of doors in Robert Bresson's *Lancelot du Lac* (1974) came to mind. Bresson's film also feels curiously flat. Yet, it seemed, for all the discarded metal that litters it, to be about the knights of King Arthur's court, and hence about the symbolic. Thus, the question of the relation of the filmic production of flatness to the withdrawal from the symbolic order appeared to be a complex one. Paul Schrader refers to Bresson's wish to flatten out the image, with a steam iron, as it were.[21] This applies to all his films, and a comparison between *Crash* and *Lancelot du Lac* will do much to illuminate the filmic means by which the symbolic is usually – and, in this film, unusually – held in place.

The means of producing flatness in *Lancelot du Lac* are a little different from those used in *Crash*. Flatness there is, but a flatness that is clearly and immediately recognisable as conceived and constructed by the director; in no way can it be taken as a straightforward representation of reality. In *Crash*, the film's construction remains in the background even as we experience the flatness. However, we will see that this difference makes no difference to the distance taken from the symbolic.

Bresson creates flatness in a number of ways. The film takes to an extreme his fondness for shooting only parts of humans, animals and objects. In *Lancelot du Lac*, we see this in the tournament sequence with the lower half of horses as they charge out for each round, an effect which is strikingly enhanced by the crosscutting with the image of the top half of Lancelot on horseback, lance held high in victory. The movement of the horses is horizontal, and that of the victorious Lancelot is vertical. It is a strange stretching of the screen that establishes the screen as a surface that may be described as, precisely, a thick surface.

The power of this effect of stretching is partly due to the repetition that makes up the tournament sequence. Lindley Hanlon describes this, and links it with an argument that reinforces the thesis of flatness:

> Action upon action is repeated at the same distance from the
> camera, at the same angle, and with similar camera
> movements: five knights in a row will mount their horses or
> close the visors of their helmets. This paratactic, repetitious
> style of listing perfectly mimics medieval sources of the
> Lancelot legend in which sentences are repeatedly strung
> together with 'and' or 'then,' without specific connection or
> subordination.[22]

Hanlon seems to be commenting on the organisation of a space of apposition, so to speak. Now a space without relative clauses is a space without nesting. This absence precisely lends itself to the flat surface I am arguing for, but we will see that, at the level of the overall organisation of the film, there *is* "nesting" that promises effects of depth. This aspect has consequences for our reading of the film, but finally it does not distinguish it from the psychical space of *Crash*.

Let us continue with the analysis of the ways in which *Lancelot du Lac* produces the flatness of the surface by noting the pictorial quality of the images. Schrader, writing on Bresson, speaks of "surface" in contrast with the realism of documentary. Bresson wants the surface and the detail of the surface, but he does not want the accompanying meaning. Note how close this sounds to the link I make between surface and a withdrawal from the space of the Other, from the symbolic. In relation to the notion of pictorial quality, Schrader speaks of certain Byzantine qualities found in mosaics; he finds something hieratic in Bresson's work.

I do not disagree with either of these accounts of pictorial quality, but want to add my own version of it. Pictures are compositions, and certainly Bresson has composed his scenes. Many of these seem to occupy the space of what looks like a painting in a classical Western tradition. Within these compositions, there is a minimum of movement, but it is only at the moment of a cut, when the picture comes to life with a large movement of a character, that it becomes clear retrospectively that one had in some sense been looking at a painting. It is at that moment that the "painting" becomes bereft of depth. While paintings are flat, they usually encourage the illusion of depth. Here the minimal depth introduced by an exit effects the opposite: we might almost say that it encourages an illusion of flatness. I am thinking in particular of a scene between Arthur and Gawain – they take up poses and, although they speak, the movement is minimal, and it is only when they suddenly move in different directions that they gain the consistency of real, live characters. The painting comes to life, as it were, but not for long. The flatness of the surface reasserts itself.

Let us add some visual detail to the scene above to enhance the argument. There are few props; the two men almost mirror each other, and the background is a continuous wall of varying colours. When a character exits, a part of this wall reveals itself to be a door. This is often true in the film where doors declare themselves as such only when a character exits; otherwise, they are present just as a difference of colour in an otherwise homogeneous-appearing wall surface. I have already suggested that these exits add to the flatness of the scenes that they close.

Paradoxically, the door in *Lancelot du Lac* has another, but opposite, function. *The door introduces depth at the same time as it flattens the scene* just played. This is not to say that Bresson changes his handling of space so that suddenly we are in the space of traditional cinema. Yet, it is this introduction of depth that distinguishes *Lancelot du Lac* from *Crash*. What is this depth? And what is its relation to psychical space?

Take the question of depth first. I found myself wondering of *Lancelot du Lac* how many scenes end with an exit. I did not need to count, for it happens all the time, whether through those surprising opportunities that open in those homogeneous walls (and almost at once close again), or through the repeated exits from tents that leave us wondering whether we are on the inside or the outside. Bresson does not offer us an escape from flatness into depth. Yet, the moment of the break with flatness does have an effect. The repeated promise of a depth repeatedly curtailed creates a framework of space around the flat surfaces of the image. This newly constructed space could not be a smooth and coherent three-dimensional space. This construction renders space heterogeneous, and this in itself produces a kind of flatness. Perhaps we can say of *Lancelot du Lac* that it sets a limit on flatness with a depth that constitutes itself through a series of flat but *nested* surfaces. I refer to this as *formal depth*.

What is the relation of formal depth to psychical space, remembering that this depth does not overcome flatness, but rather relies upon it? My thesis is that it is through this formal depth that the film establishes a symbolic framework. Flatness, for its part, serves the same purpose that it did in *Crash*, of distancing us from this order. There, desire was reduced to a minimum; what of desire in *Lancelot du Lac*? We could say that the knights of King Arthur's court are stumbling around in a symbolic that has ceased to give them direction. Love is part of the relations of the symbolic, but the central love relationship here is represented not at the level of the Other, but as an impossibility, in some recognition perhaps of what Lacan calls the lack of sexual relation. The one scene in which Lancelot gets as far as divesting himself of his armour is far from being pleasurable. In this film, chinks in the armour only let out blood, and, when Lancelot slowly strips, we have the full vulnerability of the flesh. There is the rawness of a tortoise stripped of its shell. It is as though the film offers only the symbolic and the real. The repetition, the rules and the loyalties belong to the symbolic; the bleeding bodies and the glint of armour belong to the real. Perhaps we can say that, while the social always constrains the desiring subject, at the court of King Arthur it flattens the dimension of the desiring subject to the exact measure of the symbolic. What the film portrays is the moment of the *collapse* of this symbolic. The flatness of the images conveys this to us.

What, therefore, of the formal depth that I have identified in the film? It is the way in which the symbolic can be indicated even as it may be collapsing. For, of course, the flatness of the images through which this is effected makes this collapse palpable for us. The film works by putting us at the join of the symbolic and the real.

In *Lancelot du Lac*, death is part of the symbolic order, and is a consequence also of its collapse. But we do not partake of the eternity of the death drive. Lancelot ends with a graveyard of armour followed by a blank screen. It is as close as one can get to nothingness. But there is no trace here of the desire to be a legend that is found in *Crash*. *Crash* is about the death drive and the evacuation of the field of the Other (although, of course, the subject remains desiring to the extent that it wishes to vacate the field of the Other).

In both *Crash* and *Lancelot du Lac*, there is a closing down of space. Both make use of flatness, but in some way the space of Bresson's film is more complex. What I have identified as depth in the film is not in some simple, straightforward way a cinematic construction of the space of enunciation that draws the viewer into a symbolic world. The formality of the construction at one and the same time indicates the symbolic space and its collapse. In analysing *Crash*, I made the connection between flatness and the distance from the symbolic in psychoanalytic terms. In trying to understand the effects of the formal depth of *Lancelot du Lac*, Metz's idea of how cinema usually constructs a symbolic space helps us to see how Bresson's techniques fall short of such construction.[23]

Cinema has its own ways of establishing its field of enunciation. What is "enunciation" in cinema? Metz rightly recognises that it is not a question of the deictic marks through which Benveniste establishes the field of enunciation. Rather, cinema does this through *reflexive* constructions. He says that the film speaks to us of itself, or of cinema, or of the position of the spectator. It is a doubling of the enoncé. This "fold" takes many forms – the film within the film, the address off, the address in, the subjective image, shot/counter-shot, the flashback, and much else. Reflexive constructions have the effect of bringing out the enunciative level of the film's production:

[T]he capacity that much of the enunciated has to pleat itself here and there, to appear here or there in relief, to peel itself off from a delicate film by itself, which records some indications of *another nature* (or of another level), concerning the production and not the product.[24]

For Metz, *what the enunciated announces is enunciation*. So, although he acknowledges that levels of enunciation vary from film to film, that really makes relatively little difference to him:

The only difference between the marked image, objective or subjective, and the unmarked (neutral) image (again this division admits of all degrees), is that in the former the enunciative intervention is patent and so to speak distinguishable (=overflowing music, rough framing, a strongly emphasised composition of the whole, etc.) while in the second it is everywhere and nowhere, an abstract postulate recessed from the image, 'behind' the whole film. It is deduced from the very presence of the enounced: it is the idea, already remarked upon, of an 'assumed enunciation' when confronted with the 'enounced enunciation'.[25]

What Metz claims is that, when the film is unmarked, enunciation is presupposed. "What the enunciated announces is enunciation" amounts to a claim that would always preserve for cinema a symbolic field despite the efforts of any director. But I think that both *Crash* and *Lancelot du Lac* suggest otherwise. I want to say that the level of enunciation does indeed determine flatness and depth, but that one has to respect the fact that there is such a thing as a determinate level of enunciation. For Metz, this level is, on the one hand, totally variable, subject to a number of factors such as the degree of knowledge and expertise in film, familiarity with the particular film, and so on. But, on the other hand, he posits the general function of the enunciated which is always to point to the act of enunciation. Why, therefore, does Metz need to elaborate on the reflexive mechanisms?

I think that, when there is an ample use of reflexive mechanisms, a film's level of enunciation is high. But I also think that the enunciated can fail to announce enunciation, because enunciation is not a mere matter of the visibility of the film's construction or the inescapability of the enunciative act. So we could say that it *is* the level of enunciation *per se* that determines depth or flatness.

In *Lancelot du Lac*, the reflexiveness that Metz talks of has been transformed. Far from being drawn into the picture by the mechanism of formal depth, we are subjected to a series of unending cuts. This truncated form of the Bressonian symbolic suffices to indicate a field of enunciation that has collapsed in its function.

The end of desire

Clearly the court of King Arthur is a very different psychic space from contemporary urban space. I want to end with a final set of remarks about this contemporary psychic space as it is represented in Cronenberg's film. All versions of the urban involve a certain relation between the subject, danger and technology. In the 19th century, the excitement of the city involved immediate danger. In the 1950s, the gradual rendering of the city into the safety of the suburbs required that danger reappear frequently as the car, as in the game of chicken. But this use of the car as danger could not be further from what we are speaking about with *Crash*. The world of James Dean is about the use of skill and nerve to avoid catastrophe. Even if the body is put at risk, the reward is the body unscathed. The inertia of reality is activated by introducing the threat of death. The economy of desire here is the pleasure principle in all its simplicity. Danger is used as a way of highlighting or outlining objects, and of glamourising subjects. The world of *Crash* is completely different; perhaps it corresponds to a radical change in the nature of repetition, and therefore of addiction. If addiction was used in the 1950s to heighten overly domesticated and suburbanised object relations, in the 1990s it seems that they may be being used to bring the world of desire to an end, or to find the end of the world of desire. It would not be the first time in history that this has happened.

It would be an eschatology of desire, a concern with "the last things" of desire. Or another way to put it is as the wish to end desire – as if the subject has seen through the illusions and substitutions of the object, and wishes to be precipitated beyond desire and beyond the object into the ending of desire. It is akin to being within the death drive, in which the apparatus of the subject is progressively smashed to pieces, while the residue of the subject regresses, warm and sleepy, to an inevitable assignation with death. This is the space of the death drive, an analytic road-movie. But it is not, as Cronenberg has seen, a phenomenological violence. Violence is an experience of inhabited tissue, of an experience which life suffers in its attempt to maintain itself. This is after violence; it is the wreck of the abandoned. Firstly, there were abandoned buildings, then there were abandoned cars. Now in this late, very late landscape there are abandoned limbs in an abandoned narrative. The text will be complete when we are not there.

Notes

1   These terms, "subject" and "object", are necessary for differentiating the structures of neurosis and perversion. With the entry into language, the subject makes an appearance, but something is lost. This is the Lacanian object, akin to, but not identical to, the Freudian lost object. Fantasy is the attempt to unite subject and object into a whole, but the neurotic and the pervert do this very differently. The pervert tries to achieve this by taking the place of the object. Remember that Lacan has a list of objects that includes, along with the breast, the faeces and the phallus, the gaze and the voice. The voyeur, for example, puts himself in the place of the object gaze. This is not developed here because the thesis of this essay primarily concerns the death drive, where there is no question of subject and object.

2   The Lacanian Other is the locus of language and the symbolic.

3   Bruce Fink, *The Lacanian Subject: Between Language and Jouissance* (Princeton, NJ: Princeton University Press, 1995): 112.

4   Quoted in Jacques Lacan, *The Ethics of Psychoanalysis 1959-1960: The Seminar of Jacques Lacan, Book VII*, edited by Jacques-Alain Miller, translated by Dennis Porter (London: Tavistock/Routledge, 1992): 202.

5   Ibid: 216.

[6] The argument that *Crash* is not masochistic can also be made by considering the place of the object *a* in each. The masochist puts himself in the place of the object to ensure the *jouissance* of the Other. He puts himself just there, where the Other lacks. He thus fills the gap with the object. In Lacanian theory, the object is both that which covers the gap *and* also the gap. What looms large in *Crash* is not the object in its function of cover, but its aspect of the hole. It is as if the attempt were to abolish the object altogether.

[7] J G Ballard, *Crash* (London: Paladin, 1990): 113.

[8] Ibid: 147.

[9] Translated from the French: "Un homme, une femme, une voiture, et voilà un très grand film, une forte expérience de cinéma...une plongée dans un univers radical et neuf. Un homme, une femme, une voiture, n'importe lesquels pourvu qu'il y ait triangle. Parfois, l'homme change, ou la femme; parfois, ce sont deux hommes ensemble, ou deux femmes. L'important n'est ni le sexe ni l'identité, mais le moment où les êtres se rencontrent, se cognent l'un à l'autre, se carambolent." Stéphane Bouquet, "Sweet movie", *Cahiers du Cinéma* 504 (July-August 1996): 24.

[10] Translated from the French: "*Crash* est donc un film construit sur la répétition, mais une répétition a-dramatique, non progressive, sérielle...Il n'y a pas d'accélération, pas d'urgence, pas d'affolement, pas d'enjeu qui se dévoilerait soudain. Il y a toujours le même rythme, toujours cette même lenteur, franchement bienvenue dans un film qui aurait pu facilement se laisser griser par la vitesse. Simplement, les gens font l'amour, et l'amour encore, au milieu de voitures plus ou moins accidentées." (Ibid: 24)

[11] Translated from the French: "Vaughan...travaille à déréaliser l'automobile, à la projeter dans l'espace du fantasme, à la nimber d'une aura héroïque, en reconstituant des accidents célèbres dans de clandestins théâtres de plein air. Dans une longue, minutieuse et splendide séquence bleu nuit, on le voit rejouer réellement l'accident de James Dean, présenter les voitures et les protagonistes du drame, reproduire le choc, et s'en sortir, comme si la force de l'automobile avait été d'instaurer un espace imaginaire où le désir pouvait ne jamais rencontrer le principe de réalité." (Ibid: 25).

[12] Translated from the French: "l'imagerie médicale la plus traumatisante: minerves, broches, prothèses, appareils de contention pour soutenir des plaies qui ne peuvent se fermer seules". (Ibid: 24).

[13] Jacques Lacan, *The Four Fundamental Concepts of Psycho-analysis* [Seminar XI, 1963-64], edited by Jacques-Alain Miller, translated by Alan Sheridan (Harmondsworth: Penguin Books, 1979): 197.

[14] Jacques Lacan, *Crucial Problems of Psychoanalysis, Seminar XII* (1964-65) [unpublished].

[15] Jacques Lacan, "Le temps logique et l'assertion de certitude anticipée", *Écrits* (Paris: Éditions du Seuil, 1966): 197-213.

[16]   Chris Rodley (ed), *Cronenberg on Cronenberg*, revised edition (London; Boston: Faber and Faber, 1997): 202. Emphases in original.

[17]   Dana Polan, "History in Perspective, Perspective in History: A Commentary on *L'Origine de la perspective* by Hubert Damisch", *Camera Obscura* 24 (1990): 89-97.

[18]   Ibid: 93.

[19]   Ibid. Emphases in original.

[20]   Ibid: 97.

[21]   Paul Schrader, *Transcendental Style in Film: Ozu, Bresson, Dreyer* (Berkeley: University of California Press, 1972).

[22]   Lindley Hanlon, *Fragments: Bresson's Film Style* (London: Associated University Presses, 1986): 159.

[23]   Christian Metz, *L'Énonciation Impersonnelle, ou le Site du Film* (Paris: Méridiens Klincksieck, 1991).

[24]   Translated from the French: "la capacité qu'ont beaucoup d'énoncés à se plisser par endroits, à apparaître ici ou là comme en relief, à se desquamer d'une fine pellicule d'eux-mêmes qui porte gravées quelques indications d'*une autre nature* (ou d'un autre niveau), concernant la production et non le produit". (Ibid: 20. Emphasis in original.)

[25]   Translated from the French: "La seule différence entre l'image orientée, objective ou subjective, et l'image neutre (encore cet écart admet-il tous les degrés), est que dans la première l'intervention énonciative est ostensible et pour ainsi dire isolable (=musique irruptive, recadrage brutal, composition d'ensemble fortement soulignée, etc.), alors que dans la seconde elle est partout et nulle part, postulat abstrait *en retrait de l'image*, 'derrière' le film global. On la déduit de la présence même de l'énoncé: c'est l'idée, déjà commentée, d'une 'énonciation présupposée' face à l'enonciation énoncée'." (Ibid: 168-169. Emphasis in original.)

Cronenberg and the poetics of time

Michael Grant

On the evidence of his later films, from *Dead Ringers* (1988) to *Crash* (1996), David Cronenberg may without derogation be called a literary filmmaker.[1] I have in mind not his practice of literary adaptation, but the understanding of cinema evident in the nature of the challenge with which the later work confronts us. Cronenberg intends a cinema that stands in a critical relation to what it depicts, and it is literature that points the way to the realisation of his purposes. This is to imply that films such as *Dead Ringers* and *M. Butterfly* (1993) have links with those traditions of modernism that confront the question of what it is to understand the fundamental relations we have with ourselves in terms of the relations we have with language, relations characteristically brought to the fore in literature, and especially in poetry. There is evident in much of Cronenberg's work a thematic concern with derelicts, misfits and outsiders, embodied in characters such as Max Renn, Seth Brundle, the Mantle twins, Bill Lee and René Gallimard. It is a concern linked with questions of the excess and violence of male fantasy. However, this is only the beginning of the matter. In *M. Butterfly*, for example, Cronenberg achieves a complex sense of the continually changing rhythm and tempo of Gallimard's memories and desires as he creates and re-creates the culture and people with whom he is involved. In achieving this, Cronenberg also achieves a coinherence of imagination and temporality, doing so in ways that make the search for meaning abstracted from what is specifically enacted in the film a profound misconception of its purpose. It is not thematic concerns that Cronenberg intends to bring home to us, but events in what Donald Davie has called their "eventfulness", their temporality. As Davie has said of the symbolist poetry of Eliot, Yeats and Valéry, so it might be said of Cronenberg's later films: "whatever else symbolist poems may describe or adumbrate, one thing they always describe is themselves, their own way of coming into being, comporting themselves, and coming to an end".[2] This is to achieve a condition not unlike that of music: the complex ecstasies of past, present and future make of the present time something to be dwelt in and dwelt upon, something lived. Davie describes symbolist poetry "as something which so shapes time as to make us live its elapsing, its duration, with unusual attention to each present moment".[3] In Cronenberg, this sense of complex duration is not to be separated from his sense of mortality and the transformation of the body. The result is a series of narratives that explore the limits – the lack, we might say – of what engenders them. Cronenberg has spoken of his outlook as one of "astringent romanticism", and of his characters as artists doomed to create and doomed equally to fail.[4] In them, he addresses his own condition, that of the modern artist condemned to explore, in ever-renewed transformations of failure and death, the inexorable conditions of art.

Film theory and its misconceptions

The view that the modernist achievement in poetry is to extract from language effects comparable to those produced by music is not shared by contemporary theory, as is evident from one of the founding documents of present-day criticism, Roman Jakobson's account of the poetic function, the lineaments of which were in place by 1921. The poetic function determines the essence of the poetic: it is what constitutes the poeticalness of poetry. Language is focused on the message for its own sake, so that words become, as it were, things in themselves. As a result, the poetic function promotes the "palpability" of signs and "deepens the fundamental dichotomy of signs and objects".[5] Language has, on this view, a kind of free-floating autonomy, and the ability to generate meaning out of nothing but itself. Although this may seem an almost musical conception of language, Jakobson's examples point in another direction, and tend to emphasise effects based on the foregrounding of similarities and differences, as in these lines from Wallace Stevens' "An Ordinary Evening in New Haven":

The oldest-newest day is the newest alone.
The oldest-newest night does not creak by...[6]

The word "new" is renewed, inasmuch as the palpability of the word is emphasised or promoted by a concatenation of opposites, and a repetition of similarities. It is thus tempting to say that, in this sense at least, textual organisation takes over from meaning, so serving what Jakobson and the Formalists see as the modernist poem's defining strategy, the baring of the device. Meaning becomes one element around which the defamiliarising system of style forms itself into an abstract and independent structure. The American neo-formalist Kristin Thompson has argued that the intensity and complexity of perception resulting from stylistic abstraction of this kind may well be the main end and justification of artistic experience. Poetry is less an experience shaped in time than the foregrounding of a spatially conceived paradigm, a set of choices revealing itself as such.

Jakobson's account of the poetic function depends for its efficacy upon an acceptance of the Saussurean division of the sign into signifier and signified. Later linguists and semioticians take this to justify a division of language into two planes or levels, of expression and content, which can then be extended further, as it was by Roland Barthes in *Elements of Semiology*, to incorporate the related ideas that language is "the domain of *articulations*",[7] and that "meaning is above all a cutting-out of shapes".[8] Barthes' position depends on the notion that language is determined by a double articulation comprising, on the one hand, signifiers or distinctive patterns of sound, and, on the other, concepts, thoughts or meanings. Thus, for Barthes, language is "an intermediate object between sound and thought", and "it consists *in uniting both while simultaneously decomposing them*".[9] This picture or myth of language has exercised a continuing fascination over contemporary theorists, and yet it is misconceived. Barthes has confused a description of language with what he thinks of as its reality. He has ascribed powers of causality to what is no more than an analogy. Furthermore, the notion of articulation he employs remains unclear. As Wittgenstein has pointed out, "[t]hought and intention are neither 'articulated' nor 'non-articulated'; to be compared neither with a single note that sounds during the acting or speaking, nor with a tune".[10] Barthes assumes that meaning is a process, such that meaning is caused, produced or engendered by something that goes on at the time of uttering. This something is thought to be the process of enunciation, or articulation of the signifiers, a process of differentiation which (in some way) gives rise to the enounced, the meaning. However, nothing that goes on as we speak constitutes the meaning of what we say. Our words have meaning because they are uttered by someone who intends to say something: "conversation, the application and further interpretation of words flows on and only in this current does a word have its meaning".[11] As Paul Johnston comments: "having a thought is neither like watching a telegram message gradually come through nor like laboriously stringing pearls on a necklace. No one can think half a thought or be three-quarters of the way through the process of thinking it".[12] In other words, a thought is not a process in the way in which an act of speech is a process. The act of speech has duration, with beginning, middle and end, and it can be timed. No such concept of duration or measurement is applicable to thoughts, concepts or meanings. As Wittgenstein remarks in *Zettel*, "[t]he mistake is to say that there is anything that meaning something consists in".[13] One therefore has to conclude that, inasmuch as semiotics is founded on the idea that language articulates thought, it is founded on a confusion deriving from a misunderstanding of the relation between words and meanings.

Stanley Cavell

If we are to escape from the hold which theory has over us, we need to recognise that we are not obliged to accept the assumption that human subjectivity stands in need of some overall interpretation or explanation, a need satisfied by theory. There is nothing inevitable about the model of human experience on which theory is founded, described by Michael Weston as "*governance* by what aspires to the condition of thought", and we can reject it: "Our fundamental relation to ourselves and to all else cannot lie in an understanding of their nature which can be brought to conceptual articulation and so be the subject of interpretation, for this understands that relation as *already*, although implicitly, conceptual and linguistic".[14] Hence, one may be justified in thinking that the questions raised by modern art are not ones that can profitably be addressed theoretically in terms of a universal problematics of meaning and subjectivity. As Stanley Cavell has argued, the question endemic to modern art is that of identity, and an understanding of it requires a fullness of individual response: "One cannot imagine an audience of new music before Beethoven, or viewers of the paintings or spectators of the theater of that period, as wondering, or having the occasion to wonder, whether the thing in front of them was a piece of genuine art or not. But sometime thereafter, audiences did begin to wonder".[15] The full impact of modern art depends on "a willingness to trust the object, knowing that the time spent with its difficulties may be betrayed".[16] What modern art requires is not only evaluation, but also that the notion of evaluation be extended: it is a question not only of judging the achievement of a given work, but also of deciding whether the work with which we are dealing is art at all, and this is no simple matter. It is characteristic of modernism that it forces the issue of the nature of art on us in a particularly direct and uncompromising way. It raises, as the art of earlier periods had no need to do, the question of the artist's intention, his sincerity and seriousness, and to deal with this the critic has no other recourse but to get us to see what he sees. But, as Cavell insists, "for that to communicate, you have to see it too. Describing one's experience of art is itself a form of art; the burden of describing it is like the burden of producing it".[17]

Cavell conducts his discussion of art against the background of the Romantic idea that reality is not given to us in a preordained way. Human beings create reality, and there is really no other kind of reality for us. This idea is closely related to another concept equally fundamental to Romanticism, the idea of *expression*. As Charles Taylor puts it: "To express something is to make it manifest in a given medium. I express my feelings in my face; I express my thoughts in the words I speak or write. I express my vision of things in some work of art".[18] In all these cases, we have the notion of making something manifest, and if we make something manifest we do so in a particular medium with specific properties. But, as Taylor points out, when we talk of making something manifest, at least in this context, we do not mean that what is so revealed was fully formulated beforehand. This may, on some occasions, be the case; I may finally say what I really feel about something in words I had thought out some time before. But, in the case of a poem or novel, my expression will "involve a *formulation* of what I have to say".[19] I am giving voice or expression to something that was not fully formed beforehand; my thoughts were inchoate and only partly formed, and I am discovering what it is that I intend to say in the process of saying it. The process of writing, or whatever, may be a way of discovering what one's true feelings are.

This means that we have difficulty (in relation to art) distinguishing between the medium and the message. For works of art, being in the medium they are is integral to them. We cannot distinguish meaning from how that meaning is expressed: style and meaning are one. Taylor makes it clear that, understood in this way, the creation of a work of art not only makes something manifest, but also *makes* something: it brings something into being that did not exist before. It is this way of understanding artistic creativity that is central to Cronenberg's undertaking in *M. Butterfly*. This becomes clear from an interview he gave to Chris Rodley, where he emphasises how crucial the idea of transformation is to his conception of the film: "René is creating a reality for himself and, for her own reasons, Song is helping him":

> Gallimard is in the process (unknown to him) of creating his own opera. He is creating the opera of his life, preparing to become the diva of it.[20]

The narrative of *M. Butterfly* enacts the process whereby René Gallimard discovers what he is, but what he discovers is a being he has himself created. He does not simply play the role as laid down in Puccini's opera; he creates Madam Butterfly anew, and becomes her.[21] The complexity of Cronenberg's engagement with Gallimard's transformation is evident in his style. The film has none of the gore and bodily violence of, for example, *Scanners* (1981) or *The Fly*

(1986). Nor do we find in it that critique of the norms of cinematic editing – that distanciation – which exponents of formalist and semiotic aesthetics have emphasised. Cronenberg's later style is classical, almost marmoreal, and nowhere more so than in *M. Butterfly*, the beauty of whose images is evident from the opening credits. It is from within this style of balance and detachment that the most perverse and threatening elements emerge. As Steven Shaviro has noted:

> The imposing plenitude of the image instills in the spectator a heightened sensitivity to the affections of his or her own body. The continuity of character and action binds us to a logic of nonidentity and disintegration.[22]

Cronenberg's continuity style is relentlessly attentive to Gallimard and Song as together they play out the processes of self-transcendence. The gravity of style embodies an integrity of vision that binds us to the characters, individuating their unique identities out of their unique ways of negotiating the differing conditions that confront them. This refusal to abstract from the characters, or to generalise them into types, is essential to constituting the style as a critique not only of the characters' actions, but also of the self-understanding manifest in those actions. Cronenberg does not work through rhythmic or emotive forms of editing to evoke complicity with his characters or pass adverse judgment on them. The precision of style exacts from the viewer a closeness of attention to what the characters do and how they do it, and by virtue of its very scrupulosity calls into question the Romantic desire for self-creation to which Gallimard so profoundly commits himself.

The way in which style subsumes the narrative to itself becomes evident if we place in the overall context of the film the sequence in which Gallimard leaves Song's house after his first visit to her. As he departs, he stops to watch a man catching dragonflies in a net. The man talks to him in Chinese, and gives him one of the dragonflies. Gallimard hails a rickshaw, and, as he is pulled along in it, he watches the dragonfly move across his hand, and then fly away. There is on his face an expression of quizzical amusement. Cronenberg remarks that he put this sequence into the film, a sequence not in the play or the script, "because it seemed so perfect, subtle and obscure to me: the idea that these dragonflies have come out as a result of a transformation".[23] One might say that the dragonfly is an emblem of the condition to which Gallimard finds himself being drawn: just as the dragonfly emerges from its earlier larval and pupal stages into a final condition of iridescent beauty, the imago stage beyond all metamorphoses, so Gallimard already feels the promptings of an urge to go beyond himself, an urge to personal transformation that is wholly consistent with the Romantic conception of selfhood to which Coleridge has given memorable expression: "what is the Future, but the Image of the Past projected on the mist of the Unknown, and seen with a glory round its head".[24] As George Steiner has argued, there is in Heidegger's account of human being a similar emphasis on anticipation as that which makes us authentically what we are. The authentic nature of man is manifest in the way in which we are shaped by the future: the past does not lie behind me, it awaits me and is yet to come. I run ahead to the past and make it my own, and, in the process of so coming towards myself, my true nature is revealed. It is a process that leads me to break with what is familiar, with the everyday world of clocks, appointments and deadlines, in an act that projects me towards self-fulfilment.[25] For Gallimard, however, self-fulfilment is not accessible on these terms. In telling his story to his audience of prisoners – his captive audience – Gallimard seeks to achieve sanction and fulfilment in death. And, since the story is about love, for Gallimard to tell the story is for him to seek to ground the love of which he speaks – his own love – in a similar sanction and consummation. And yet, this sanction is empty: René's death leads on to nothing. The only identification he can achieve with the role of Butterfly is as a masquerade, a mask, returned back on him by his own image in a mirror. To present the final scene in these terms is, for Cronenberg, to subvert the claim implicit in Gallimard's telling of his story, that he has transformed his life into an equivalent of what in the dragonfly or butterfly is the perfection of the imago. When Gallimard tells his story, the story collapses, due not to effects of self-distancing or estrangement, but to the unflinching way in which Cronenberg's direction forces us to confront its absurdity. Gallimard is grotesque, and nowhere more so than in the farcical quality of his self-dramatisation. His death, far from accomplishing a mysterious and creative transformation of his life, merely emphasises the absurdly theatrical and operatic excesses of his story.

The *Sight and Sound* reviewer, John Harkness, finds the last scene unsatisfactory. He is unable to relate it to the rest of the film, finding it "miles removed from the world of the film that we've seen".[26] But this is to mistake its purpose. Gallimard's grotesque make-up and costume, so different from how Song Liling used make-up and clothing in her equally suspect role-playing, together with the plangency of his speech and the emotively inflected music, combine to express a piercing sense of sadness and loss. It is characteristic of the dispassion of Cronenberg's presentation of the scene that these feelings are exposed to scrutiny, one that effects a critique of Romantic ambition by employing the very procedures that Romanticism made possible. We see that René's vision of the world – of human reality – is a vision sustained heroically by nothing other than its internal energies of transformation, and yet we see also that what this heroism of creative and imaginative effort achieves is ultimately fraudulent. Gallimard is deluding himself as to the significance of his actions. Cronenberg renders void the kind of meanings to which Gallimard's narrative lays claim, and yet he does not invite us to dismiss him or take his sufferings as unreal. We are left in no doubt that the pain and suffering which Gallimard has endured on account of his love are genuine: nevertheless, our response to this strength of feeling is equivocal. The film's movement is such that it requires us to decide where we stand in relation to him, and yet it offers only indeterminate points of reference by which to do so. The equivocation with regard to the character folds back onto our relation with the film itself: we are left suspended, irresolute, and in a state of apparent incompletion.

Walter Benjamin and the novel

The point at issue here, which brings into relief the critical challenge posed by Cronenberg's art, can be captured by reference to some remarks of Walter Benjamin in his essay, "The Storyteller". Benjamin points out that, in the Middle Ages (and in what remains today of traditional societies), there was no house, hardly a room, in which someone had not died. Death was integral to life, as mourning and celebration found expression in the great religious festivals and the passage of the seasons. However, in modern times, dying has been pushed further and further out of the perceptual world of the living. Today we live in rooms that have never been touched by death, and, when our deaths approach, we are stowed away in hospitals or sanatoria, out of sight and out of mind. Nevertheless, it is "characteristic that not only a man's knowledge or wisdom, but above all his real life...assumes transmissible form at the moment of his death".[27] As someone's life comes to an end, the unforgettable emerges in his gestures and expressions; it imparts to "everything that concerned him that authority which even the poorest wretch in dying possesses for the living around him".[28] Death, insists Benjamin, is the very source from which the traditional form of the story, the folk tale, the chronicle, draws its authority. For the storyteller (from Chaucer to Kipling), death is recognised and accepted as a natural part of life. Life can only be meaningful if we accept the fact that we die and the world goes on.

In this, the traditional story or tale differs from the novel, which Benjamin assimilates to the Romantic tradition. The novel, he argues,

130

is the only art form that includes time amongst its constitutive principles. There is a duality between the inwardness or subjectivity of the protagonist and the outside world which can only be overcome for the hero when he is in a position to comprehend the unity of his life, a unity encompassed in memory. Benjamin quotes from Georg Lukács' *Theory of the Novel*: "The insight which grasps this unity… becomes the divinatory-intuitive grasping of the unattained and therefore inexpressible meaning of life".[29] The novel in the 19th and 20th centuries is concerned to exorcise the terrors of death for both the writer and the reader. As Benjamin remarks: "What draws the reader to the novel is the hope of warming his shivering life with a death he reads about".[30] This suggests that there is something of the religious still attaching to the practice of the novel. The novel came into the ascendant at a time when religious forms could no longer satisfy the Romantic ambition to find human experience itself an incarnation of the sacramental. Romantics such as Blake and Shelley sought to achieve through the imagination an intimacy and spirituality powerful enough to challenge established religion on its own ground. In the novel, we are encouraged to identify with the hero, so that when the hero dies, either literally or figuratively (marriage or passing into some other wholly new state), the presentation of his death impresses upon the reader the sense that what is being revealed is the true meaning of life. The hero of the novel is removed from the continuum of life and given an exceptional destiny, which condenses into itself a meaning and significance beyond the ordinary, a meaning and significance that are, for the protagonist, otherwise inexpressible. The same holds true of many Hollywood films: consider the last sequence of *Duel in the Sun* (1947). Here the deaths of the hero and heroine, who have fatally wounded each other in a final shootout, give meaning and purpose to their lives. Cradled in each other's arms and united by death in a kind of marriage, the final crane shot gathers them into a mystical union with the American wilderness.

But *M. Butterfly* is not organised in accordance with the principles of the novelistic continuum. The significance of the film lies elsewhere, in Cronenberg's understanding of the critical role played by modern art in relation to the forms of modern life. Cavell has argued that it is not merely the threat of fraudulence and the necessity for trust that has become characteristic of the modern, "but equally the reactions of disgust, embarrassment, impatience, partisanship, excitement without release, silence without serenity".[31] There is a dynamic of spiritual life present in Romantic art, but not the fulfilment, and this tradition of provocation and failure has been handed on to the moderns. Cavell's remarks on modern art give what might be called grammatical facts, facts that tell us what kind of object a modern work of art is, and what that work means for us. They find support from J G Ballard. In an interview concerned with Cronenberg's film of his novel *Crash*, Ballard argues that the emphasis on what he calls the "sacramental aspect" of the car crash is far more pronounced in the film than it is in the book. The crashes are performed like profane versions of the Mass:

> Bertolucci, whom I know slightly, called the film 'a religious masterpiece' and I know what he meant. The compulsive rehearsal of the same scenario – these endless crashes being planned and executed – is in fact no more than the sort of repetitions you find in religious observance. The same mantras are recited, the same knees are bent before the same bleeding Christ up on his cross.[32]

Ballard finds in the car wash sequence in *Crash* – which he considers one of the great scenes of cinema – the same quality of the ritualistic, in which the characters are made aware of some sort of transcendent experience taking place, lying outside their comprehension or grasp. It is in this sense that *Crash* may be described as critical: the evocation of religious iconography serves to make clear the failure of that evocation to connect with a living tradition, or to speak with authority on behalf of the individual. An unbridgeable rupture opens between the individual's experience and the traditional forms that once served to make sense of that experience. And this is Cavell's point: poetry in the 19th and 20th centuries has altered in such a way that the issues of sincerity, intention and seriousness are forced on the reader by the poem itself. This does not require the reader to respond in ways that are somehow fuller or more complex than those asked of us by earlier writing, but it does require a response that is more personal. Modern poetry "promises us, not the re-assembly of community, but personal relationship unsponsored by that community; not the overcoming of our isolation, but the sharing of that isolation". If modern art expresses a religious impulse, it does so insofar as it promises "not to save the world out of love, but to save love for the world, until it is responsive again".[33]

These matters come to a focus on the question of sexuality. For Cronenberg, human sexuality, having become detached from the needs of reproduction, is now almost abstract: it has become an art form in its own right. "Only a man knows how a woman is supposed to act". This is the explanation given by Song to her Communist controller, a large and masculine woman, as to why men play women's roles in the Beijing opera. It is, says Cronenberg, the line in the script that attracted him to making the film. In casting John Lone as Song, Cronenberg chose an actor who could play the role of a woman while still remaining a man. The balance was delicate: "There must be this transformation into a man, and you can't get that if you get someone that is such a perfect woman that you can't transform them".[34] At the same time, there had to be sufficient femaleness in the Song character to allow Gallimard to create his fantasy of femaleness out of her:

> I don't want [Gallimard] to be a total fool. I want the audience to understand why he doesn't twig to it. By the end of the movie you should realize that there's a will involved in this; he's determined not to accept that Song is a man and he has his own reasons for that. Several of them. So it's complex.[35]

Song has to be neither man nor woman, but suspended between both conditions: neuter. Sexuality is thus abstracted or distanced from the body, and, in the resulting condition of formal possibility, becomes the material of Gallimard's art, an art of sexuality in precisely Cronenberg's sense. Hence, Gallimard cannot accept Song as a man: to do so would be to close off the possibilities of transformation on which his fantasy depends. Gallimard, as Jeremy Irons presents him, is not fooled. He *wants* to be fooled. There is in him, says Cronenberg, echoing Coleridge, "a willing suspension of disbelief". Song creates a fake Chinese culture, a fake ancient Chinese culture of love and sexuality. Gallimard enters into it, goes along with it, as one would a work of art, a work of art of which, retrospectively, he himself is to become the creator. To insist on the singularity of the body, on the maleness of Song's body, would short-circuit Gallimard's imaginative drive and deprive him of what he and Song in their complicity have created together. The artist in Gallimard refuses to abandon to mere reality the supreme fiction of his love. In the sequence of their final separation, in the police van after the verdict of the court has been delivered on them, Song strips naked, and exposes himself, appealing to Gallimard as a man who loves him: "I am your Butterfly". Gallimard replies: "How could you, who understood me so well, make such a mistake?". Speaking with a kind of introspective intensity, he says: "I'm a man who loved a woman created by a man". Song touches him, gently and with love; at first, Gallimard responds, touching his skin, but then he shrinks back and moves hurriedly to the other end of the wagon, a wire mesh seeming to come between them. "Anything else simply falls short" is his response, and he curls into a corner, turning in on himself. Song has shown Gallimard his "true self", when all he loved was "the lie, a perfect lie". In offering himself, Song has destroyed the lie and so proved, as Gallimard has it in the final sequence, "not worthy".

To present the film in these terms is to align it with the problem of status or identity which Cavell sees as central to modern art: what kind of film is it, and how is it to be understood? The undecidability that lies at the heart of *M. Butterfly*'s representation of sexuality is familiar to modern criticism from Barthes' theory of the Text. It therefore seems plausible to think that the problematics of sexuality as represented in the film also represent the problematics of the filmic text itself. For Barthes, the work is that manner of production (often identified as "19th-century realism") which "closes on a signified",[36] and represents a civilisation based on the Sign – that is, religious or transcendental meaning. The Text, however, is dilatory, deferring meaning, playing with it. The Text, Barthes says, is radically symbolic, a term he takes over from Lacan to describe language as a system displaced from itself, without closure or centre. The Text participates in, and reveals, the fundamentally ungraspable nature of language, exhibiting not ambiguity of meaning, but plurality: "the *stereographic plurality* of its weave of signifiers".[37] The reader, confronted by something as indefinable and ungraspable as the Text, remains suspended amongst the possibilities of meaning, possibilities that nevertheless require of the reader an active collaboration and involvement in the Text's processes of discourse. Barthes identifies the plurality of the Text with sexual plurality in *S/Z*, his study of *Sarrasine* (completed 1830), which, like *M. Butterfly*, tells the story of a man who is taken for a woman.

However, to read the film in similar terms would be to pass over the fact that the final sequence is concerned not with textuality in general, but with apostrophe and invocation in particular. Gallimard invokes and apostrophises his love, and, in doing so, becomes both its object and its inspiration: it is in him that the pure love of which he dreams finds realisation. The constitutive power of the creative act is thus brought to the fore as the central theme and organisational principle of the film, a position it occupies also in the major poetry of the Romantics:[38]

O Goddess! hear these tuneless numbers, wrung
    By sweet enforcement and remembrance dear,
And pardon that thy secrets should be sung
    Even into thine own soft-conchèd ear:
Surely I dreamt to-day, or did I see
    The wingèd Psyche with awakened eyes?[39]

Here Keats presents the goddess Psyche as both the inspiration of the poem and its addressee or recipient. The poem's invocation of her constitutes her, creating a world of poetic suspension (not unlike that described by Barthes in relation to the Text) in which the two lovers, Psyche and Cupid, embrace:

I wandered in a forest thoughtlessly,
   And, on the sudden, fainting with surprise,
Saw two fair creatures, couchèd side by side
   In deepest grass...
They lay calm-breathing on the bedded grass;
   Their arms embraced, and their pinions too;
Their lips touched not, but had not bade adieu...[40]

Timothy Clark has argued that "Ode to Psyche" enacts "the poetic or creative process itself as a movement of self-transcendence or becoming, for the ode unfolds itself as the act of dedication to a deity who is both its inspiration and its projection".[41] According to Clark, the ode conflates poem and subject, inspiration and addressee, poet and audience:

So let me be thy choir, and make a moan
   Upon the midnight hours;
Thy voice, thy lute, thy pipe, thy incense sweet
   From swingèd censer teeming...[42]

Drawing on Heidegger, Clark makes it clear that the temporality of the poem is futural, projecting itself towards "a conjunction with Psyche that would be at once the summation of a human poetic yet, at the same time, also its annihilation".[43] In such a summation, the poet achieves a silence beyond poetry: "*No one can take the Other's dying away from him*".[44] For Heidegger, it is the fundamental truth of human being, *Dasein*, that each one of us must die for himself:

Dying is something that every Dasein itself must take upon itself at the time. By its very essence, death is in every case mine, in so far as it 'is' at all.[45]

He goes on to insist that mineness and existence are ontologically constitutive for death, or, as George Steiner puts it, that "[t]he essence, the motion, the meaning of life are totally at one with being-towards-death, with the individual's 'assumption'...of his own singular death".[46] Death is the possibility of our impossibility, of our no longer being able to be there. In anticipating the indefinite certainty of death, we open ourselves to a threat arising out of the fact of our own being "there", and, if we are to develop an authentic being-towards-death, we must maintain ourselves in this very threat. But it is possible for this constant threat to be genuinely disclosed to us only when we achieve that state of mind in which we are capable of taking upon ourselves our thrownness into the world:

> *But the state-of-mind which can hold open the utter and constant threat to itself arising from Dasein's ownmost individualized Being, is anxiety.* In this state-of-mind, Dasein finds itself *face to face* with the 'nothing' of the possible impossibility of its existence.[47]

For Heidegger, being-towards-death, human being, is in essence anxiety. And anxiety (*Angst*) is inseparable from an anticipation which reveals to Dasein the possibility of being itself in an "impassioned FREEDOM TOWARDS DEATH – a freedom which has been released from the illusion of the 'they', and which is factual, certain of itself, and anxious".[48]

The anxiety of which Heidegger speaks is not neurotic fear or psychological dread, but the liberating capacity to take upon oneself the nearness of nothingness, and to recognise the contingency of the possibilities that make up our contingent lives. This is manifest in the interplay of apostrophe, invocation and negation that make up the stylistic energies of Keats' "Ode to Psyche". The poet, who would be the choir, the lute, the pipe of the goddess, apostrophises her through a series of negatives ("temple thou hast none/...No voice, no lute, no pipe"), a contradictory dialectic of negation and affirmation in which the possibilities of poetic creation are revealed for the contingencies they are: what poetry creates and what it negates are internal to poetry itself. The goddess is a creation of the poem addressed to her. Keats' paradoxical achievement is an achievement of style: it is through style that "Ode to Psyche" achieves the extreme reach of sympathetic imagination, of negative capability, on which it concludes, and it is through style that it attains the temporality characterised in "Ode on a Grecian Urn": "And, happy melodist, unwearièd,/For ever piping songs for ever new".[49] The contradictory and paradoxical interplay between negation and affirmation is inseparable from rhythm and movement: we see a sustained tension between the demands of the stanzaic form, of the movement of one line to the next, and the dismemberment of the line from within. The apostrophe tends to delay the movement forward, through an effect of stasis arising from repetition:

O latest born and loveliest vision far
Of all Olympus' faded hierarchy!
Fairer than Phoebe's sapphire-regioned star,
Or Vesper, amorous glow-worm of the sky;
Fairer than these, though temple thou hast none...[50]

As the movement forward is inhibited, so each line and the discrete parts of each line come to the fore. The repetitions enable an effect of slackening, as the onward momentum is halted, and the lines and their constituent phrases achieve a status independent of the stanza. "Ode to Psyche" enacts a temporality of anticipation: I am "what I shall have been for what I am in the process of becoming".[51] For Heidegger, it is a temporality that underpins authentic being-towards-death, and it finds expression here, in a poetry of invocation, in which the name assumes qualities proper to the verb.

It seems clear that the temporality of anticipation is that of symbolist poetry also. As Davie's article is at pains to argue, the poetry of Mallarmé, Yeats and Eliot attends to time in a way that renders the verbal event of the poem simultaneous with the event it describes. The time of the narrative is identified with, or made indistinguishable from, the time of the telling of the narrative. Davie gives as an example some lines from "A Game of Chess", section II of "The Waste Land":

In vials of ivory and coloured glass
Unstoppered, lurked her strange synthetic perfumes,
Unguent, powdered, or liquid – troubled, confused
And drowned the sense in odours;[52]

The ambiguity of "troubled, confused" is evident: they are both taken by the reader in the first place as adjectival participles, like "powdered". But, as Davie points out, after coming around the line-ending and reaching "drowned", "the reader realizes them for what they are, past indicatives".[53] We are, as it were, suspended between two possibilities, and what we have to recognise is that "troubled, confused" are participles as we come up to them, and in retrospect active verbs as we move away from them. Davie concludes that ambiguities such as these operate to drive the reader on from line to line, and by so doing "force home to him just how poetry moves and must move always forward through time".[54] Insofar as Eliot's lines may be seen as characteristic of symbolist writing (and Davie provides corroborating examples from Mallarmé and Yeats), one may say of symbolist syntax that it enacts the futural anticipation that, for Heidegger, constitutes human being:

This running ahead is nothing other than *the authentic and singular future of one's own Dasein.* In running ahead Dasein *is* its future, in such a way that in this being futural it comes back to its past and present. Dasein, conceived in its most extreme possibility of Being, *is time itself*, not *in* time.[55]

Heidegger describes a temporal movement that, in poetry such as Eliot's, becomes indistinguishable from the act of reading: to read the poem is to enact the very process of its coming into being.

However, Cronenberg's *M. Butterfly* does not identify its time of presentation with the time represented in it. The depicted events take place over some five years, while the film's running time is about 100 minutes. One might remark at this point that the identification of the two times, which cinema delivers automatically in the continuous take, has been seen by André Bazin, and those influenced by him, as a precondition of realism. This means that if one is to characterise the film's symbolist temporality one will have to look elsewhere. In *M. Butterfly*, Cronenberg's artistic purposes are inseparable from an exploration of the instabilities of identity, and the film engages with them from the moment of Gallimard's first encounter with Song Liling at the Swedish Embassy. She is singing the aria "Un bel dì, vedremo..." from Puccini's *Madama Butterfly* (*Madam Butterfly*, 1904), in which the Japanese girl gives passionate voice to her belief that "one fine day" her American lover will return to her. Later, in the grounds of the embassy, Song confronts Gallimard with the irony of her situation (which, she tells him, is "lost on you"). Speaking as a Chinese woman taking on the role of a Japanese woman in an opera written in the West for the entertainment of Westerners, she insists on the fact that during the last war the Japanese used "thousands of our people for medical experiments". Gallimard is confused, and unable to reply; Song plays on his discomfort, giving an ironic inversion of the story of the opera by recasting it in terms of an American girl who falls in love with, and kills herself for, a Japanese businessman. Such a girl, she says, would be regarded in the West as mad. Gallimard's confusion continues, until she relents to the extent of telling him that what matters is not the ridiculous story, but the music. Retrospectively, this scene takes on a different aspect when we learn that Song is a man. The position from which Song speaks can no longer be seen as one of assurance; as a homosexual and an artist, he is, at best, in an ambiguous position with respect to the Communist Party, and, as we also learn later, the idea of China that he embodies is one which he has created himself, for Gallimard's benefit and for his own, inasmuch as his love for Gallimard depends upon Gallimard's accepting his version of Chinese culture as a reality.

A similar use of retrospective disclosure arises with respect to Gallimard's knowledge of Song's sexual identity. According to Cronenberg, an opening prologue was originally shot for the film, in which the audience was told that Song turned out to be a man. However, this was dropped in the interests of a more complex purpose. Cronenberg points to this when he discusses the reaction shot during the trial in which we view Gallimard's response to seeing Song as a man for the first time:

> We were playing several things with that reaction shot. One of them was, 'Why is she dressed that way? Why is she pretending to be a man?' A little laugh and then a little confusion and then a little feeling of, 'I knew anyway but I didn't want to know.' It's very complex.[56]

Song's sexual identity is, therefore, not something which Gallimard did not know, but which is finally revealed at the trial. (It is worth noting here the ambiguity of the film's title. *M. Butterfly* may stand for either Monsieur or Madame Butterfly.) We might at this point shift our ground and go on to ask: when does the film want the viewer to know of Song's real identity? One might say that there is no final answer to this question, and that the concern of the film is with questions far removed from the revelation of a hitherto concealed secret. Cronenberg is not interested in posing the question of Song's sexual identity in terms of knowledge (one of the many points on which this film contrasts with *The Crying Game* [1992], for example): the significance of Song's sexuality remains internal to the film, emerging for the viewer, as well as for Gallimard, only as a consequence of the retrospective understanding inseparable from the film's onward movement. The question of Song's being a man is crucial from the beginning, but that this is so emerges only as the subsequent development of the film turns back onto its beginning, inverting the past into the future and showing it in a new light. Retrospective disclosure of this kind accomplishes a mode of understanding similar to that which symbolist poetry achieves as it brings complex torsions of syntax home to the reader. Ambiguities enfolding the meaning and significance of Song's identity are so realised within the film's duration that readings based on a choice between either knowing or not knowing are without crucial pertinence to it. The question of knowledge is not at the film's imaginative centre: its engagement with sexual identity is creative and exploratory, and Cronenberg invites us into an understanding that is given inseparably from our experience of the film through time. Sexuality is explored in terms of a succession of related events, which overlap and qualify each other, and it is from this intertwining of events that a sense of things emerges that is different from anything we see onscreen. We are to respond to a complex attitude towards sexuality which we cannot define independently of the film itself, although recognisable attitudes form the material out of which it has been created. The truth of *M. Butterfly* is not that of fact, but of the imagination: Gallimard calls this "the perfect lie".

M. Butterfly and the Romantic image

The creation of attitude in this way results in part from Cronenberg's refusal to force readings of the characters' actions onto the viewer, and this refusal is, as we have seen, a matter of style. Style in Cronenberg embraces not only the organisation of the image on the screen (the *mise en scène*), but also (and most significantly) the movement and rhythm of the film as a whole, including the presentation of the constitutive elements of the narrative. Such a concept of style makes it appropriate to evoke the "Conclusion" to *The Renaissance*, where Pater insists that "[n]ot the fruit of experience, but experience itself, is the end". In a famous passage, he continues:

> To burn always with this hard, gemlike flame, to maintain this ecstasy, is success in life...Not to discriminate every moment some passionate attitude in those about us, and in the very brilliancy of their gifts some tragic dividing of forces on their ways, is, on this short day of frost and sun, to sleep before evening.[57]

There is a certain contradiction here: although Pater speaks of burning with a "hard, gemlike flame", there is, as F R Leavis has pointed out, "nothing answering in his prose".[58] Leavis advances a highly adverse judgment on the writing, considering it "cloistral, mannered, urbane, consciously subtle and sophisticated and actually monotonous and irresponsive in tone, sentiment and movement", and yet one might respond by saying that, in Pater, we find an early realisation of that paradoxical sense of life-in-death, of death-in-life, which crucially informs the imaginative achievement of later modernist poetry. Frank Kermode cites a passage from Pater's story, "Emerald Uthwart" (1892), in which a case-hardened and experienced doctor removes a ball of shot from the dead body of a young man whose beauty moves him profoundly: "This expression of health and life, under my seemingly merciless doings...touched me to a degree very unusual in persons of my years and profession...The flowers were...hastily replaced, the hands and the peak of the handsome nose remaining visible among them; the wind ruffled the fair hair a little; the lips were still red. I shall not forget it".[59] As Kermode points out, by making a dead face stand for what is most "vital" in art, Pater was providing an early type of the paradoxical emblems by which Yeats was later to define art in a poem such as "Byzantium": "I hail the superhuman;/I call it death-in-life and life-in-death".[60] It is this paradox that informs Pater's style: he sought for the living phrase in which to embody the "speech of the soul", and yet "it is a commonplace that Pater wrote English like a *dead* language, laying out every sentence, as Max Beerbohm says, 'in a shroud'".[61]

The style of *M. Butterfly* is similarly paradoxical: shot length is measured in pace, even "cloistral", employing deliberate and unhurried pans and tracks, together with relatively long-held takes, while shot composition shows a marked predilection for balance, with what is often a self-conscious attention to patterning, shape and colour. As with Bresson, an effect of contemplative stillness is achieved, reinforced in this case by the music, and yet the pace of the narrative is not allowed to slacken, or to digress into irrelevancies. In other words, we do not find in Cronenberg a division between narrative control and stylistic autonomy such that these might constitute opposed realms, with one achieving dominance over the other. Cronenberg's style is not formalist or "parametric", nor is it reified into mannerism. Narrative is an aspect of style, and it works to create a sense of time that is the primary expression of the director's vision of the creative act. Hence, the film's success in large part derives from its disclosing to us a sense of what an authentic experience of the proximity of nothingness might mean in terms of one man's life, a disclosure never stated as such, but which emerges as a consequence of the retrospection and onward thrust integral to the film's vitality and movement. As the result of his affair with Song, Gallimard's world is fragmented past redemption, and much of the film's power lies in the way in which it shows his acceptance of this rupture as a process of bitterly achieved release from the illusions of the "they" (perhaps illusory notions of patriotism, diplomacy and duty; perhaps illusory notions of love). His refusal in the penultimate sequence in the police truck to acknowledge Song's body is a failure to acknowledge Song's love, and yet it is through this refusal that we come to see something of what authentic freedom towards death might amount to. The failed, farcical quality of Gallimard's death is transformed not by morally redemptive qualities of feeling or emotion, but by what his performance, in all its ludicrous excess, allows him to assume: his death as singular, as uniquely his.[62] As Irons plays him, Gallimard is ridiculous and, at the same time, possessed of humour and a delicately assured poise of tone, a balance through which his certainty of himself is made a palpable and moving reality. It is against the background of this reality that Gallimard's vision of himself in the mirror takes on its force: Narcissus-like, he is drawn to his own image, but it is an image of himself as *made up*. Having put on face-paint and lipstick, and having inscribed parodic cupid's bows on his lips that make of his face a grotesque mask, and wearing a wig, he looks at himself. The image he sees is a reflection of all that remains to him of himself: an image anticipating death. As he sees the reflection, he utters almost inaudibly the word "nothing", and his voice trails away, the utterance seemingly unfinished. In creating himself as art, as the diva of the opera into which he has transformed his being, he has transformed creation also into an act endowing nothingness with presence. Gallimard has become at last neither himself nor someone else: he is no one.[63]

Seen in this way, the film seems to have much in common with what Cavell understands modern art to be: *M. Butterfly* is less a representation directed towards the truth than an intervention into our accepted ways of thought. Cronenberg's wit and detachment work to prevent a recuperation of his characters and motifs into a general thematic, whether of the body or of the subject, and require of the viewer a response in terms of the existing individual he or she is. Thought about life must be our own, and will have no value for us unless it has the character of thought we direct upon ourselves. *M. Butterfly* may well share something of what Michael Weston has characterised as essential to what the texts of Kierkegaard may come to mean for us – namely, that through our responses to them we gain insight into ourselves, into the "how" of our own lives.[64] Cronenberg's cinema requires a first-person response, as does the literature of the Romantic and modern traditions, and this involves self-reflection, in which notions such as "subject", "self", "transformation", "imagination" and "problem" have uses other than those they have in the pursuit of theoretical or intellectual inquiry. We are thrown beyond, or outside, the boundaries of theoretical formulation into a disclosing of our ownmost possibility. And this for Cronenberg, as for Heidegger, is death.

However, Cronenberg does not leave matters here. There is a further aspect to the film, and this bears on the place of Song in the film after Gallimard's death. "I have a vision of the Orient. That deep within her almond eyes there are still women, women willing to sacrifice themselves for the love of a man. Even a man whose love is completely without worth." Gallimard dreams of an ideal woman, a woman of the Orient who will sacrifice herself for the love of a man, but he has no way of realising his ideal, other than by becoming her. And yet, Gallimard's self-immolation can take place only after he has turned from Song, repudiating his human reality as the prelude to his own death and consummation. After Gallimard has declared himself to be "René Gallimard, also known as Madam Butterfly", he cuts his throat not with a dagger or knife, but with the mirror which earlier reflected his image as Butterfly, an image anticipated in the dragonfly sequence. In Puccini's opera, Butterfly dies for Pinkerton, the American lover who has deserted her, but, in Cronenberg's film, Song leaves Gallimard, the Westerner, as he sacrifices himself for an ideal love that exists only as the two of them together have created it. Gallimard's death is intercut with shots of Song being taken aboard a plane. Wearing Western-style clothes, he is placed in a seat, surrounded by men who are (presumably) Chinese agents or security police, and he stares forward, unblinking, expressionless. The sequence is difficult to read: we may see Song as a figure embodying renunciation and resignation, or he may appear locked into the bitterness of his memories; or we may place him beyond either of these, and come to understand him in terms of the "strangeness of that existence" of which Maurice Blanchot speaks, an existence "which being has rejected and which does not fit into any category".[65] The film seems to invest Song's very body, as he remains there, unmoving and cut off from social and verbal expression, with a mode of existence that is neither being nor nothingness. In contrast to Gallimard, whose death is now accomplished, Song appears to be in the grasp of what Blanchot describes as "an impersonal power that does not let him either live or die".[66]

That this complex movement of doubling and reversal, resulting in ambiguity and suspension, is itself the meaning of the film is made memorably clear in the last shot, showing the closing of the door of the airliner carrying Song back to China. The camera is mounted on the steps leading up to the plane, positioned so that the rails of the steps are symmetrical on either side of the frame. The door is locked, and, as the steps draw back, the camera moving with them, we continue to hear the climactic moments from "Un bel dì, vedremo...", which Gallimard first heard at the Swedish Embassy, the tape of which he plays in the prison to accompany his performance and death. The aria is particularly pertinent here: Butterfly is invoking a future of which she is herself the voice, and the placing of the aria at this point in the film brings home to the viewer a temporality analogous to that informing the film as a whole. It is as though Cronenberg were using the aria to replicate his own procedures, and to identify the aesthetic of his film with the temporal expressiveness of music and song. "Un bel dì, vedremo..." is thus not merely an expressive accompaniment to Gallimard's performance: it circulates between Gallimard and Song, linking them and keeping them apart. Gallimard wills and achieves his transformation, grotesque though it is, into Butterfly. Song is condemned to realise the void.[67] It is, therefore, Song's failure as an artist, an artist whose very name indicates his role, that is constitutive of the film's meaning. The image fades to black and the soundtrack to silence, and, as they do so, a phrase from Wallace Stevens comes forcibly to mind: "Nothing that is not there and the nothing that is".[68] Cronenberg has created here an overwhelming sense of irreducible doubleness, and he has brought us to see, in its disclosure, the central event of the time-span which is the duration of the film. He has made of his film the evident presence of the force that has engendered it. *M. Butterfly* may thus be seen as the narrative of its own futural temporality, and it is this that makes it plausible to say that Cronenberg has extended the domain of symbolist poetics to the cinema.

Notes

[1]   His literary interests are attested to by his biographer, Peter Morris: "Even today, he maintains no more than a lively, intelligent interest in other people's films, while his understanding of literature and literary criticism is prodigious". See Peter Morris, *David Cronenberg: A Delicate Balance* (Toronto: ECW Press, 1994): 17.

[2]   Donald Davie, *The Poet in the Imaginary Museum: essays of two decades*, edited by Barry Alpert (Manchester: Carcanet, 1977): 98.

[3]   Ibid: 103.

[4]   In an interview with David Breskin, cited in Morris: 129.

[5]   Roman Jakobson, *Language in Literature*, edited by Krystyna Pomorska and Stephen Rudy (Cambridge, MA; London: Belknap Press of Harvard University Press, 1987): 70.

[6]   Wallace Stevens, "An Ordinary Evening in New Haven", *Selected Poems* (London: Faber and Faber, 1953): 136.

[7]   Roland Barthes, *Elements of Semiology*, translated by Annette Lavers and Colin Smith (London: Jonathan Cape, 1967): 57. Emphasis in original.

[8]   Ibid.

[9]   Ibid: 56. Emphasis in original.

[10]   Ludwig Wittgenstein, *Philosophical Investigations*, translated by G E M Anscombe (Oxford: Basil Blackwell, 1967), Part II: 217.

[11]   Ludwig Wittgenstein, *Remarks on the Philosophy of Psychology, volume 1*, edited by G E M Anscombe and G H von Wright, translated by G E M Anscombe (Oxford: Basil Blackwell, 1980): §240.

[12]   Paul Johnston, *Wittgenstein: Rethinking the Inner* (London; New York:

Routledge, 1993): 87.

[13] Ludwig Wittgenstein, *Zettel*, edited by G E M Anscombe and G H von Wright, translated by G E M Anscombe (Oxford: Basil Blackwell, 1967): §16.

[14] Michael Weston, *Kierkegaard and Modern Continental Philosophy: An Introduction* (London; New York: Routledge, 1994): 133. Emphases in original.

[15] Stanley Cavell, *Must we mean what we say?: A Book of Essays* (Cambridge; London; New York; Melbourne: Cambridge University Press, 1969): 176.

[16] Ibid: 188.

[17] Ibid: 193.

[18] Charles Taylor, *Sources of the Self: The Making of the Modern Identity* (Cambridge: Cambridge University Press, 1989): 374.

[19] Ibid. Emphasis added.

[20] Chris Rodley (ed), *Cronenberg on Cronenberg*, revised edition (London; Boston: Faber and Faber, 1997): 174.

[21] This point is reinforced by the film's title, *M. Butterfly*, which is an abbreviation of "Monsieur Butterfly".

[22] Steven Shaviro, *The Cinematic Body* (Minneapolis; London: University of Minnesota Press, 1993): 156.

[23] Rodley: 174.

[24] Samuel Taylor Coleridge, letter to Charles Aders, quoted in George Steiner, *Heidegger* (London: Fontana, 1978): 107.

[25] Steiner: 109-111. See also Stephen Mulhall, *Heidegger and* Being and Time (London; New York: Routledge, 1996): 144-146.

[26] John Harkness, "M. Butterfly", *Sight and Sound* 4: 5 (May 1994): 45.

[27] Walter Benjamin, *Illuminations*, edited and with an introduction by Hannah Arendt, translated by Harry Zohn (London: FontanaPress, 1992): 93.

[28] Ibid.

[29] Quoted in ibid: 98.

[30] Ibid: 100.

[31] Cavell: 229.

[32] "Dangerous Driving" [J G Ballard interviewed by Ralph Rugoff], *Frieze* 34 (May 1997): 50.

[33] Cavell: 229.

[34] Rodley: 180.

[35] Ibid: 181.

[36] Roland Barthes, "From Work to Text", in *Image Music Text*, essays selected and translated by Stephen Heath (London: Fontana/Collins, 1977): 158.

[37] Ibid: 159. Emphasis in original.

[38] This theme is explored by Earl R Wasserman, *The Subtler Language: Critical Readings of Neoclassic and Romantic Poems* (Baltimore: The Johns Hopkins Press, 1959), and by Taylor: especially 368-390.

[39] John Keats, "Ode to Psyche", *The Complete Poems*, edited by John Barnard, second edition (Harmondsworth: Penguin Books, 1977): 340.

[40] Ibid: 341.

[41] Timothy Clark, "By Heart: A Reading of Derrida's 'Che cos'è la poesia?' through Keats and Celan", *The Oxford Literary Review* 15: 1-2 (1993): 55.

[42] Keats: 341-342.

[43] Clark: 56.

[44] Martin Heidegger, *Being and Time*, translated by John Macquarrie and Edward Robinson (Oxford: Basil Blackwell, 1973): 284. Emphasis in original.

[45] Ibid.

[46] Steiner: 101, 106. Emphasis in original.

[47] Heidegger: 310. Emphases in original.

[48] Ibid: 311. I follow the translation of this passage given in Steiner: 106. Emphasis in original.

[49] Keats: 345.

[50] Ibid: 341.

[51] This phrasing is derived from Jacques Lacan, *Écrits: A Selection*, translated by Alan Sheridan (London: Tavistock Publications, 1977): 86.

[52] T S Eliot, "The Waste Land", *The Complete Poems and Plays of T. S. Eliot* (London: Faber and Faber, 1969): 64.

[53] Davie: 101.

[54] Ibid.

[55] Martin Heidegger, *The Concept of Time*, translated by William McNeill

(Oxford; Cambridge, MA: Blackwell, 1992): 13E-14E. Emphases in original.

⁵⁶ Rodley: 181.

⁵⁷ Walter Pater, *The Renaissance: Studies in Art and Poetry* (London: Macmillan, 1910): 236-237.

⁵⁸ F R Leavis, *Revaluation: Tradition & Development in English Poetry* (London: Chatto & Windus, 1962): 259.

⁵⁹ Cited in Frank Kermode, *Romantic Image* (London: Routledge and Kegan Paul, 1957): 64.

⁶⁰ W B Yeats, "Byzantium", *W. B. Yeats: Selected Poetry*, edited by A Norman Jeffares (London; Basingstoke: Macmillan, 1962): 153.

⁶¹ Kermode: 65. Emphasis in original.

⁶² Cronenberg remarks of *Crash* in an interview with Amy Taubin in *The Village Voice* (25 March 1997): 80, that he sees the film as an "existentialist romance": "To say that all love ends in death is not to say anything that's untrue, although it might be unbearable at times. But as a card-carrying existentialist, one accepts this as part of the bargain".

⁶³ For a different reading of this scene, in terms of the Lacanian notion of the gaze or look, see Rey Chow, "The Dream of a Butterfly", in Diana Fuss (ed), *Human, All Too Human* (New York; London: Routledge, 1996): 61-92.

⁶⁴ Weston: 135.

⁶⁵ Maurice Blanchot, *The Gaze of Orpheus and other literary essays*, translated by Lydia Davis, edited by P Adams Sitney (New York: Station Hill, 1981): 58.

⁶⁶ Ibid.

⁶⁷ For a reading of *M. Butterfly* in terms of feminism and postcolonial theory, see Asuman Suner, "Postmodern Double Cross: Reading David Cronenberg's *M. Butterfly* as a Horror Story", *Cinema Journal* 37: 2 (winter 1998): 49-64. For Suner (62), Song represents the unspoken voice of the Other, "whose presence radically unsettles the sovereign, self-integrated, and unified status attributed to the Western, white, male subject".

⁶⁸ Wallace Stevens, "The Snow Man", in Stevens: 15.

The mysterious disappearance of style: some critical notes about the writing on *Dead Ringers*

Andrew Klevan

This essay focuses on four substantial pieces of writing concerning *Dead Ringers* (1988), a prestigious film directed by David Cronenberg.[1] All four pieces differ in approach and critical standpoint, but the prominence of these differences makes their similarities worthy of attention. They are similar in that they all fail to sustain a discussion about the film's style. The avoidance of an analysis of film style is a tendency in modern film scholarship, and, because these pieces concentrate on a renowned film and are by a cross-section of notable film scholars, I felt this to be an occasion to draw attention to some prevalent evasions.

I consider the sensitive scrutiny of film style to bring intensity and discipline to film study. I am sympathetic, however, to the difficulty of the task: scrutinising the visual and aural significance of films is demanding; there are few exemplary models from which to learn; the institutional environments and the pressure to publish unreasonably force all manner of short cuts and contrivances; and, beyond that, there is simply the challenge, often heartbreaking, often ending in defeat, to find *any* appropriate words which fit one's sense of a moment in a film.[2]

Filling in the colour

The following quotations below are taken from three separate, sustained pieces of writing on *Dead Ringers*:

Beverly ties Claire to the bed with surgical tubing and clamps. The room is bathed in a bluish light, sounds of deep breathing fill the room: it is as if a birth were taking place.[3]

The pervasive blue, which informs much of the film, contrasting with the striking reds of the operating theatre sequences, suggests both a commentary by the director on the world of the Mantles, and an evocation of their shared attitude of mind. Blue suggests something of how the world they inhabit seems to them, while at the same time it suggests the severe limitations of vision to which such an attitude subjects them...[I]n the final separation sequences...the use of blue serves to construct Elliot and Beverly's world in terms of an emotional quality that is at once distorted and intense, unifying them and marking them off from others as singular and unique.[4]

The stylized ritualistic presentation of the *mise-en-scène*...the cold blue and steel sombre tones of the Mantle twins... Cronenberg further reinforces the sterility of the environment through colour: blue/grey tones, a monochromatic palette, the ashen makeup used on Jeremy Irons.[5]

Although these quotations are taken out of their overall discursive context, in no case is that context an extended rumination on the matter of colour in the film. In each case, the quotation represents the greater part of each article's devotion to the subject of the colour blue. The remaining references to colour in the film refer to the red gowns worn by the Mantle twins, Beverly and Elliot (both played by Jeremy Irons), and amount to little more than another sentence or so in each case.[6] Each of the writers quoted above considers the colour blue to be of some significance in the film, and all three pieces mention it in some regard, but none of them considers the feature to warrant more than an occasional remark.

Of course, length of discussion is not necessarily indicative of quality of observation, and, as well as mentioning the occurrence of the colour, the authors do provide an interpretation of its function. For Barbara Creed, the presence of blue in the particular scene to which she refers, along with the deep breathing, allows the film to evoke the moments of birth, and this is consistent with her taking the film, beyond this scene, to be concerned with the culture of gynaecological treatment, childlike regression and the impossibility of a stable, mature masculinity. Creed does not exactly specify what aspect of "birth" she understands the colour blue to be expressing, but she may be thinking along the lines of Pam Cook, in her short review of the film in *Monthly Film Bulletin*. Cook writes: "Much of the action appears suffused with blue as though taking place in a sea of amniotic fluid".[7]

It is possible that the film's deployment of the colour blue is amply described in a single, terse sentence because the feature of style has a uniform effect throughout the film: for Creed, perhaps, something

149

like "amniotic fluid" flowing around, or surrounding, other aspects of the film. This sense of *surrounding* is suggested by Michael Grant when he writes about the "pervasive blue", and hints at the colour "unifying" the Mantles and "marking" them off. The use of the word "informs", however, as in "[t]he pervasive blue, which informs much of the film", keeps the role of colour obscure, partly because it is unclear in what way a colour "informs". The piece is not forthcoming, furthermore, on why the colour blue particularly, rather than the repeated use of another colour, might "construct Elliot and Beverly's world in terms of an emotional quality that is at once distorted and intense", or why the presence of blue "suggests something of how the world they inhabit seems to them", or why blue "suggests the severe limitations of vision to which such an attitude subjects them".

Assessing how *this* colour creates its distortions is important, and the way in which the colour is "intense" is also a pertinent inquiry, especially as Grant contrasts the "pervasive blue" to the "*striking* reds of the operating theatre sequences [my emphasis]". His comparison suggests that the use of "pervasive blue" is actually alleviating, or offsetting, some of the intensity created by the "striking reds", while the blue is also expressing a different quality of intensity, perhaps as a consequence of its constancy. The presence of "striking reds" as against the more "pervasive blue" begs the question regarding the contrast, and particularly the extent to which the colours are distributed across an image, across a scene, or across the film as a whole.

This failure to address the colour's distribution results in some confusion: is it the critic or the film which is being vague, and, if the film is being vague, is this a strength or a weakness? Take the full sentence, for example: "The pervasive blue, which informs much of the film, contrasting with the striking reds of the operating theatre sequences, suggests both a commentary by the director on the world of the Mantles, and an evocation of their shared attitude of mind." Is it the "pervasive blue" alone that "suggests both a commentary by the director on the world of the Mantles, and an evocation of their shared attitude of mind", or is it the "pervasive blue...contrasting with the striking reds" that is doing the suggesting? The sentence is not clarified because the piece does not attend to the colour's patterning, and the reader is provoked to suppose that the film's use of colour is lazy or even crude. Its use will be neither, however, if the effect is one of vague presence, perhaps expressing drowsiness, iciness or refrigeration of some kind, but the critic needs to be exact about the colour's achievement by specifying the character of its imprecision. In fact, Grant understands the use of blue as expressing "a *commentary* by the director on the world of the Mantles [my emphasis]", proposing that the colour's meaning evolves, differently inflecting our feelings towards the unfolding drama of the Mantles – in the sense of a "running commentary" and as distinct from a single comment. Drawing out the flexibility of an aspect of style, such as the developing expressive possibilities of a colour, might be necessary to this appreciation which wishes to persuade us that *Dead Ringers* is a film of some distinction because it is capable of its own distinctions.

I draw attention to these passages to illustrate a characteristic tendency in the writers' treatment of film style, rather than to take them to task for failing to concentrate their pieces on the subject of colour. A tendency to summarise, to assess quickly rather than to discriminate, pervades the pieces, as the colour they speak of pervades the film. The discussion of the music, for example, is more cursory even than the treatment of colour, despite, once again, the writers' claims that this aspect of style, like colour, is crucial to the film's meaning. Creed writes:

> In a discussion of *Dead Ringers*, Cronenberg stated that he did not show the parents of the twins because he was trying to suggest that, as in a classical Greek tragedy, their lives are pre-determined' [sic]. Certainly Cronenberg gives a sense of classical drama to his narrative, particularly in the haunting, elegiac music which has played throughout the narrative and is clearly heard in the film's final scene.[8]

If there is anything "pre-determined" here, it is those words "haunting" and "elegiac", words frequently – too frequently perhaps – exploited to describe the effects of music in film (to the extent that it is difficult for the words to summon anything distinct or distinctive for the reader). Their effect is reduced further by the fact that they appear, as usual, as a pair – if "haunting", then certainly "elegiac". Creed writes of "the haunting, elegiac music which has played *throughout the narrative* [my emphasis]", but the music has not played "throughout the narrative". It has played through the narrative periodically, the particular manner and moments of its playing (and not playing) being crucial here, and crucially ignored. She goes on to say that the music is "clearly heard in the film's final scene", but her "clearly" again conflates – indeed confuses – very different effects of style. Is the music clearer because it is louder, relative to other scenes, clearer because of a changed relationship to other elements in the scene, or clear as against the possibility of distortion?

"*Certainly* Cronenberg gives a *sense* of classical drama [my emphasis]": which "sense" of classical drama is expressed by "haunting, elegiac" music, and, with only "a sense", what is there to be

151

certain of? Grant comments on the music as follows:

> Music is also used, often in a highly self-aware manner, to evoke moods and emotional states of mind, particularly in the final separation sequences, where the feeling of sadness called up by Howard Shore's music implies the profundity of the loss which the twins are about to suffer.[9]

We will find few films where the music does not "evoke moods and emotional states of mind", and the comment shows how a writer capable of perspicacious interpretations elsewhere in the piece becomes strangely evasive about style. The substance of the sentence may be "in a highly self-aware manner", although the writer's use of "highly" invites interest into not only how this music achieves an awareness of itself, but also how the level of awareness might be heightened or reduced. It is an important critical claim, similarly, that Shore's music "*implies* the profundity of the loss [my emphasis]" as distinct, perhaps, from asserting "the profundity of the loss", but Grant does not establish why the music, weighted against other aspects of style, would allow him to propose this discrimination.

The words "highly" or "implies" themselves imply that the film has a few sophisticated methods of varying its dramatic register, but Grant's use of "in a highly self-aware manner" might provide the clue as to why the writers are reluctant to make some moves towards scrutinising these methods. The writers resist emphasising stylistic nuance because they might be drawn to understanding "style" in the film to be operating by broad brush strokes, sending single-issue messages: understood in this way, blue in the film is "pervasive", and the music achieves "*the feeling* of sadness [my emphasis]". Grant's piece, however, would not wish to present a view of the film's music, for example, as *one-note*, and therefore we are no closer to understanding the particular handling or consequences of this film's "self-aware" style, especially when every good film contains varying facets of self-awareness.

Music is a notoriously difficult aspect of film style to discuss sensitively or in detail, but such hesitations in the criticism about the overall execution of style in *Dead Ringers* may mean that even Grant is betraying an unacknowledged ambivalence regarding its quality. Florence Jacobowitz and Richard Lippe condemn the style of the film as exhibiting a "stylized ritualistic presentation of the *mise-en-scène*... its lustrous aesthetic polish...a perfected style comfortably signifying High Art".[10] They also write:

*Dead Ringers...*takes on a complex of social and cultural issues that are at the forefront of theoretical chic: the body as site of horror and the grotesque, the appropriation of the body as a declaration of power and control, suspicions surrounding the sacral omnipotence of the medical profession, etc. These are dressed within a sophisticated, controlled style of filmmaking which heightens and validates the significance of what the film appears to take on.[11]

Bearing in mind that even an admirer of the film such as Grant implies that certain important aspects of the film's style are *blanket*, the possibility proposed by Jacobowitz and Lippe, that the film is "dressed", is neither perverse nor obscure. The possibility may be wrong, but one would expect it to be a relevant, even pressing, concern in any critical treatment.

"Constructing a coherent critical position"

Jacobowitz and Lippe, however, also assert these generalisations concerning style without sustained attention to a particular sequence which might lend force to their case. At one stage, they proclaim some advice for critical practice:

[T]he critic's responsibility should be to explore a response *within* the context of the whole work (i.e., Where did I get this idea from? Why am I responding this way?) and to identify the values which shape the reading. This inevitably leads to a discussion of valuation and pleasure.[12]

They then reduce the possibilities of the advice in the following sentence, turning it into further licence for critical summary:

If one finds offensive films which exploit and denigrate women and have no respect for the human body, then one cannot support *Dead Ringers* as a significant work. In fact, its lustrous aesthetic polish only contributes to the film's formidable achievement in its indiscriminate disdain and revulsion for the human body and physical expressions of the most fundamental aspects of human interaction.[13]

There is not much scrutiny of personal response – "Why am I responding this way?" – in the asserted "[i]f one finds offensive...". The writers go on to explain in what way the film "exploits" and "denigrates", but this assertion so early in the piece does not bode well with regard to their own pedagogical criteria: "discussion", critical "responsibility" and a reading with "shape". They later refer to the film being "unquestionably, impressive",[14] but, in the light of the writers' evident dislike for crucial elements of the film, it is indeed questionable why it would be "impressive". The film's impressiveness seems to be achieved by its "obvious technical sophistication"[15] and by "technical sophistication" they are possibly referring to the film overcoming "technical" difficulties, particularly concerning the performance of the Mantle twins by the same actor. Yet, once again, "technical sophistication" is "obvious", and so the piece does not refer directly to performance, or to any other aspect of style at this point. The reader may be forgiven for confusing "technical sophistication" with the adjacent disdainful reference to "lustrous aesthetic polish". The precise sense in which the style is "lustrous" or has "polish" is never elucidated. Once again, the writers have not met their criteria – "Where did I get this idea from? Why am I responding this way?".

Jacobowitz and Lippe devote much of their article to what they see as problems in "subject matter", but each time they make a critical or interpretive claim they beg a question concerning style:

> In addition to its subject matter, the film imparts meaning through a variety of elements often neglected in current criticism such as tone, humour, attitude and processes of empathy and identification, star presence as well as the director's domain of *mise-en-scène*.[16]

"[T]one, humour, attitude" are "often neglected" precisely because they are conceived "[i]n addition to...subject matter": these elements are the subject-matter, or else adjust what we take the subject-matter to be. There are benefits, for the purposes of developing a critical discussion, in separating these elements, but the use of "as well as" later in the sentence signals some worrying consequences arising from such a separation: one essential element of the "director's domain of *mise-en-scène*" is, for example, "star presence".

It is common for the "director's domain of *mise-en-scène*" to find itself languishing on the far side of some phrase such as "as well as". This comment is in reference to the character of Claire, played by Geneviève Bujold:

> Given this disparaging, blatantly sexist representation of a modern woman, one must take a closer look at the sleight-of-hand being effected: under the guise of a sexually open career woman of the '80s, one finds the familiar and pejorative stereotype of the nymphomaniac.[17]

154

The film may indeed present Claire as a "stereotype", but the "pejorative...representation" does not depend on it being "familiar". Good films are full of "familiar" types: the gunslinger, the gangster with a heart, the moll, the fallen woman, the bored housewife.[18] Note Stanley Cavell's remarks in *The World Viewed*:

> I would find it hard to believe that anyone admires *Grand Illusion, Rules of the Game, Zero for Conduct* and *L'Atalante* more than I, but it seems to me more accurate to their intention and effect to say that they are explorations of types rather than explorations of characters...just think of the obvious surface of their content. The figures in both of the Renoir films are insistently labelled for us: the Aristocrat, the Jew, the Officer, the Professor, the Good Guy, the Poacher, the Wronged Wife, the Impetuous Lover. The shared subjects of the films depend upon this; both are about the arbitrariness and the [inevitability] of labels, and thence about the human need for society and the equal human need to escape it, and hence about human privacy and unknownness.[19]

For Cavell, the richness, or *individuality*, of "type" is found in the human being's relationship with the camera; furthermore, the scrutiny of the camera makes the human being in front of it not always well-described by the term "actor", because they are also, more deeply, *subjects* of study, albeit subjects who have a more or less active participation in the way films present them. The ontology of film allows for this rendering of characterisation because it tends to taunt the detail of real filmed human individualities against types, or more precisely *within* types.[20]

This does not mean that Bujold's presence in front of the camera will transform a lazy "stereotype" into a scrutiny of a type, but the necessary distinction between a type and a stereotype cannot be made by the article because her relationship to the camera is not examined. Such a relationship is hinted at when the writers say: "Geneviève Bujold's persona contributes an intelligence, wit and knowingness that threatens to foreground the sexist conception of the character, but ultimately, is unable to counter Cronenberg's usage of her".[21] The word "persona" is having to do too much work because it is condensing many of the actress' relationships with other aspects of style which require individual assessment, aspects which are themselves being squashed into "Cronenberg's usage" (for example, camera presence and placement, composition, colour, lighting, fellow actors and locations). The relationship between her face and the camera is touched upon with regard to the scene in the make-up trailer, but it does not form part of a discussion about the visual and aural presentation of the character/actor. This would be necessary to substantiate their critique of her role, but instead they rest much on the claim that "the film's *project* is not committed to developing the woman's story".[22]

The word "project" is therefore an important one for Jacobowitz and Lippe, and they use the word on two other occasions: "the type is complicated by the casting of an actress whose star persona is at odds with the film's ideological project",[23] and later they write, "[h]aving thus justified the male character's suspicions of the Woman's deceptive nature and inherent duplicity...the film can then luxuriate in its manifest project".[24] I associate the word "project" with work done by schoolchildren, or students, or else by advertising agents or social planners (for example, housing "projects"), but the writers seem to be using "project" disparagingly, suggesting something stronger than simply organised for a purpose. *Dead Ringers* is therefore stringently planned, determinedly pursuing a "manifest" strategy, and the film has closed down a range of imaginative possibilities.

This negative appropriation of the word, however, does not fit easily with another of their frequently used words, "critique", the use of which indicates the writers' own desire for a "project". The article says: "the film has the potential to produce a trenchant critique",[25] "[t]he critique is completely undermined as the scene progresses",[26] and "*Dead Ringers* does not deliver the necessary critique demanded of the issues set forth"[27] – the use of "deliver" and "necessary" suggesting the desire for the "manifest" *results* "demanded" of a "project". This sense of "critique", furthermore, is carried over into the words "critical" or "criticism": "This is all, potentially, audacious had the film persisted in developing a criticism of these gender politics",[28] or "the film avoids the construction of a coherent critical position towards Eli and Bev".[29] The "critical position" to be adopted is not characterised by a lively, fluid, intelligent and felt engagement by the film – or the viewer. As well as being "coherent", it is a "construction" (more housing projects again) and the "position", as in "what is your position on this 'issue'", is, of course, "demanded".

The word "coherent" is used again in the next paragraph: "Like so much of the film, these scenes do not allow for a coherent reading".[30] The type of "coherent reading" that Jacobowitz and Lippe require is something like this:

> When Eli later questions Bev in private about the examination, Bev's perspective is made clear. 'There is nothing wrong with the instrument. It's the body – the woman's body was all wrong.' Within a critical context this statement could give full

recognition to the manner in which the patriarchal underpinnings of the medical system entrenches its control through the utilisation of late capitalist technology.[31]

This "recognition" might make a "coherent" conclusion to an undergraduate social policy "project", or a leader in a newspaper, but it will not constitute a "critical context" for the film. The film's quality is here assessed in terms of "issues" which, if we recall, "demanded" the "necessary critique",[32] but the language of "issues" circumscribes the possibilities for the film's expression by reducing it to the demonstrations, more or less subtle, of public communication (suitable for the arena of newspapers, current affairs television and political activism). The writers, therefore, say at one point, not surprisingly, "*Dead Ringers* never acknowledges overtly the reality that the love relationship which the twins cannot live without is their own",[33] but a film of quality may not wish "overtly" or "coherently" to acknowledge its matters of significance. It may acknowledge them tactfully, subtly or ambivalently; it may deliberately keep them vague, or hesitate over them.

The writers' failure to "acknowledge" the film as a sequence of sound and images ensures that they are without the stylistic detail to explicate which specific aspects of the film they would like to be overt. Film melodrama, for example, in order to modulate its effects, balances aspects of style which are overt with those that are less so, perhaps placing a prominent piece of dialogue alongside a modest or unobtrusive physical gesture. Would the overtness which Jacobowitz and Lippe require be provided by a piece of music played "throughout the narrative", or the "pervasive" use of a colour perhaps? In general, if we think of filmmakers as creating, thinking, feeling or working with a series of sound and images, and we think of ourselves, as viewers, feeling and thinking in front of a series of sound and images, remarks such as "the film avoids the construction of a coherent critical position" do not provide a fair "representation" (to borrow Jacobowitz and Lippe's word) of the sensitivities involved in the engagements.

The excitations of persuasion

There is a quality in *Dead Ringers* which drives those who appreciate it into expressing their appreciation with an apocalyptic vocabulary. The accounts of Michael Grant and Steven Shaviro are similar in that they both provide an intelligently reasoned interpretation of the film followed by a series of comments which, contrary to their own measured responses, tell us that the viewer will experience a "loss of control",[34] or will find the film "hard to master".[35] It should be recognised that Shaviro's analysis of the film is embedded in a general refutation of the major tenets of prevalent strands of film theory, and, at the close of his section on Cronenberg in general, and a couple of paragraphs after his specific discussion of *Dead Ringers*, he writes:

> When the possibilities of fantasy and appropriative identification are destroyed for the male protagonists of these films, they are equally destroyed for the spectator... Cronenberg's strategy is continually to up the ante of shock... We are pushed to the limits of vision and of representation, compelled to witness what we cannot bear to see. Exploding and multiplied flesh, the violent or insidious violation of bodily integrity, is crucial to Cronenberg's project formally as well as thematically...The imposing plenitude of the image instills in the spectator a heightened sensitivity to the affections of his or her own body...Identification (of the spectator with the protagonist, or with the gaze of the camera) leads to a loss of control, a shattering of the ego.[36]

An initial observation to make here is that Shaviro, despite criticising much film theory earlier in his book, quite happily adopts much of its language here for his own ends: "fantasy", "appropriative identification", "limits of...representation", "plenitude of the image", "spectator", "gaze" and "ego". (Indeed, many prominent film scholars who have made noisy attacks on film theory have then gleefully deployed the enemy's paradigms, their methods of analysis, or their vocabulary and expression.) Note, furthermore, the level and extent of the hyperbole involved: "pushed to the limits of vision", "[t]he imposing plenitude of the image" and the "shattering of the ego". I confess that I fail to experience these fantastic sensations while viewing the film, and one would expect, given the extremity of the claims, that the writer would feel the need to persuade me of their possibility.

Shaviro's own preceding interpretation, moreover, does not lead to his own conclusions. The following is one of his perceptive interpretations of the film, and one that involves the acknowledgment of an aspect of style, namely performance:

> The uncanniness of the situation is perfectly captured in Jeremy Irons's double performance. The mannerisms of Elliot and Beverly are subtly different, so that we can nearly always tell which one of them is which. But these differences are not enough to negate our awareness that the same actor, the same body, is rendering both. (The film wouldn't work with two

actors as the brothers, even if the actors were themselves twins.) Because of their excessive physical similarity, the characters of Beverly and Elliot are more like different performances than like different selves. Neither of them is able convincingly to dislodge his interiority from its reflection in the other; neither can ever be self-sufficient or self-contained. They are unable even to live apart from one another, although Beverly tries at times to escape. Nonetheless, such dependency does not guarantee communion. Because their bodies are two, and separated in space, it is also impossible for them to ever fully to coincide...These seemingly opposed impulses are in fact mutually cohesive manifestations of the same situation of excessive proximity. The Mantle twins can achieve neither absolute union nor complete differentiation.[37]

Shaviro's cogent and vivid discussion alerts us to a pivotal tension in the film, but at what point does he make us realise that we have been "compelled to witness what we cannot bear to see"? Equally, how has Shaviro, as a "spectator", after discerning the consequences of a double performance (but not necessarily the particular consequences of Jeremy Irons' double performance), experienced a "loss of control, a shattering of the ego"? I am reminded also of "[t]he imposing plenitude of the image", but, because the writer does not scrutinise a specific "image" of the film, it is difficult to grasp how any "image" might be "imposing". In the absence of an account of which particular elements are filling up the "image", it is a similar problem for a reader to assess the claim of "plenitude". The further question which arises is: how can the images of the film, for Shaviro, be expressing the precise negotiations or vacillations of separation and intimacy for the Mantle twins, while at the same time "destroying", "shattering", "violating" and "imposing"?

The magical achievement of *Dead Ringers'* style is that it performs extraordinary feats on the viewer separately from the meaning it expresses at any particular moment. Shaviro writes of "formally as well as thematically" (see quotation above), and therefore this magic is probably being conjured secretly in that mysterious zone innocuously entitled "as well as". This should remind us of Jacobowitz and Lippe's "*as well as* the director's domain of *mise-en-scène* [my emphasis]". Grant writes something similar when he announces "that there is in Cronenberg's art a redemptive power, which derives not from what it depicts but from the aesthetic organisation of the depiction".[38] It will need to be a bewitching "power" indeed which authorises or stimulates me to experience the "what" of the depiction separately from the depiction's "organisation".

Connections and their compressions

Barbara Creed has long passages in her article on Sigmund Freud, Egyptian art, Elaine Showalter and Julia Kristeva, while also including references to Jacques Lacan and Greek tragedy. Grant sees both John Donne and T S Eliot as crucial reference points for the film, while also developing connections with Oscar Wilde, Otto Rank and Shakespearian tragedy. The nature of the connections differs, but these other writings are crucial to the writers' critical perspectives. Grant quotes a couple of lines from John Donne's poem, "The Flea" (1635), and then writes:

> *Dead Ringers* is no less 'metaphysical' a film than *The Fly*: the play of wit across themes of identity and selfhood is its structuring principle. Throughout the film, we discover occult resemblances in things apparently unlike, and we see the violent revelation of dissimilarity or difference in what seems most similar. Wit, we might say, defines the essential mode of being of the Mantle twins, and their relations with those around them. The dynamic interactions which are central to the idea of the double permit exactly the play of paradox and wit found in the poetry of the 17th century.[39]

The link to 17th-century poetry, and John Donne's poetry in particular, is alluring and provocative. The use of "exactly" in the last sentence of the passage, however, ensures a strong claim, and it is unlikely that the "dynamic interactions...of the double" in the film permits "*exactly* the play of paradox and wit found in the poetry of the 17th century [my emphasis]". The association seems provocative because a Donne poem does not "exactly" mirror *Dead Ringers*, but the piece fails to address the particular "play" of "paradox and wit" in any of the film's sequences. There would be profit, however, in attending to how aspects of poetic style illuminated aspects of film style – for example, assessing the ways in which the Mantle twins might be *rhymed*. I refer to the two lines quoted by Grant:

> This flea is you and I, and this
> Our marriage bed, and marriage temple is[40]

Note the use of "this", which both begins and closes the first line. The potent transformation of the "marriage bed" is achieved by breaking the line at the second "this" so that it is emphasised and rhymed, through repetition, with the first "This" which is directly associated with the "flea". The second "this", at the same time, takes its place in a bouncy, beckoning roll-call, consisting of "you and I, and this", delivered too quickly to quarrel with; meanwhile, the presence of "is" is mischievously sewing up the whole conceit, by weaving across both lines, beginning with "Th*is*", and snaking irresistibly through "*is* you", "and th*is*", and "temple *is*". I only touch on the deft and seductive shifts in tone and attitude in these two lines, but enough has been evoked for us to inquire how such deft and seductive shifts might "exactly" occur in *Dead Ringers*.

Grant also likens the film, as Creed does, via the quotation from Cronenberg, to forms of Greek tragedy, the lives of the Mantle twins being "pre-determined",[41] and to the poetry of T S Eliot, especially "Ash-Wednesday" (1930), which is characterised by "loss, failure and incomprehension".[42] How does the film encompass all these tones?: for example, how might it achieve Donne's witty flexibility while also expressing the dark tragedy of the "pre-determined"? Which aspects of the film's style positively "play" like "The Flea", and which convey "failure" and "incomprehension" like "Ash-Wednesday"? I have the sense here of the film inevitably triggering concepts or ideas: the film gives off a diffuse aura which then surrounds it – rather like the "pervasive blue" – within which the authors float, and *coast*, orbiting the film, intoxicated and light-headed, fearful of touching down.

Generalisations are useful to us insofar as they aid the distinguishing of the particular. We feel the necessity of according respect to the individual personality of human beings, and, when we consider similarity across works and across mediums, we might ask ourselves what constitutes this film as opposed to what constitutes another film, poem, book, play or piece of philosophy. I welcome the use in film study of the works of Freud, Kristeva or Lacan as much as I do those of Donne, Eliot or Shakespeare, but I become wary of their usefulness when, surrounded by many thousands of words discussing and quoting their work, Creed writes this paragraph, which is instructive enough to quote at length:

The representation of male hysteria in Hollywood cinema has taken various forms and differs from genre to genre. In the woman's film (*Random Harvest* [1942]) and the suspense thriller (*Spellbound* [1945]), male hysteria is represented in terms of a mental problem such as a loss of memory. Female hysteria in these genres is constructed more in relation to the body and displayed as a physical symptom such as a brain tumour (*Dark Victory* [1939]), a loss of speech (*The Spiral Staircase* [1946]), or a facial disfigurement (*A Woman's Face* [1941]). A more recent film, *Paris, Texas* (1984), explores male hysteria in relation to amnesia and sexual desire. The representation of male hysteria as arising from a disturbance of gender occurs most frequently in comedy: hysteria is displayed not only in sequences of crossdressing but also in the breakneck speed of these films – as, for instance, in *Some Like It Hot* (1959), the films of Jerry Lewis, and the sex comedies of Howard Hawks. Not only are these films about male hysteria, the texts themselves also become 'hysterical', probably because of the disruptive nature of their subject-matter. Recently, cinema has attempted to deal with a different form of male hysteria, one which is displaced onto a male body through which masculinity is represented as in excess, over-present. The films of Arnold Schwarzenegger and Sylvester Stallone display the male body as a living phallus: hysterical images of masculinity such as these point to the impossible nature of the phallic ideal, made even more so by the demands of the patriarchal·cult of masculinity. In science fiction, male hysteria has found expression in the theme of *couvade*: in these texts (*Frankenstein* [1931], *Altered States* [1980], *The Fly* [1986]), the 'mad' male scientist attempts to take up the position of woman by creating life in a 'womb' of his own. The mise-en-scene [sic] of the laboratory...in these films has become increasingly fanciful: in *The Fly* the scientist creates two large womb-like 'teleporters' in which he deconstructs and reconstructs himself.[43]

The word "hysteria" is used nine times in this paragraph alone, and one wonders how all the complex psychoanalytical writing has facilitated such a reduction in the range of observation (the words "represented" and "representation" also experience heavy repetition, and therefore keep substituting for an analysis of the methods of "representation" in each case). Within the paragraph, the word "hysteria" is used in connection with films as varied as *Dark Victory*, *Some Like It Hot* and *Paris, Texas*. The relationship between Joan Crawford's character and her disfigurement in *A Woman's Face* is reduced to a simple external expression of "hysteria", but the finest parts of that film are precisely concerned with scrutinising, or complicating, such behavioural labels (we might ponder the earlier quotation by Cavell concerning the arbitrariness and inevitability of labels). The benefit of Creed's psychoanalytical research, for the purpose of film study, should be that it refines our notion of "hysteria" in relation to these different films. The behaviour of performers/ characters might require varied descriptions such as distraught, neurotic, frantic, compulsive or calculating, and, suitably adjusted by an expressive rapport with other aspects of film style, the performers may convey forms of hysteria by agitation or distraction, by panic or worry, or by being overwrought or complacent.

Even though it is unclear which "sex comedies of Howard Hawks" are being considered, only a backhanded dismissiveness could explain Creed's use of the description of "sex comedies" (as in *Confessions of a Palaeontologist*, starring Katharine Hepburn and Cary Grant?). The reference to "sex comedies" nevertheless might explain the use of "about" in "these films about male hysteria", as in "Have you heard the one *about* the repressed professor, the madcap heiress and the leopard mix-up?". Even this gag version of the film cannot reduce it, as does "male hysteria", to only two elements. Without the author revealing to which specific films she is referring, and without a selection of appropriate evidence, it is hard to know what is at stake in the "not only" construction of "Not only are these films about male hysteria, the texts themselves also become 'hysterical'". What kindly act is "about" performing in this sentence that it rescues "these films" from becoming "texts", and which aspects of style in these films are actually "hysterical" and which aspects have the more restrained capacity to be simply "about...hysteria"? Creed's article is more precise about the nature of "hysteria" in *Dead Ringers*, and this is, after all, the film under attention ("it constructs male hysteria in relation to the uterus, to castration anxieties, and to male narcissism...the impossible nature of the masculine quest for wholeness and totality"),[44] but this recognition only further presses the problem of *critical* focus: the place, purpose and weighting of "external" references.

*   *   *

It might be said that this piece is in part making a request for some old-fashioned "close reading", or what has become known as "close textual analysis". This would be acceptable to me providing that "close reading" was not presented as the occupation of an eccentric cult. I am worried by the neutral – and occasionally pejorative – use of the word "close", as if "far-away" might be considered an equally advantageous position. The wish to be *close* arises out of the desire to give intense, felt attention. "Close" in this sense carries a quality of attachment, if not necessarily affection, and this state of commitment should ensure the search for relevant and eloquent detail. The claims for a film or filmmaker may be more or less positive, but the writers of these pieces on *Dead Ringers* do unquestionably *devote* many of their words to the film. The striving for particular words, however, those which do justice to the visual and aural specifics of a film's expressive personality, is an arduous one, sometimes thankless, and this may be why they are keen to avoid it. Yet, in a book such as this, *dedicated* to the work of a single filmmaker, it is especially urgent to ask: how discriminating are the devotions of those who are so easily distracted?

Postscript

During and after the writing of this piece, I was compelled to consider two possible charges which could be brought against it: the first charge would be that it is too negative; the second, which is connected to the first, would be that it does not concentrate positively on any film by the director David Cronenberg. As the piece appears in a book subtitled *The Films of David Cronenberg*, both these criticisms seem fair and appropriate enough to be worth addressing. The piece I have written is not on Cronenberg's films *per se*, but on my estrangement from much of the academic criticism on these films. Since it appears in a book *of* academic criticism, I hoped that the piece would permit me to be critical and useful. I felt incapable of presenting a specific interpretation of a Cronenberg film – and considered that the collection probably did not require another one – but thought I could facilitate other viewers' interpretations, and their articulation of them. I take it that the collection will be read by many people familiar with the literature I address, or familiar enough – too familiar perhaps – with the language and paradigms deployed by that literature. Although I hope that the analysis will cast light on modern film writing more generally, I also hope, more specifically, that teachers, students, specialists and fans of Cronenberg's films will take the piece to be of particular relevance: they will find themselves now challenged to check themselves when searching for approaches, terms and vocabulary to use in their interpretations and evaluations of the director's films. The piece is asking, in effect, what sensible and sensitive ways are we able to talk about, or write about, Cronenberg's work within the ways in which it might be, and has been, talked and written about: in terms of, for example, psychoanalytical formulation (Creed), literary tradition (Grant), sociopolitical challenge (Lippe and Jacobowitz) or paradigm-busting euphoria (Shaviro). In what ways do the words of these approaches allow us to talk sense, make sense, of the workings and effects of this film – that is to say, *make sense of its style*? Hoping to encourage this investigation, I have made the piece a touch provocative, and possibly agitating, precisely so that its consequences will not be negative.

Notes

1. The substance of the analysis is directed towards these particular writings, not towards any other work, teaching or concerns of the writers involved in the discussion. I would like to thank Edward Klevan for help with this piece.

2. V F Perkins writes of the "problem with oneself, of finding the words that fit one's sense of the moment or the movie". (V F Perkins, "Must We Say What They Mean?: Film Criticism and Interpretation", *Movie* 34/35 [winter 1990]: 4.) At this point, I should acknowledge the influence of the writing and teaching of V F Perkins. He is not, however, specifically associated in any way with this piece. With regard to a related point, I do not offer my own interpretation of *Dead Ringers*, or a specific analysis of its style, in this piece because I have never felt the urge to persuade anyone, unlike the writers analysed here, of the significance of the film. (See also Postscript.)

3. Barbara Creed, "Phallic panic: male hysteria and *Dead Ringers*", *Screen* 31: 2 (summer 1990): 135.

4. Michael Grant, *Dead Ringers* (Trowbridge: Flicks Books, 1997): 36, 37, 42.

5. Florence Jacobowitz and Richard Lippe, "*Dead Ringers*: The Joke's On Us", *CineAction!* spring 1989: 65, 68.

6. In a discussion, for example, of the "ritualistic" quality of the film, Grant (42) mentions that "the brothers are robed in crimson, presiding like priests over a ceremony in which the scientific and the atavistic seem intermingled", while Creed (142) explains how "[t]he notion of castration anxiety...helps to explain the twins' puzzling predilection for red surgical gowns, masks, and gloves. By wearing red clothing, traces of woman's blood – the sight of which might awaken castration anxiety – are rendered invisible to their eyes".

7. Pam Cook, "Dead Ringers", *Monthly Film Bulletin* 56: 660 (January 1989): 4.

8. Creed: 143. The quotation by Cronenberg comes from an interview with Alan Stanbrook, "Cronenberg's Creative Cancers", *Sight and Sound* 58: 1 (winter 1988/89): 54-56. Grant also draws on this quotation (see note below).

9. Grant: 36-37.

10. Jacobowitz and Lippe: 65, 68.

11. Ibid: 65.

12. Ibid. Emphasis in original.

13. Ibid.

14. Ibid.

[15]   Ibid.

[16]   Ibid.

[17]   Ibid: 66.

[18]   Some of these categories are listed by Stanley Cavell, *The World Viewed: Reflections on the Ontology of Film*, enlarged edition (Cambridge, MA; London: Harvard University Press, 1979): 36.

[19]   Ibid: 175-176.

[20]   Ideas here are taken from William Rothman, analysis of Stanley Cavell's *The World Viewed* (unpublished).

[21]   Jacobowitz and Lippe: 66.

[22]   Ibid: 67. Emphasis added.

[23]   Ibid: 66.

[24]   Ibid: 67.

[25]   Ibid.

[26]   Ibid.

[27]   Ibid: 68.

[28]   Ibid: 66.

[29]   Ibid: 68.

[30]   Ibid.

[31]   Ibid

[32]   Ibid.

[33]   Ibid: 67.

[34]   Steven Shaviro, *The Cinematic Body* (Minneapolis; London: University of Minnesota Press, 1993): 156.

[35]   Grant: 19.

[36]   Shaviro: 155-156.

[37]   Ibid: 150-151.

[38]   Grant: 18-19.

[39]   Ibid: 17.

[40]   Quoted in ibid.

[41] Ibid: 21. This is the same quotation by Cronenberg from the interview with Stanbrook on which Creed draws. Grant quotes it as follows: "[I]n *Dead Ringers* I don't show the parents of the twins, because I am trying to suggest that, as in a classical Greek tragedy, their lives are predetermined". This quotation is confusing as it stands here, because the connection between not showing parents and the "predetermined" is obscure, especially because the "predetermined lives" of many protagonists in classical Greek tragedy has much to do with the presence of their parents!

[42] Ibid: 19.

[43] Creed: 133-134.

[44] Ibid: 134.

Logic, creativity and (critical) misinterpretations: an interview with David Cronenberg

Conducted by Xavier Mendik

With the release of *Shivers* (1976), David Cronenberg established himself as a leading figure in horror cinema. The film's theme of a breed of scientifically manufactured venereal parasites infecting a group of bourgeois condominium dwellers indicated the director's willingness to use the human body as a vehicle for wider social and sexual examinations.[1] Certain critics hailed his vivid concentration on the violent corruption of the human form as an advance in the genre's depiction of subjectivity. Other commentators pointed to his background in experimental film production as a rationale for the complex and multilayered style of his work.

However, the release of *Shivers* also initiated a sharp division surrounding the critical reception of the director's work. Indeed, it is noticeable that those "oppositional" voices critical to the "disgust" factor in Cronenberg's early depictions of sexuality and human physiology were still very much in evidence with the recent controversy surrounding his adaptation of *Crash* (1996). While much of this derision has traditionally come from journalistic sources, it is also important to recall Robin Wood's theoretical placement of Cronenberg in horror's "reactionary" wing. In his influential essay, "An Introduction to the American Horror Film", Wood made a sustained critique of the director's depiction of female and "queer" sexualities, which he felt failed to challenge existing social and ideological values.[2]

By utilising a mixture of Freudian and Marxist criticism,[3] Wood's analysis reveals the prominence of a "symptomatic" tendency which, as David Bordwell argues, has informed recent paradigms in film theory.[4] This method exceeds (presumed) biographical information as a motivating factor behind the filmmaker's work in favour of an approach incorporating prevailing modes of critical theory.

To this extent, the historical importance of the director's work can be judged by the reciprocal emergence of a body of ideas that can be termed "Cronenberg theory". These notions (which dominate the writings of both critics and defenders of Cronenberg) work to "explain" the director's motivations while linking specific readings to dominant theoretical paradigms. In its positive form, "Cronenberg theory" draws on many of the established notions around authorship, genre, textual (and sexual) analysis which this volume employs.

In the accompanying interview, Cronenberg discusses how such ideas provide an important framework through which his films can be discussed. The quotations which punctuate his comments are included to show a development in the richness and diversity of "Cronenberg theory". While the director's statements during the interview reiterate the need for what he terms "playful and intelligent criticism", they also indicate the complexity of his narratives as requiring a *plurality* of interpretation.

Of particular importance here is the need to counterbalance any textual understanding of political and ideological modes of representation with an understanding of the economic imperatives underpinning contemporary film production beyond the Hollywood canon. Equally, while acknowledging the historical importance of both Marxist and psychoanalytical methods of criticism, Cronenberg's remarks point to the need for his work to be contextualised in the light of other factors, such as those affecting definitions of national identity.

The requirement for a "reflexive" theory of the director's cinema is made all the more important by the fact that Cronenberg is so clearly a filmmaker who actively *engages* with the theory that surrounds his work. While this awareness confirms Michael Grant's recent conclusion of Cronenberg's cinema as fusing intellect within the unique act of creation,[5] it has also lead to an interpretive conundrum: that of the critically aware filmmaker who is always one step ahead of the theory which purports to explain him. This ability to shift between different registers of critical interpretation has been further complicated by the distinctive phases through which the director's career has moved. No sooner were definitions of Cronenberg as the king of "body horror" in circulation than he had already begun to reinvent himself as a master of literary and cinematic adaptation (*The Dead Zone* [1983] and *The Fly* [1986]). This phase of his filmic development was itself replaced by interests which took him increasingly away from those themes traditionally associated with the horror genre (*Dead Ringers* [1988] and *M. Butterfly* [1993]), while also charting his evolution as a visual interpreter of "difficult" avant-garde literary works (for example, Burroughs in *Naked Lunch* [1991] and Ballard in *Crash*).

The following interview was conducted while Cronenberg was in the post-production stages of his latest film, *eXistenZ* (1999). The narrative concerns a virtual-reality game that produces alterations in both consciousness and physiology for its users. As the director indicates here, the theme of the film can be seen more as an extension of interests explored in earlier productions such as *Scanners* (1981) and *Videodrome* (1982), rather than as a continuation of the recent narrative explorations of *Naked Lunch* and *Crash*. What this latest production points to is yet another phase of the director's career, and one which will ensure his continued placement at the forefront of both fantasy film production and its related theoretical debates.

On theory and the relationship between critic and filmmaker

In many ways, a psychoanalytical approach to Cronenberg's films seems a fairly obvious ploy...it is no novelty to treat the 'horror' genre through the theories of psychoanalysis, for like the surrealists, one imagines that in many cases the source of the material, either the director or the writer of the film, or both, is a 'knowing' one, in contrast to, say, the pre-Freudian nightmare landscapes of Bosch or Goya.[6]

Xavier Mendik: *Your work has traditionally been interpreted using psychoanalysis. Frequently, critics have linked elements of disgust in your films to repressed sexual tensions or monstrous representations of the mother. Are you happy with these accounts, or reluctant to have your films associated with any one line of interpretation?*

David Cronenberg: I guess it's the "classical" thing to do, but psychoanalytical criticism of the arts has really had its day, as have Marxist interpretations and those traditions that have been thought of as defining the politically correct. Therefore, to me it is just another fashion in criticism. I don't necessarily mean that in a totally negative way, because that line of thought is a very human thing to do, and it is not necessarily unilluminating either. The problem only comes when you find that your film is analysed in terms of a filmmaker who is absolutely not me! Obviously most of the people who are writing from that perspective don't know me at all.

Do you feel that it presumes that, as a filmmaker, you are not in control of what you are creating?

Yes, not only that you are not in control, but that this is the right set of critical and surgical tools through which to make a very meaningful anatomical inspection of the film.

You are clearly a director with an awareness of film debate and film theory. Do you feel that film theory has provided a interesting and valid way of understanding your films in a wider context?

I tend to like some of the French critics who write for journals such as *Cahiers du Cinéma*, and even then it is because I feel they

170

are more accurate in some way. They may be very intense, but they are also very playful. Importantly, the spectrum of their analysis is also very broad. They are very capable of bringing in cultural references, political references and psychoanalytical ones when they need to. They also employ literary references, as well as very cinematic ones. I find the breadth of this approach very rich and very stimulating.

Have these theoretical trends in any way been an influence on your work?

Criticism is not in itself a tool for me to make films, though I know that there are some critics who think that there is a neat fit between the two. Some critics believe that theory allows a complete understanding of where the inspiration of your film has come from. Yet, they often then go and stick an entirely different meaning over yours. That's where we have a purely psychoanalytical approach, which disbelieves and questions your intention. Which is very funny and yet kind of bizarre. In this way, I suppose there is a relationship between the art and psychology. The filmmaker has become like a very interesting patient to the critic as a kind of analyst!

I would very much place you in that tradition of European horror filmmakers who have an acute awareness of elements of film theory and philosophy, yet are resistant to its excesses. When you were talking, I was reminded of Jess Franco's comments to me that "theory can become a prison when making films".[7]

His comment is interesting, but it depends on what type of film criticism you are talking about. The type that we are exposed to daily is the normal newspaper journalistic features which are more fact- or information-based usually for commercial purposes. This type of information is often not very helpful, often difficult for the filmmaker's views, and frequently compromising for writers who want to express serious views. Therefore, at one level, I welcome any criticism that is really imaginative and lively and not just an extension of Hollywood marketing. As I say, this is a pattern that one finds. Unless one reads specialist magazines or books like the one you are working on, you are really getting an extension of studio marketing mentality. And the problem is also that it is very star- or personality-oriented, you know. It's more interested in questions like how well-developed are Demi Moore's assets in this movie! Therefore in this respect I have to qualify anything that I have said with an appreciation of any truly deep, intellectual, or even just very playful and intelligent criticism, because there is a real lack of it now.

On the Gothic and the role of genre

His formal stylistic and structural concerns, wit and clear sense of philosophical inquiry, allows his work to achieve the aboriginal impact of the Gothic novel itself. Cronenberg has moved away from conventional, outworn iconography and replaced it with contemporary, culturally appropriate images which allow for the reactivation of a hitherto effaced arena for debate.[8]

Thinking about some of these possible misinterpretations, you have frequently been labelled as the "king of body horror", a label which gives your movies a very contemporary feel. However, the themes of your work fit into a longer tradition of Gothic literature, particularly the well-documented split between the mind and the body found in works such as Shivers, Rabid *(1977) and* Videodrome.

I studied the Gothic and read books like *The Monk* [1796] by Lewis, but I don't necessarily feel part of the Gothic tradition. I think that the Gothic tradition is very retro at this point anyway, and it doesn't match my interests. Right now, I do have a real appreciation of the laws of logic, and logical progression. This is because I have recently been reading a lot of Wittgenstein and Nietzsche, which tells you to be logical to the point of madness. But Gothic literature, of course, is a form where logic is not really a major factor.

It's interesting that you mention Wittgenstein, because, as you will have seen from the outline of this book, this is exactly the approach that Michael Grant has been using to the consideration of films such as Crash *and* M. Butterfly.[9]

Yes, I noticed.

Does your interest in Wittgenstein's ideas then translate into your interest with male scientific figures?

Yes, once again it has to do with what we have just discussed: logic, reason, rationality and the possession of the mathematical mind. These are embodied in the figure of the scientist, they represent the achievements of what distinguishes us from other creatures and beings. So I enjoy creating characters who embody all of that, but at the same time *are* human and contradictory.

On "biography" and the role of the scientist

Though his focus is biological, and usually sexual, Cronenberg does involve technology in his plots...he always gives us a culprit, and that culprit is always a scientist – in fact, a doctor his doctors never intend the catastrophic effects of their research and inventions, and are always destroyed by them... Cronenberg's doctors are in the grip of a technological enthusiasm stronger than human will or discretion, and their zealous tinkering with Nature reaps from her a calamitous revenge.[10]

Critics have been quick to scuttle for an autobiographical reason behind your interest in the figure of the contradictory male scientist. They have presumed that, in depicting compromised figures such as Hobbes, Keloid and Raglan, you are commenting on tensions which relate to your own scientific background.

To be honest, I had a very minimal scientific background. I mean I had science tutors at high school and science tutors at university, but not for very long. However, they were of interest to me as individuals, they were real characters. They were what you would call "proto-Wittgensteins", although most people just saw them as a lot of strange men! I myself came to view them as "truncated humans" in the way that they interacted with people. They were very insular, very in control, but totally unable to communicate. But beyond this, these scientific figures are part of my imagination, my inventing and my feelings, rather than being personal in the normal autobiographical sense. This is something that is extremely hard for someone analysing one of my films at a "personal" level to comprehend. Critics often take this reply as my being evasive.

Therefore, when talking about a theory of Cronenberg's cinema, one should be wary of either attaching an "unconscious" meaning to one of your narratives, or latching onto one aspect of a production and then extrapolating an autobiographical meaning across both the film and the rest of the body of your work?

Yes. However, I do feel some empathy for those critics, because I do the very same thing myself. Say, for example, when I am reading Nietzsche, I want to fuse with Nietzsche, I wish I had known him, had been able to have a conversation with him, had been able to see a taped interview with him or something. It seems to me to be a very humanistic impulse to want to get to know the creative person in a very deep, detailed way, the way you might know a very close personal friend and their confidences. Therefore, in a way, I don't deride this type of autobiographical criticism, it only becomes awkward when they feel that they know your inner psyche without actually ever having met you. I think the basic problem is also that this approach does not recognise how complex the relationship is

173

between the artistic creator and what he creates. It is *very* complex, it is just not a simple one-to-one kind of thing. I do feel that the synthesising power of the imagination is really quite awesome, and it shouldn't be downplayed or simplified.

Over the years you must have been quite unnerved by some of the supposed "biographical" interpretations of your work.

One example that comes to mind is of a famous female Canadian broadcaster who by accident ended up (for some reason and I can't even remember why) sitting in a theatre where I was screening *Stereo* [1969] to my parents. She was sitting behind us and was really struck by the fact that here is a young filmmaker showing a very difficult, arcane, intellectual film to his parents. As a result, she became obsessed with the topic of my parents for the next twenty years, and brought it up every time I did an interview with her. And then my parents died, which she thought confirmed her view that my films were dark and death-laden because of my relations with them. All of this coming from the moment when she was at that screening! I did explain that I was thinking about all the type of stuff in *Stereo* when I was twelve years old when they were both vital and healthy. The fact that my parents died only confirmed what I had anticipated about human existence. I suppose I was a tiny existentialist in the making!

On male and female sexuality

Both *The Fly*...and *Dead Ringers* prominently feature men of science whose hubristic control over advanced technologies epitomizes what might be called 'phallic' power – the power that...relegates nature, matter, and the female to a position of inferiority, otherness, and objecthood that is nevertheless potentially dangerous and therefore must be controlled through the complex institutions of dominion.[11]

Although not necessarily as personal an interest as some believe, your depiction of the logical, and yet emotionally limited, scientists is interesting. When you were talking, I was instantly reminded of the image of Seth Brundle with identical jackets in a cupboard and a real fear of communication and sexual contact. In a way, he and your other male scientists are very asexual.

I suppose asexual is part of that, but it is more to do with how a character such as Seth Brundle orders his own sense of reality and consciousness. His awareness is evolved from a straightforwardly existential approach, recognising that there is no order and that we basically have to make it up, to order our own reality in a way that makes us feel that our lives are meaningful. This is a point that really interests me – indeed, I have to do this myself as a filmmaker when I am creating these characters. This is also what Brundle does, but he uses science to achieve this order. It is not that he is totally asexual, just that he only has enough energy to be successful in one line of thinking: that of scientific thinking. Therefore what he will do is strip away anything extraneous to that: that means fashion and it also means women. So it is just not accurate to say that he is sexually deficient, or that he hates women or that he is a repressed homosexual or anything like that. Rather, it is just that he wills himself to be just what he is – a man of one thing, a man of rational thinking. This is the only way he can perform and function.

However, it is interesting that you refer to Seth's apparent disinterest in women, because it is a trait that does make many of your male scientists.

I know that some people have argued that my scientists actually hate women, but this is based on a total misunderstanding. I am creating male characters because I am very interested in seeing what happens to someone who has deliberately divested themselves from the sexual element of human experience in order to achieve something. This is because the habits of anyone who has achieved anything in the creative field (whether it is science, entertainment, arts or music) have often led that person to divest himself or herself from certain emotional bonds. You are focusing on a certain thing, an event, then your life is not long enough – which of course is another existential concern, that there is too much to learn and too much to do in life. Therefore my scientists are examples of people who deliberately divest themselves of emotional bonds in order to achieve something. However, they are also people who are faulted because they do this to extremes and, as a result, they go over the edge.

On "Cronenberg's women"

David Cronenberg's *Shivers*...is a film single-mindedly about sexual liberation, a prospect it views with unmitigated horror... If the film presents sexuality in general as the object of loathing, it has a very special animus reserved for female sexuality...throughout, sexually aroused preying women are presented with a particular intensity of horror and disgust.[12]

I can understand your unease about how some critics have interpreted the role of females in your films. However, I do want to push you on the issue of "Cronenberg's women". In particular, your

1970s films presented women as a source not only of desire, but also of infection (Shivers, Rabid) and disgust (The Brood [1979]). What comment do you think these films are making on female sexuality?

I don't think they *are* making a comment on female sexuality as a source of disgust. I think they are making a comment on the men and the scientists who have created this feeling of disgust for themselves. You see, this is a perfect example of how people have misinterpreted these women *and* my films. I often get really distressed to see people thinking "well, we really have figured out Cronenberg, and somewhere in his past he must have been traumatised by women, probably by his mother during toilet training or something!". Yet again, what they are doing is misinterpreting what I am doing.

And again fusing the theoretical with presumptions about the biographical.

Yes, I have to say to myself, I do know what my life has been like, and the relations with the women in my life have just not been like that. To me, it seems like I have had a very simple past! I have often been confronted by such questions, and it always puts me in an awkward situation because I feel obligated to explain that if you talk to these women you will see that there is no disgust factor. I have no fear of women and have no repulsion or objection to the female sexual organ. To find that you are having to defend yourself against such a misinterpretation is very demeaning. The other thing, of course, which I find kind of amusing is that some of my male characters like the Mantles are not reacting to the female body with disgust, but with real curiosity. Often I find it is actually the viewer's response that is one of disgust, and that's not my doing. In fact, I am often very surprised at the reaction of my audiences to some of the things I have done because it is *their* response which is projected back onto me, which, as we discussed, is a very humanistic pursuit.

Let's reverse the question. You frequently depict your heroines as possessing bodies that transform and alter. Frequently they take on aggressive and even phallic qualities in the case of Rose in Rabid. *With such depictions, do you think that your films have managed to overcome criticisms that the horror film trades on passive and regressive images of women?*

Let's remember that my men have bodies that alter and take on feminine qualities, too. However, I am interested in representations of the female body, and one of the things that people frequently ask me as a creative artist is if I am engaged in a politics of filmmaking while I am making a film. I must admit that I don't set out to do that at the time of filming. However, in *Rabid*, as you know, its main character is a woman, and I have to tell you that just by doing that you are engaging in a kind of politics because you are making your movie a much more difficult thing to actually make. It made *Rabid* harder to finance and harder to cast. I have to say that I am now heading back to the same thing with *eXistenZ*. This is because once again the main character and driving force behind the film is a woman. Those problems have been made very clear to me in the way I have had to make the film!

Therefore is there still a long way to go in the way in which gender and genre films are received by financiers and audiences?

Yes, but in this case it's nothing to do with the genre, but the current nature of filmmaking in general. Maybe the aforementioned Demi Moore might be one of the few women able to trigger off the financing of a female role in, say, an action movie, but there are very, very few actresses able to do that. Although *eXistenZ* is not really an action film – more of a sci-fi film – to have a lead that is a woman means that when you talk to many male stars they are reluctant to play in the film. This is because they know they will be playing second fiddle to a woman who will be the focus of the movie – it's a very macho thing still. These problems existed even as far back as *Rabid*, so to find myself branded as a misogynist is such an irony for me.

Also you imply that more critical attention should be directed towards the economics of filmmaking.

Yes. Once again, what it points to is that some of the critics would like to find a purely personal motive for my depiction of women, and they just don't understand the realities of filmmaking. That is another curious thing about the relationship between critic and filmmaker: a lot of critics have no idea about *how* films are made. There is conflict there, but it is not necessarily *within* the director but between people, such as the power struggles involved in getting your film financed and all the rest of it. Now, I'm not saying that critics have to know, anymore than you have to know the technology of an automobile in order to be able to say why you like or don't like driving it. But if you're going to analyse the design of that automobile – you bloody well better know how automobiles were made! If you're going to go under the bonnet and examine each feature and dissect what it means, then you really should know something about how it was made. Those factors affecting how the film is made may often seem very pragmatic, and are often not of interest to many critics. But if you're going to get into the psychology of a filmmaker, you owe it to the filmmaker to understand the psychology of filmmaking, and the experiences they had when they were making that movie. That's why, as I say, I like a lot of the French critics, because they do consider that.

Given these interests in both female power and a critique of male sexuality, were you surprised by Robin Wood's high-profile attacks on your work?

I was, even after I was up onstage debating my work with him. Where is Robin Wood these days?

I believe that he is now back teaching in Canada.

I only ask because I did quite like the man when I knew him, though I didn't know him extremely well. And in a way I didn't necessarily oppose his stance, because at least it was criticism at a very interesting and intellectual level. But I have to say that when you boil it all down the basis of his argument was very simplistic in its fusion of critical and political analysis. It just entails you taking a stand and proclaiming your credentials through gay, Marxist, feminist theory. Everything is examined using those specific points of view. It is interesting because, although they would hate to admit it, a critic like that is exactly like one of my scientists. They have the understanding of a very broad spectrum of knowledge, but use this to drill only a very small hole, which makes criticism of their position harder. As you reach down that small hole you feel you can congratulate yourself on how "deep" you are, but there is no breadth to it whatsoever. Therefore, there really is no truth to it, it is merely a construct.

The one film to which he particularly objected was Shivers.

The problem here was that he saw *Shivers* as the triumph of the middle class and patriarchal power structures over women, wildness and rebellion. Yet, to me, it spoke to the audience that I know, and his reading was just not correct, and I told him so many times. The end of the film *is* a triumph, a weirdly, twisted, happy ending with the crazies running through the hall and leaving the tower. I have to say that throughout the film I identify with them, not with the "good" people stuck in their little cubicles. Again, this also points to the need to know the actual experience of the filmmaker making the film, because the whole film crew were actually stuck, living in those actual apartments. And I have to tell you that we were going completely stir-crazy; we ourselves would run through the halls, causing a stir and making trouble because we totally identified with the sex crazies in that film. However, it is such a neat political construct for him that he wanted to ignore all that and go with this Party line examination of the film. It is nonsense, I think he got it completely backwards. He didn't understand that, for me, those crazy people represented the artist and the creative mind.

On film style and construction

> Cronenberg's attacks on the sensibilities and framework of reference of the spectator are reinforced through narrative and structural experimentation...Such structure is perhaps best exemplified in *Rabid* which has an extraordinary episodic tangential plot consisting of set pieces held together by a central theme – the spread of the disease – rather than character or action in an accepted sense.[13]

*Your early productions (*Stereo, Crimes of the Future *[1970]) were often seen as experimenting with narrative structure. Do you feel that you have managed to retain this stylistic complexity in later, more commercial productions?*

Yes, I believe I have, and I think this has occurred in a kind of innate fashion, rather than at a purely conscious level. When I make these films, I am not thinking "I am now going to build a scene with stylistic, experimental elements or *vérité* moments, or whatever". But I can tell you that the script I did for *eXistenZ* was rejected by MGM because they thought it "wasn't linear enough" quote!. I thought that statement was very interesting because, after all these years, such opposition comes down to a structural problem. They were very afraid of the film because it deals with shifting planes of reality. Despite the fact that it was a science-fiction film, they felt it wasn't linear enough. So I have to assume that I am doing something right with my experimentations!

One recent film where your stylistic experimentation is marked is Dead Ringers, *the structure of which is very unclassical. Rather than pursuing a point of resolution, one becomes aware that the narrative must work backwards, back to that initial scene where the twins are identical in dress and nature.*

Yes, what I wanted to do here is to avoid thinking in terms of the three-act structure, with rising and falling planes of action. I do believe that if your film is to come alive you have to understand there cannot be an ultimately fixed structure; it is more the result of evolution and struggle. I am often amused by certain critics who ask me in almost confrontational terms, "Why have you done this?". The most accurate reply I can give is to say that when you start up, you just don't know what the end result of your filmmaking will be. That's the joy of it, it is very much like a journey, a creative and experimental expedition.

Continuing with Dead Ringers, *the film marked the beginning of your relationship with Jeremy Irons. What do you think he adds to your cinema?*

Again, it's very difficult to articulate an answer to this. In fact, it is another question that I am often asked. Just in terms of a film's production, people frequently ask "why did you cast that actor?". Therefore, rather than appear illusive, what I tend to do is come up with the same answer for each actor I have used! But the truth is that it is more of a textural thing, it is beyond generalisation and often just down to pragmatics. This is the case with *Dead Ringers*; I think the story is well-known. The reason I cast Jeremy is because he really wanted the role. I did approach a number of other actors who turned it down. The first person I tried to get for that role was Michael Moriarty, who is a Canadian actor and had returned to live in Canada, but Michael turned it down. In fact, one of the reasons that Jeremy was not my first choice was the fact that he was English and I hadn't written the part for an English actor. That's what I mean when I say that my casting often comes down to pragmatics. Often you do end up with the actor that you should have had, but it is a very fortuitous route by which the choice is made, and that actor might not have been the first choice.

On the controversy over *Crash*

The British press campaign against *Crash* started with a review of the movie by Alexander Walker in the *Evening Standard*, 3 June 1996. Having seen the film at Cannes, he described it as containing 'some of the most perverted acts and theories of sexual deviance I have ever seen propagated in mainstream cinema,' under the juicy headline, 'A movie beyond the bounds of depravity'. This latter phrase would be recycled endlessly over the next few months, whenever *Crash* was mentioned in print.[14]

How would you defend Crash *against claims that it is pornographic – or are you happy with the label?*

I get very pedantic when the word "pornography" is used in connection with the film. This is because pornography is a very specific thing. In fact, it really annoys me when people talk about the "pornography" of politics or the "pornography" of terrorism, because all these things are metaphors, not literal things. I do believe that pornography is that which is created to arouse the viewer or reader sexually. By using that literal definition, *Crash* is not pornographic. What confused me about the way the film was received was that people accused it of being pornographic, only then to say that they were even more offended because they felt it was absolutely not sexy in any way. What does this mean? Is the film failed pornography, or something that escapes this definition?

If anything, it seems to me that the film is denaturalising porn conventions: every act of pleasure is complemented by an act of displeasure and a constant equation with death.[15]

Yes, by doing this, the film is *anti*-pornographic. Pornography is a medium that wants you to feel comfortable in your arousal, and how it tries to do so is by portraying characters who very sexually healthy – even if they are perverse. Often my characters are nothing like that, and therefore I see the label of pornography as an easy tar-brush that just does not fit the film. Don't get me wrong, that the film should be sexually arousing to me is fine, I think that it is understood. I think that is one of the reasons why it disturbed a lot of people: they could not believe that they *were* being sexually aroused given what they were seeing on the screen, which, as I said, was not a traditional pornographic setting at all. What I wanted to do was to try and make it difficult for sexual arousal while still presenting imagery that technically should be arousing at least in terms of the psychology of such images. Therefore I think the film makes for a complex and difficult experience for a lot of people.

Extending your comments on the film as anti-pornography, one of the things that Crash *does that porn strictly tries not to do is to mix heterosexual and homosexual scenes of intercourse. This seems to be blurring presumed pornographic markets that traditionally are viewed as being separate.*

Of course, it's the male homosexuality that is so taboo in the film. Female homosexuality has become a staple element of male heterosexual pornography, which is why it is not central to the development of the film. However, by showing two guys getting it on together, the film was again difficult for many people, and they felt very threatened by this. I do believe it is at that point where we lost or truly shocked a lot of our audience.

One of the things that disturbed me about the film was not the explicit nature of the sex scenes, but the inability of the characters to relate to one another in an emotional way.

In many respects, this is an important element of the film because it works with the difficult images of sex that the film portrays. For desire to work you have to have not only a sexual impulse or a concept of sex, but in order to carry it through you have to have an emotion of sex because it tells you that you are alive. But if the underlying emotion of sex is missing, then so is the pleasure that goes with it, and that is why I said it is anti-pornographic. When people are repulsed by the film they tend to bounce off the surface of it, rather than being able to penetrate why those elements of disgust are there – especially it seems in Britain!

On Canadian identity and the future of the genre

Although film culture knows him as a cultish horror director, David Cronenberg is also a Canadian filmmaker. Yet, his nationality carries no resonance, nor has it drawn any but the scantiest attention from film critics, Canadian or not. When we attempt to discover the potential ramifications of Cronenberg's nationality, moreover, we discover instead that questions of authorship, genre cinema and nationality are fraught with problems.[16]

To close, I want to ask you about the issue of national identity. Do you think that your status as a Canadian director has had an important bearing on the way you direct films?

Yes, I am sure that it does, in the same way that Marshall McLuhan felt that being Canadian allowed him to have a perspective on the United States, its society, media and culture, that he wouldn't have had if he had been writing from the American backwaters. I don't feel that his comments relate only to the US, but obviously when it relates to film, the film forum is obviously dominated by Hollywood, Hollywood directors and the formulas that they have. The problem is obviously that if you come from outside that American context, the films that you produce are often seen as difficult, complex and not fitting within these formulas. This is something that I have found with *eXistenZ*. Although there are these problems with the Hollywood model of interpretation, I think it is very important that I am a Canadian director, and, in fact, I think we have some real filmmaking talent here, among the best in the world.

By way of conclusion, I wondered how you see a film such as eXistenZ *fitting into future horror trends? You have been pushing the boundaries of horror forward for over 30 years: do you feel that you will continue to do so with this new film?*

Right now, it's difficult for me to predict, because when making a film you focus your attention on its actual production, rather than how you feel it will extend the boundaries of a genre. It's almost as if you go into a kind of trance when you are making a film. I don't mind talking about how it might push barriers forward when it is finished and being shown, but until then it is difficult. However, it certainly seems from the reaction that I have had that the film relates back to the period of films such as *Scanners* more than it does to, say, my last couple of films. By this I mean that it is a definite genre picture. As I said earlier, it is a science-fiction movie, but one which has horror elements in it. I don't think it was necessarily a conscious thing, I wasn't thinking that I have to get back to my horror roots, but it might be legitimately perceived as that. I think people will definitely see it as my return to genre filmmaking, but hopefully in an interesting way – a non-linear way that MGM were so upset by!

Notes

I wish to offer my sincere thanks to David Cronenberg for both agreeing to the interview, and for offering his encouragement and support for this book. I would also like to express my gratitude to Sandra Tucker of David Cronenberg Productions, without whose assistance and patience the interview would not have been possible.

[1]   The role of the Starliner Towers as a metaphor for the body is established in the promotional footage of the building which forms the pre-credit sequence of the film. Here a voice-over (revealed to be that of hotel manager Merrick) informs the viewer that the tower is a division of "General Structures Incorporated". It is pertinent that the collapse of these established structures is mirrored by a corruption in the bodies' presumed form and mode of behaviour.

[2]   Arguably, Wood's view is problematised by the *method* through which wider social structures are represented in Cronenberg's cinema. It is not that the director is uninterested in examining the interrelations between the individual and wider social systems. Rather, it is the fact that his protagonists have reached such a level of alienation as to sever any fruitful connection to such networks. This pattern is present as early as *Shivers*, which, in its opening montage sequence, introduces the "Starliner" as a locale that is separate from the chaos of the wider social landscape. In *Rabid*, the spread of the infection that Rose provokes forces a separation of self from wider social interactions in the form of the emergency measures imposed by the authorities to limit the contagion. As recently as *Crash*, one again finds the theme of financially stable protagonists who remain separated from wider social affiliations by an increase in road and communication networks.

[3]   Wood's essay is reproduced as "An Introduction to the American Horror Film", in Bill Nichols (ed), *Movies and Methods volume II: An Anthology* (Berkeley; Los Angeles; London: University of California Press, 1985): 195-220. He employs notions of "surplus" repression derived from the Frankfurt School critics such as Gad Horowitz in order to show how social and ideological forces create a series of additional repressions upon those "basic" mechanisms which Freud defined as a necessary component of

psychological development. Wood goes on to argue that one cinematic focus of these additional pressures is the contradictory figure of the monster that the horror genre depicts.

[4]   David Bordwell, *Making Meaning: Inference and Rhetoric in the Interpretation of Cinema* (Cambridge, MA: Harvard University Press, 1989): 71-104. What is of interest to Bordwell is how filmic "meaning" has become increasingly abstracted from its modes of production via advanced theoretical interventions. Equally, in the chapter entitled "Rhetoric in Action: Seven Models of *Psycho*", Bordwell indicates how changes in theoretical perceptions of popular cinema can dramatically alter the critical reception of a work. He exemplifies this point by charting the changes in the theoretical reception of Hitchcock's film. Although mid-1960s accounts stress its artistic value in exploring themes central to the human condition, later 1970s criticism derides the film as containing a sadistic quest to punish its female protagonists. As Bordwell notes, this gender reading (resulting from critical advances in feminist and Lacanian theory) is itself displaced by later 1980s readings, which see the film as a critique of the economic excesses of American culture.

[5]   Michael Grant, *Dead Ringers* (Trowbridge: Flicks Books, 1997): 19. In a break with psychoanalytic interpretations of the filmmaker, Grant picks up on Cronenberg's well-documented interest in literature as a means of understanding the complex and often difficult images that the director produces. As with the most gifted of writers such as Eliot and Burroughs, Grant sees Cronenberg as conceiving the act of creation as a structural journey which both artist and audience often find hard to comprehend.

[6]   Michael O'Pray, "Primitive Phantasy in Cronenberg's Films", in Wayne Drew (ed), *BFI Dossier 21: David Cronenberg* (London: British Film Institute, 1984): 48.

[7]   Xavier Mendik, "A Sadeian Speaks: An Interview with Jesus Franco", in Andy Black (ed), *Necronomicon Book Two* (London: Creation Books International, 1998): 22.

[8]   Wayne Drew, "A Gothic Revival: Obsession and Fascination in the Films of David Cronenberg", in Drew (ed): 22.

[9]   See his contributions to this volume.

[10]   Mary B Campbell, "Biological Alchemy and the Films of David Cronenberg", in Barry Keith Grant (ed), *Planks of Reason: Essays on the Horror Film* (Metuchen, NJ; London: The Scarecrow Press, 1984): 308-309.

[11]   Helen W Robbins, "'More Human Than I Am Alone': Womb envy in David Cronenberg's *The Fly* and *Dead Ringers*", in Steven Cohan and Ina Rae Hark (eds), *Screening the Male: Exploring masculinities in Hollywood cinema* (London; New York: Routledge, 1993): 134.

[12]   Wood in Nichols (ed): 216.

[13]   Drew in Drew (ed): 20-21.

[14] Mark Kermode and Julian Petley, "Road Rage", *Sight and Sound* 7: 6 (June 1997): 16.

[15] The equation between sexuality, death and displeasure underpinning the film confirms my earlier placement of Cronenberg within European traditions of filmmaking. For instance, in the frequent sexual encounters between Catherine and Ballard, the potential visual pleasure of their nakedness is diminished by the incongruity of the dialogue accompanying these couplings. Their constant references to relations with other lovers, as well as an obsessive need to verbalise confirmation of orgasm as a sign of sexual pleasure, are reminiscent of the techniques used by Godard in some of his explicit 1970s experimentations.

[16] Bart Testa, "Technology's Body: Cronenberg, Genre and the Canadian Ethos", http://www.netlink.co.uk/users/zappa/testa1.html, 21 August 1998.

David Cronenberg: filmography

Compiled by Michael Grant

The following abbreviations have been used in this filmography:

ad	art director	*dist*	distributor
bw	black and white	*ed*	editor
CBC	Canadian Broadcasting	*ep*	executive producer
	Company	m	minutes
CFDC	Canadian Film	*m*	music
	Development Corporation	*p*	producer
col	colour	*pc*	production company
comm	commentary	*ph*	cinematographer
d	director	*sc*	scriptwriter
DC	David Cronenberg		

All films are directed by David Cronenberg.

Transfer
Canada 1966 7m col 16mm
sc, ph, ed DC
cast Mort Ritts, Rafe Macpherson.

From the Drain
Canada 1966 14m col 16mm
sc, ph, ed DC
cast Mort Ritts, Stephen Nosko.

Stereo
Canada 1969 65m bw 35mm
pc Emergent Films *p* DC, with Stephen Nosko, Pedro McCormick, Janet M Good *sc, ph, ed* DC
cast Ronald Mlodzik, Iain Ewing, Jack Messinger, Clara Mayer, Paul Mulholland, Arlene Mlodzik, Glenn McCauley.
dist The Other Cinema

Crimes of the Future
Canada 1970 65m col 35mm
pc Emergent Films, with the participation of the CFDC *p* DC, with
Stephen Nosko *sc, ph, ed* DC
cast Ronald Mlodzik (Adrian Tripod), John Lidolt, Tania Zoltry, Jack
Messinger, Iain Ewing, Rafe Macpherson, Willem Poolman, Donald
Owen, Norman Snider, Stephen Czernecki.
dist The Other Cinema

[In 1971 and 1972, Cronenberg scripted, directed and photographed nine
16mm fillers for Canadian Television]

Secret Weapons
Canada 1972 27m col 16mm
pc Emergent Films, for CBC (*Program X*) *ep* Paddy Sampson *sc* Norman
Snider *ph* DC *comm* Lister Sinclair
cast Barbara O'Kelly (motor cycle gang leader), Norman Snider (the
scientist), Vernon Chapman (the bureaucrat), Ronald Mlodzik, Bruce
Martin, Tom Skudra, Moses Smith, Michael D Spencer, G Chalmers
Adams.

Shivers
aka *They Came from Within*
aka *The Parasite Murders*
Canada 1976 87m col 35mm
ep Alfred Pariser *pc* DAL Productions, with the participation of the CFDC
p Ivan Reitman, John Dunning, André Link *sc* DC *ph* Robert Saad
ed Patrick Dodd *m supervisor* Ivan Reitman *special make-up and
creatures* Joc Blasco
cast Paul Hampton (Roger St Luc), Joe Silver (Rollo Linksy), Lynn Lowry
(Forsythe), Alan Migicovsky (Nicholas Tudor), Susan Petrie (Janine
Tudor), Barbara Steele (Betts), Ronald Mlodzik (Merrick), Barry Baldero
(Detective Heller), Camille Ducharme (Mr Guilbault), Hanka Posnanska
(Mrs Guilbault), Fred Doederlein (Dr Emil Hobbes).
dist Target

The Victim
Canada 1975 27m col 2" VTR
pc CBC (*Peepshow*) *ep* George Bloomfield *p* Deborah Peaker *sc* Ty
Haller *ph* Eamonn Beglan, Ron Manson, John Halenda, Dave Doherty,
Peter Brimson *VT ed* Garry Fisher *ad* Nickolai Soliov
cast Janet Wright (Lucy), Jonathan Welsh (Donald), Cedric Smith (man
on park bench).

The Lie Chair
Canada 1975 27m col 2" VTR
pc CBC (*Peepshow*) *ep* George Bloomfield *p* Eoinn Sprott *sc* David Cole
ph Eamonn Beglan, George Clemens, Tom Farquharson, Peter Brimson
set designer Rudi Dorn
cast Richard Monette (Neil), Susan Hogan (Carol), Amelia Hall (Mildred),
Doris Petrie (Mrs Rogers).
[Shown on Canadian Television, 1976]

The Italian Machine
Canada 1976 28m col 16mm
pc CBC (*Teleplay*) *ep* Stephen Patrick *sc* DC *ph* Nicholas Evdemon
ed David Denovan *m* Patrick Russell *ad* Peter Douet
cast Gary McKeehan (Lionel), Frank Moore (Fred), Hardee Linehan
(Bug), Chuck Shamata (Reinhardt), Louis Negin (Mouette), Toby Tarnow
(Lana), Geza Kovacs (Ricardo), Cedric Smith (Luke).

Rabid
Canada 1977 91m col 35mm
pc Cinema Entertainment Enterprises (for DAL Productions), with the
participation of the CFDC *ep* Ivan Reitman, André Link *p* John Dunning
sc DC *ph* René Verzier *ed* Jean Lafleur *m supervisor* Ivan Reitman
ad Claude Marchand *special make-up design* Joe Blasco Make-Up
Association
cast Marilyn Chambers (Rose), Frank Moore (Hart Read), Joe Silver
(Murray Cypher), Howard Ryshpan (Dr Dan Keloid), Patricia Gage (Dr
Roxanne Keloid), Susan Roman (Mindy Kent), J Roger Periard (Lloyd
Walsh), Lynne Deragon (nurse Louise), Terry Schonblum (Judy
Glasberg), Victor Désy (Claude Lapointe).
dist Alpha

Fast Company
Canada 1979 91m col 35mm
pc Quadrant Films, with the participation of the CFDC *ep* David M
Perlmutter *p* Michael Lebowitz, Peter O'Brian, Courtney Smith *sc* Phil
Savath, Courtney Smith, DC *original story* Alan Treen *ph* Mark Irwin
ed Ronald Sanders *m* Fred Mollin *ad* Carol Spier
cast William Smith (Lonnie Johnson), Claudia Jennings (Sammy), John
Saxon (Phil Adamson), Nicholas Campbell (Billy Booker), Cedric Smith
(Gary Black), Judy Foster (Candy), George Buza (Meatball), Robert
Haley (P.J.), David Graham (Stoner), Don Francks ("Elder").
dist/video Quality Video/VCL

The Brood
Canada 1979 91m col 35mm
pc Mutual Productions and Elgin International Pictures, with the
participation of the CFDC ep Victor Solnicki, Pierre David p Claude
Héroux sc DC ph Mark Irwin ed Alan Collins m Howard Shore ad Carol
Spier special make-up Jack Young, Dennis Pike
cast Oliver Reed (Dr Hal Raglan), Samantha Eggar (Nola Carveth), Art
Hindle (Frank Carveth), Cindy Hinds (Candice Carveth), Henry Beckman
(Barton Kelly), Nuala Fitzgerald (Juliana Kelly), Susan Hogan (Ruth
Mayer), Michael Magee (Inspector Mrazek), Joseph Shaw (Dr
Desborough, coroner), Gary McKeehan (Mike Trellan).
dist Alpha

Scanners
Canada 1981 103m col 35mm
pc Filmplan International, with the participation of the CFDC and
Famous Players ep Victor Solnicki, Pierre David p Claude Héroux sc DC
ph Mark Irwin ed Ronald Sanders m Howard Shore ad Carol Spier
main cast Jennifer O'Neill (Kim Obrist), Stephen Lack (Cameron Vale),
Patrick McGoohan (Dr Paul Ruth), Lawrence Dane (Braedon Keller),
Michael Ironside (Darryl Revok), Robert Silverman (Benjamin Pierce),
Adam Ludwig (Arno Crostic), Mavor Moore (Trevellyan), Fred
Doederlein (Dieter Tautz).
dist New Realm

Videodrome
Canada 1982 87m col 35mm
pc Filmplan International, with the participation of the CFDC and
Famous Players ep Victor Solnicki, Pierre David p Claude Héroux sc DC
ph Mark Irwin ed Ronald Sanders m Howard Shore ad Carol Spier
special make-up design Rick Baker
cast James Woods (Max Renn), Sonja Smits (Bianca O'Blivion), Deborah
Harry (Nicki Brand), Peter Dvorsky (Harlan), Les Carlson (Barry
Convex), Jack Creley (Brian O'Blivion), Lynne Gorman (Masha), Julie
Khaner (Bridey), Reiner Schwarz (Moses), David Bolt (Raphael).
dist Palace
award Genie Award 1984: best achievement in direction

The Dead Zone
USA 1983 100m col 35mm
pc Dead Zone Productions, in association with Lorimar Productions
ep Dino De Laurentiis p Debra Hill sc Jeffrey Boam novel Stephen King
ph Mark Irwin ed Ronald Sanders m Michael Kamen pd Carol Spier
cast Christopher Walken (Johnny Smith), Brooke Adams (Sarah
Bracknell), Martin Sheen (Greg Stillson), Sean Sullivan (Herb Smith),

Jackie Burroughs (Vera Smith), Herbert Lom (Dr Sam Weizak), Tom Skerritt (Sheriff Bannerman), Anthony Zerbe (Roger Stuart), Nicholas Campbell (Frank Dodd), Peter Dvorsky (Dardis).
dist Columbia-Emi-Warner

The Fly

Canada 1986 92m col 35mm
pc Brooksfilms, for 20th Century Fox *p* Stuart Cornfeld *sc* Charles Edward Pogue, DC *story* George Langelaan *ph* Mark Irwin *ed* Ronald Sanders *m* Howard Shore *pd* Carol Spier *the fly created and designed by* Chris Walas Inc
cast Jeff Goldblum (Seth Brundle), Geena Davis (Veronica [Roni] Quaife), John Getz (Stathis Borans), Joy Boushel (Tawny), Les Carlson (Dr Cheevers), George Chuvalo (Marky), Michael Copeman (second man in bar), Carol Lazare (nurse), Shawn Hewitt (clerk).
awards American Academy Awards® (Oscars) 1986 for Best Make-up: Chris Walas, Stephan Dupuis
dist 20th Century Fox

Dead Ringers

Canada 1988 115m col 35mm
pc The Mantle Clinic II Ltd, in association with Morgan Creek Productions Inc. With the participation of Telefilm Canada *ep* Carol Baum, Sylvio Tabet *p* DC, Marc Boyman *sc* DC, Norman Snider based on the book, *Twins* by Bari Wood and Jack Geasland *ph* Peter Suschitzky *ed* Ronald Sanders *m* Howard Shore *pd* Carol Spier *motion control programmer* Randall Balsmeyer *optical effects supervisor* Lee Wilson *ad* Alicia Keywan, James McAteer
cast Jeremy Irons (Beverly Mantle/Elliot Mantle), Geneviève Bujold (Claire Niveau), Heidi von Palleske (Cary Weiler), Barbara Gordon (Danuta), Shirley Douglas (Laura), Stephen Lack (Anders Wolleck), Nick Nichols (Leo), Lynne Cormack (Arlene), Damir Andrei (Birchall), Miriam Newhouse (Mrs Bookman), David Hughes (superintendent), Richard Farrell (Dean of Medicine).
dist Rank
awards Genie Awards 1989: best achievement in direction, best motion picture; National Society of Film Critics Award (USA) 1991: best director

The Faith Healer

USA 1988 26m col
[Episode 12 of the television series *Friday the Thirteenth*]
pc Paramount Television Inc. *ep* Frank Mancuso, Jr *p* Iain Paterson *sc* Christine Cornish
cast Christopher Wiggins (Jack Marshak), Miguel Fernandez (Stewart Fishoff), Robert Silverman (Jerry Scott), John D LeMay (Ryan).

[In 1989, Cronenberg directed four commercials for Ontario Hydro; in 1990, he directed two commercials for William Neilson Ltd, and five commercials for Nike]

Regina Versus Horvath
Canada 1990 48m col Betacam
pc CBC in association with Scales of Justice Enterprises Inc. *ep* Carol Reynolds *p* George Jonas *sc* Michael Tait, George Jonas *ph* Rodney Charters *ed* Ronald Sanders *m* Howard Shore *pd* Carol Spier
cast Justin Louis (John Horvath), Les Carlson (Larry Proke), Len Doncheff (John Molnar), Kurt Reis (Mr Justice Gould), Michael Caruana (Mr R D Schantz, Crown), David Gardner (Mr D G G Milne, defence), James Edmond (Dr Gordon Stephenson, psychiatrist), Frank Perry (Dr Coady, coroner).

Regina Versus Logan
Canada 1990 44m col Betacam
pc CBC in association with Scales of Justice Enterprises Inc. *ep* Carol Reynolds *p* George Jonas *sc* David Emmanuel, George Jonas *ph* Rodney Charters *ed* Ronald Sanders *m* Howard Shore *pd* Carol Spier
cast Barbara Turnbull (as herself), Richard Yearwood (Cliff), Desmond Campbell (Hugh) Mark Ferguson (Warren).

Naked Lunch
Canada 1991 115m col 35mm
pc Recorded Picture Company, with the participation of Telefilm Canada and the Ontario Film Development Corporation *p* Jeremy Thomas *sc* DC, based on the novel, *Naked Lunch* by William S Burroughs *ph* Peter Suschitzky *ed* Ronald Sanders *m* Howard Shore *creatures created and designed by* Chris Walas Inc. *pd* Carol Spier *special effects supervisor* Jim Isaacs
cast Peter Weller (Bill Lee), Judy Davis (Joan Lee, Joan Frost), Roy Scheider (Dr Benway), Ian Holm (Tom Frost), Julian Sands (Yves Cloquet), Michael Zelniker (Martin), Nicholas Campbell (Hank), Monique Mercure (Fadela) Joseph Scorsiani (Kiki).
dist First Independent
awards National Society of Film Critics Awards (USA) 1991: best director, best screenplay; Genie Award 1992: best achievement in direction

M. Butterfly
Canada 1993 102m col 35mm
pc Geffen Pictures in association with M. Butterfly Productions Inc.
ep David Henry Hwang, Philip Sandhaus *p* Gabriella Martinelli *sc* David Henry Hwang, based upon his play *ph* Peter Suschitzky *ed* Ronald

Sanders *m* Howard Shore *pd* Carol Spier
main cast Jeremy Irons (René Gallimard), John Lone (Song Liling), Barbara Sukowa (Jeanne Gallimard), Ian Richardson (Amabassador Toulon), Annabel Leventon (Frau Baden).
dist Warner Bros

Crash
Canada 1996 110m col 35mm
pc Alliance Communications Corporation *ep* Robert Lantos, Jeremy Thomas *co-ep* Andras Hamori, Chris Auty *co-p* Stephane Reichel, Marilyn Stonehouse *sc* DC *novel* J G Ballard *ph* Peter Suschitzky *ed* Ronald Sanders *m* Howard Shore *pd* Carol Spier *ad* Tamara Deverell
main cast James Spader (James Ballard), Holly Hunter (Helen Remington), Elias Koteas (Vaughan), Deborah Kara Unger (Catherine Ballard), Rosanna Arquette (Gabrielle), Peter MacNeill (Colin Seagrave).
dist Columbia TriStar
awards Cannes Film Festival 1996: Special Jury Prize; Genie Awards 1997: best adapted screenplay, best achievement in direction

eXistenZ
Canada 1999 96m col 35mm
pc Alliance Atlantis and Serendipity Point Films, in association with Natural Nylon, with the participation of Telefilm Canada *p* Robert Lantos, Andras Hamori, DC *sc* DC *ph* Peter Suschitzky *ed* Ronald Sanders *m* Howard Shore *pd* Carol Spier *visual and special effects supervisor* Jim Isaac
main cast Jennifer Jason Leigh (Allegra Geller), Jude Law (Ted Pikul), Ian Holm (Kiri Vinokur), Willem Dafoe (Gas), Christopher Ecclestone (seminar leader), Don McKellar (Yevgeny Nourish), Callum Keith Rennie (Carlaw), Sarah Polley (Merle).
dist Alliance Releasing (UK)
award winner of the Silver Bear for outstanding artistic achievement, Berlin Film Festival 1999.

Cronenberg's film roles
Black Zero (1967), *Stereo* (1969), *Crimes of the Future* (1970), *Into the Night* (1985), *The Fly* (1986), *Nightbreed* (1989), *Blue* (1992), *Henry and Verlin* (1994), *Boozecan* (1994), *Trial by Jury* (1994), *To Die For* (1995), *Blood and Donuts* (1995), *Moonshine Highway* (1996), *Crash* (1996), *The Stupids* (1996), *Extreme Measures* (1996), *The Grace of God* (1997), *Last Night* (1998), *Resurrection* (1999), *Dead by Monday* (2000).

David Cronenberg: selected bibliography

Compiled by Michael Grant

Primary bibliography

A: Published screenplays and adaptations

Cronenberg, David. *Crash* (London; Boston: Faber and Faber, 1996).

Jack, Martin. *Videodrome: a Novel Based on a Screenplay by David Cronenberg* (New York; Sevenoaks: Kensington Publishing Corporation and New English Library, 1983).

King, Stephen. *The Dead Zone* (New York: New American Library, 1980).

Priest, Christopher. *eXistenZ* (New York: HarperEntertainment, 1999) [novelisation].

Starks, Richard. *The Brood* (London; Toronto; Sydney; New York: Granada Publishing/Mayflower Books; Toronto: Virgo, 1979) [novelisation].

—————————. *Rabid* (Toronto: Virgo, 1979) [novelisation].

Whiteson, Leon. *Scanners* (New York: Tower, 1980) [novelisation].

Wood, Bari and Jack Geasland. *Dead Ringers* (London: Sphere Books, 1988) [re-release of the original novel, *Twins*, on which the film was based. First published in the United States in 1978 by Signet Books, and simultaneously in Canada by Longman Canada].

B: Interviews with Cronenberg

Andrew, Geoff. "Fender bender", *Time Out* 6-13 November 1996: 18-20.

Ayscough, Susan. "David Cronenberg: Sex... Porn... Censorship... Art... Politics... And other terms", *Cinema Canada* 102 (December 1983): 15-18.

Braun, Eric. "The gentle art of mind boggling", *Films* 1: 7 (June 1981): 22-25.

Breskin, David. "Cronenberg: The Rolling Stone Interview", *Rolling Stone* 6 February 1992: 66-70.

—————————. *Inner Views: Filmmakers in Conversation* (Boston; London: Faber and Faber, 1992): 201-267.

Brown, Mick. "Secrets of his excess", *Daily Telegraph Arts* 3 May 1999: A5 [on *eXistenZ*].

Burdeau, Emmanuel. "La différence entre Cronenberg", *Cahiers du Cinéma* 534 (April 1999): 66.

Case, Brian. "China", *Time Out* 4-10 May 1994: 18-19 [on *M. Butterfly*].

Case, Brian. "Schlock tactics", *Time Out* 12-19 April 1995: 155.

Cazals, Thierry and Charles Tesson. "Quelque chose qui n'a jamais existé", *Cahiers du Cinéma* 391 (January 1987): 28-30 [on *The Fly*].

Combs, Richard. "David, we must do Lunch", *The Sunday Times* 19 April 1992: Sec. 6: 14-15 [on *Naked Lunch*].

Delorme, Gérard. "Le double jeu de Cronenberg", *Première* 266 (May 1999): 99-101.

Edwards, Phil. "The Cronenberg Tapes", *Starburst* 22 (2: 10) (1980): 40-44.

———————. "Inside Cronenberg [part 1]", *Starburst* 36 (3: 12) (1981): 40-43.

———————. "Inside Cronenberg [part 2]", *Starburst* 37 (4: 1) (1981): 36-39.

——————— and Randy Lofficier. "The Cronenberg Tapes 1984: Part One – *Videodrome*", *Starburst* 69 (6: 9) (May 1984): 20-23.

——————————————————. "The Cronenberg Tapes 1984: Part Two – *The Dead Zone*", *Starburst* 70 (6: 10) (June 1984): 8-12.

Floyd, Nigel. "Gynaecology, Symbiosis and Foetal Pigs...", *Shock Xpress* 2: 5 (winter 1988/89): 12-15 [mainly on *Dead Ringers*].

Fuller, Graham. "A Womb With a Brood", *The Listener* 22 October 1988: 6-7.

Gaitskill, Mary. "David Cronenberg", *Interview* 22: 1 (January 1992): 80-82.

Gilbey, Ryan. "Cars, death, sex", *The Independent* 10 October 1996: 4-5 [on *Crash*].

Grünberg, Serge. "Entretien avec David Cronenberg", *Cahiers du Cinéma* 453 (March 1992): 15-25.

——————————. "Entretien avec David Cronenberg", *Cahiers du Cinéma* 504 (July-August 1996): 26-30.

Hickenlooper, George. "The Primal Energies of the Horror Film: An Interview with David Cronenberg", *Cineaste* 17: 2 (1989): 4-7.

————————————————. *Reel Conversations: Candid Conversations with Film's Foremost Directors and Critics* (New York: Citadel, 1991).

Hodgkiss, Ros. "Prince of darkness", *The Guardian Friday Review* 2 April 1999: 8-9.

Hultkrans, Andrew. "Body Work: Andrew Hultkrans talks with J.G. Ballard and David Cronenberg", *Artforum* March 1997: 76-81, 117-118.

Jaehne, Karen. "David Cronenberg on William Burroughs: *Dead Ringers* Do *Naked Lunch*", *Film Quarterly* 45: 3 (spring 1992): 2-6.

Jaworzyn, Stefan. "*Nightbreed*. Clive Barker Makes Religious Epic Shock!", *Shock Xpress* 3: 1 (summer 1989): 22-25 [interviews with Clive Barker and Cronenberg].

Kennedy, Douglas. "Shock Trouper", *The Independent Magazine* 7 May 1994: 34-36, 38.

Kenny, Glenn. "The Filmmaker Series: David Cronenberg", *Premiere* 10: 8 (April 1997): 67-70.

Kermode, Mark. "David Cronenberg", *Sight and Sound* 1: 11 (March 1992): 11-13.

──────────. "David Cronenberg Invites you to Lunch", *Shivers* 1 (June 1992): 8-10 [on *Naked Lunch*].

Linklater, Alex. "On a Collision Course", *The Sunday Times* 11 August 1996: Sec. 10: 6-7 [on *Crash*].

Lucas, Tim. "No concessions", *Fear* 4 (January-February 1989): 16-18 [on *Dead Ringers*].

──────────. "Cronenberg and the Flesh", *Video Watchdog* 36 (1996): 40 [concludes with a round-up of new video releases of *Shivers* and *Rabid*, and laserdisc releases of *Shivers* and *Dead Ringers*, each being accompanied by a short critical review: 42-45].

Malcolm, Derek. "I fear, therefore I am", *The Guardian* 29 December 1988: 21.

Martin, Bob. "*The Brood* and Other Terrors", *Fangoria* 3 (December 1979): 12-15.

──────────. "David Cronenberg's *Scanners*", *Fangoria* 10 (January 1981): 7-9.

Martin, Gavin. "The Sickest Man in Movies?", *New Musical Express* 7 January 1989: 16-17 [includes brief reviews by Edwin Pouncey of *Rabid*, *The Brood*, *Scanners*, *Videodrome*, *The Dead Zone* and *Dead Ringers*].

Mathews, Tom Dewe. "Crash landing", *The Guardian* 21 April 1997: Sec. 2: 8-9.

Newman, Kim. "Unzipping the Fly: An Interview with David Cronenberg", *Shock Xpress* 2: 1 (summer 1987): 20-22.

Peachment, Chris. "Clean-cut guy with a dirty mind", *The Sunday Telegraph* 8 May 1994: 4.

Pizzello, Stephen. "Driver's Side", *American Cinematographer* 78: 4 (April 1997): 43-47.

Pullinger, Kate. "Undressing for lunch", *Evening Standard Magazine* April 1992: 80-81.

Rodley, Chris (ed). *Cronenberg on Cronenberg* (London; Boston: Faber and Faber, 1992; revised edition 1997).

Rowe, Michael. "A New Level of eXistenZ", *Fangoria* 191 (April 1999): 12, 15-17.

Scorsese, Martin (as told to Jay Cocks). "Scorsese on Cronenberg", *Fangoria* 32 (January 1984): 46-47.

Shelley, Jim. "Always crashing in the same car", *The Guardian (Weekend)* 2 November 1996: 12, 15-17.

Smith, Gavin. "Cronenberg: Mind Over Matter", *Film Comment* 33: 2 (March-April 1997): 14-15.

Tadros, Jean-Pierre. "David Cronenberg", *Le Film Français* 9 April 1999: 13.

Taubin, Amy. "Crash test", *The Village Voice* 25 March 1997: 80.

Tesson, Charles, Iannis Katsahnias and Vincent Ostria. "Entretien avec David

Cronenberg", *Cahiers du Cinéma* 416 (February 1989): 12-13, 62-64.

Weisel, Al. "David Cronenberg's *Naked Lunch*", *Gay Times* May 1992: 35-38.

Wiater, Stanley. "David Cronenberg", in *Dark Visions: Conversations with the Masters of the Horror Film* (New York: Avon Books, 1992): 57-65.

Wise, Damon. "Dr Benway Rides Again! David Cronenberg Interviewed", in Stefan Jaworzyn (ed), *Shock Xpress 1* (London: Titan Books, 1991): 60-66.

——————. "One on One: David Cronenberg", *Empire* 120 (June 1999): 104-106, 108.

Wolf, Matt. "Seen any good accidents lately?", *The Times* 28 May 1997: 39.

Secondary bibliography

A: Books and special journal issues devoted to Cronenberg and his films

Artese, Alberto (ed). *David Cronenberg: La rabbia della forma* (Rimini: Cinema Quaderni, 1987) [filmography, with programme notes from various sources].

Deleolanis, Yiannis. *Mesa apo to Skoteino Kathrefti* (Athens: Futura, 1997).

Drew, Wayne (ed). *David Cronenberg (BFI Dossier 21)* (London: British Film Institute, 1984).
Contents: "Introduction", by Wayne Drew (iv); "Counter-Introduction: Limits of Auteurism", by Colin McArthur (1-2); "Interview with David Cronenberg", by Jill McGreal (3-15); "A Gothic Revival: Obsession and Fascination in the Films of David Cronenberg", by Wayne Drew (16-22); "Stereo, Sex and Crimes for the Future", by Chris Rodley (23-27); "'The Brood'", by Stephen Schiff (28-30); "A Post-Modern Cronenberg", by Michael Silverman (31-34); "V.D. O'Nasty", by Julian Petley (35-40); "'The Victim': New Rules for an Old Game", by Bernard Thomas (41-42); "Cronenberg's Television Work", by Paul Taylor (43-44); "'Fast Company': The Machine Movie", by Kim Newman (45-47); "Primitive Phantasy in Cronenberg's Films", by Michael O'Pray (48-53); "Internal Metaphors, External Horror", by Martin Scorsese (54); "Filmography" (55-56); "Appendix: Festival of Festivals' Science Fiction Retrospective", by David Cronenberg (57).

Grant, Michael. *Dead Ringers* (Trowbridge: Flicks Books, 1997).

Grünberg, Serge. *David Cronenberg* (Paris: Éditions Cahiers du Cinéma, 1992).

Haas, Robert (ed). Special Issue: David Cronenberg. *Post Script* 15: 2 (winter/spring 1996).
Contents: "Introduction: The Cronenberg Monster: Literature, Science, and Psychology in the Cinema of Horror", by Robert Haas (3-10); "Lost and Gone Forever: Cronenberg's *Dead Ringers*", by William Beard (11-28); "Somatic Ideas: Cronenberg and the Feminine", by Mary Pharr and Lynda Haas (29-39); "Cronenberg's 'Only Really Human Movie': *The Dead Zone*", by Tony Magistrale (40-45); "Festering in Thebes: Elements of Tragedy and Myth in Cronenberg's Films", by Leonard G Heldreth (46-61); "Medicine, Surrealism, Lust, Anger, and Death: Three Early Films by David Cronenberg", by Michael J Collins (62-69); "Creating a New Reality: Cronenberg on Cronenberg", by Mark Chamey (70-74); "David Cronenberg Filmography" (75-78).

Handling, Piers (ed). *The Shape of Rage: The Films of David Cronenberg* (Toronto: General Publishing Co.; New York: New York Zoetrope; 1983).
Contents: "Introduction", by Piers Handling (vii); "Biography" (viii); "The

Visceral Mind: The Major Films of David Cronenberg", by William Beard (1 79);
"The Comedy of Cronenberg", by Maurice Yacowar (80-86); "The Word, The
Flesh and David Cronenberg", by John Harkness (87-97); "A Canadian
Cronenberg", by Piers Handling (98-114); "Cronenberg: A Dissenting View", by
Robin Wood (115-135); "Cronenberg Tackles Dominant Videology", by Geoff
Pevere (136-148); "The Image As Virus: The Filming of 'Videodrome'", by Tim
Lucas (149-158); "The Interview", conducted by William Beard and Piers
Handling (159-198); "Filmography", established by D. John Turner (199-210);
"A Select Bibliography" (211-214).

Handling, Piers, and Pierre Véronneau (eds). *Le horreur intérieure: les films de
david cronenberg* (Montreal: La Cinémathèque Québécoise, 1990; Paris: Les
Éditions du Cerf, 1990) [translation into French of *The Shape of Rage*, with
some additional material].
Contents: "Introduction: L'effet Cronenberg", by Pierre Véronneau (7-9);
"Entretien avec David Cronenberg", by William Beard, Piers Handling, Pierre
Véronneau (11-55); "L'esprit viscéral: les films majeurs de David Cronenberg",
by William Beard (57-135); "Monstration et démonstration", by Pierre
Véronneau (137-158); "La comédie de Cronenberg", by Maurice Yacowar (159-
166); "Le mot, la chair et David Cronenberg", by John Harkness (167-177); "Un
Cronenberg canadien", by Piers Handling (179-196); "Un point de vue dissident
sur Cronenberg", by Robin Wood (197-214); "Cronenberg s'attaque à la
vidéologie dominante", by Geoff Pevere (215-227); "L'image comme virus", by
Tim Lucas (229-239); "Bibliographie", by René Beauclair (241-246);
"Filmographie", by D J Turner (247-255).

Koliodymos, Dimitris (ed). *David Cronenberg* (Athens: The 34th Thessaloniki
Film Festival, 1993).
Contents: "Apo ton exoteriko tromo ston psychologiko [From internal terror to
psychological]", by Robert Collison (7-17); "Olethria gnosi [Infernal
knowledge]", by Michael O'Pray (19-23); "Esoterikes metaphores, exoterikos
tromos [Internal metaphors, external terror]", by Martin Scorsese (25-26); "Mia
gothiki anaviosi [A Gothic revival]", by Wayne Drew (27-44); "Y komodia ston
Cronenberg [The comedy of Cronenberg]", by Maurice Yacowar (45-52); "Mesa
apo to skoteino kathrefti: i eikones, i idees, kai i skies tous sto ergo tou David
Cronenberg [Through the dark mirror: images, ideas, and their shadows in the
work of David Cronenberg]", by Yiannis Deleolanis (53-81); "Bio-filmographia",
by Dimitris Koliodymos (83-107).

Morris, Peter. *David Cronenberg: A Delicate Balance* (Toronto: ECW Press,
1994).

Müller, Marco (ed). *David Cronenberg: Transformatie van een horrorfilmer/A
horrorfilmer in transformation* (Rotterdam: de Volkskrant, 1990) [containing
material from *The Shape of Rage* and *David Cronenberg (BFI Dossier 21)*].
Contents: "Introduction/Inleiding", by Jan Blokker (6-9); "The Interview/Het
Interview", by William Beard and Piers Handling (10-41); "Interview with David
Cronenberg/Interview met David Cronenberg", by Jill McGreal (42-59);
"Cronenberg's television work/Het televisiewerk van David Cronenberg", by
Paul Taylor (60-65); "Internal metaphors, external horror/Innerlijke metaforen,
uiterlijke horror", by Martin Scorsese (66-67); Appendix/Appendix (68-89);
"Filmography/Filmografie" (70-73) [dual text, in English and Dutch].

Oetjen, Almut and Holger Hacker. *Organischer Horror: Die Filme des David
Cronenberg* (Meitingen: Corian-Verlag Heinrich Wimmer, 1993).

Sinclair, Iain. *Crash: David Cronenberg's Post-mortem on J.G. Ballard's*

'*Trajectory of Fate*' (London: British Film Institute, 1999).

Yates, James N. *David Cronenberg as Mythmaker: An Archetypal Interpretation of His Films, 1975-1991* (Ann Arbor, MI: Dissertation Abstracts International, 1996).

B: General articles and essays on Cronenberg in journals and books

Auty, Chris and Steve Woolley. "'A Terror So Complete That It's Almost A Kind Of Peace'", *Time Out* 576 (1-7 May 1981): 34-35.

Badley, Linda. "David Cronenberg's Anatomy Lessons", in *Film, Horror, and the Body Fantastic* (Westport, CT; London: Greenwood Press, 1995): 125-136.

Beard, William. "Cronenberg, Flyness, and the Other-self", *Cinémas* 4: 2 (winter 1994): 153-173.

Campbell, Mary B. "Biological Alchemy and the Films of David Cronenberg", in Barry Keith Grant (ed), *Planks of Reason: Essays on the Horror Film* (Metuchen, NJ; London: The Scarecrow Press, 1984): 307-320.

Carroll, Michael Thomas. "The Bloody Spectacle: Mishima, The Sacred Heart, Cronenberg, and the Entrails of Culture", *Studies in Popular Culture* 15: 2 (1993): 43-56.

Chute, David. "He Came from Within", *Film Comment* 16: 2 (March-April 1980): 36-39, 42.

—————. "Twelve New Movies: The Latest from Cronenberg and Venice", *Film Comment* 18: 1 (January-February 1982): 2-4.

—————. "David Cronenberg", in Jack Sullivan (ed), *The Penguin Encyclopedia of Horror and the Supernatural* (New York: Viking, 1986): 103-106.

Fischer, Dennis. *Horror Film Directors, 1931-1990* (Jefferson, NC; London: McFarland & Company, 1991): 268-285.

Freeland, Cynthia A. "Monstrous Flesh", *The Naked and the Undead: Evil and the Appeal of Horror* (Boulder, CO: Westview Press, 2000): 87-120.

Govier, Katherine. "Middle-class shivers", *Toronto Life* July 1979: 50-51, 56-58, 61-62.

Hanke, Ken. "David Cronenberg", in John McCarty (ed), *The Fearmakers: The Screen's Directorial Masters of Suspense and Terror* (New York: St. Martin's Press, 1994): 176-185.

Harkness, John. "David Cronenberg: Brilliantly Bizarre", *Cinema Canada* 72 (March 1981): 8-17.

—————. "The word, the flesh and the films of David Cronenberg", *Cinema Canada* 97 (June 1983): 23-25.

Hofsess, John. "Fear and Loathing to Order", *The Canadian* 26 February 1977: 14-17 [reprinted in Seth Feldman and Joyce Nelson (eds), *Canadian Film Reader* (Toronto: Peter Martin Associates, 1977): 274-278].

Humm, Maggie. "Cronenberg's Films and Feminist Theories of Mothering", in *Feminism and Film* (Edinburgh: Edinburgh University Press; Bloomington and

Indianapolis: Indiana University Press; 1997): 58-89

Kauffman, Linda S. "David Cronenberg's Surreal Abjection", in *Bad Girls and Sick Boys: Fantasies in Contemporary Art and Culture* (Berkeley; Los Angeles; London: University of California Press, 1998): 115-145.

Lewis, Brent. "Nightmare Man", *Films and Filming* 389 (February 1987): 17-19.

Lowenstein, Adam. "Canadian Horror Made Flesh: Contextualising David Cronenberg", *Post Script* 18: 2 (winter/spring 1999): 37-51.

Lucas, Tim. "David Cronenberg: from *Shivers* to *Dead Ringers*", *Video Watchdog* 36 (1996): 26-39.

McCarty, John. *Splatter Movies: Breaking the Last Taboo of the Screen* (New York: St. Martin's Press, 1984): 73-87.

McGregor, Gaile. "Grounding the Countertext: David Cronenberg and the Ethnospecificity of Horror", *Canadian Journal of Film Studies* 2: 1 (spring 1992): 43-62.

McLarty, Lianne. "'Beyond the Veil of the Flesh': Cronenberg and the Disembodiment of Horror", in Barry Keith Grant (ed), *The Dread of Difference: Gender and the Horror Film* (Austin: University of Texas Press, 1996): 231-252.

Newman, Kim. "King in a Small Field – David Cronenberg", *Monthly Film Bulletin* 54: 637 (February 1987): 64.

—————. *Nightmare Movies: A Critical History of the Horror Film, 1968-88* (London: Bloomsbury, 1988): 116-121.

————— [updated by John McCarty]. "Cronenberg, David", in Laurie Collier Hillstrom (ed), *International Dictionary of Films and Filmmakers – 2: Directors*, third edition (Detroit; New York; Toronto; London: St. James Press, 1997): 202-204.

Nutman, Philip. "The Exploding Family", in Christopher Golden (ed), *Cut! Horror Writers on Horror Film* (New York: Berkley Books, 1992): 171-182.

O'Neill, Edward R. "David Cronenberg", in Geoffrey Nowell-Smith (ed), *The Oxford History of World Cinema* (Oxford: Oxford University Press, 1996): 736.

O'Pray, Michael. "Fatal knowledge", *Sight and Sound* 1: 11 (March 1992): 10-11.

Parker, Andrew. "Grafting David Cronenberg: Monstrosity, AIDS Media, National/Sexual Difference", in Marjorie Garber, Jann Matlock and Rebecca L Walkowitz (eds), *Media Spectacles* (New York; London: Routledge, 1993): 209-231.

Pevere, Geoff. "Cliffhanger: Cronenberg and the Canadian Cultural Consciousness", *Take One* 3 (autumn 1993): 4-9.

Porton, Richard. "The Film Director as Philosopher", *Cineaste* 24: 4 (1999): 4-9.

Sage, Victor. "The Gothic, the Body, and the Failed Homeopathy Argument", in Xavier Mendik and Graeme Harper (eds), *Unruly Pleasures: The Cult Film and its Critics* (Guildford: FAB Press, 2000): 139-153.

Sammon, Paul M. "David Cronenberg", *Cinefantastique* 10: 4 (spring 1981): 20-35.

Sarner, Mark. "Telepathy is Just an Excuse", *Time Out* 6-12 April 1973: 17-20.

199

Sharrett, Christopher. "The Shape of Rage: The Films of David Cronenberg", *Journal of Popular Film and Television* 11: 4 (winter 1984): 172-174.

—————————. "Myth and Ritual in the Post-Industrial Landscape: The Horror Films of David Cronenberg", *Persistence of Vision* 3/4 (summer 1986): 111-130.

Shaviro, Steven. "Bodies of Fear: David Cronenberg", in *The Cinematic Body* (Minneapolis; London: University of Minnesota Press, 1993): 127-156.

—————————. "David Cronenberg", in *Doom Patrols* (London; New York: Serpent's Tail, 1997): 110-121.

Sutton, Martin. "Schlock! Horror! The films of David Cronenberg", *Films and Filming* 337 (October 1982): 15-21.

Testa, Bart. "Technology's Body: Cronenberg, Genre, and the Canadian Ethos", *Post Script* 15: 1 (autumn 1995): 38-56.

Thomson, David. *A Biographical Dictionary of Film*, revised and enlarged edition (London: André Deutsch, 1994): 158-159.

Toubiana, Serge. "L'homme tout bête", *Cahiers du Cinéma* 453 (March 1992): 8-9.

Tuchman, Mitch. "Fish gotta swim...", *Monthly Film Bulletin* 51: 605 (June 1984): 192.

Williams, Linda Ruth. "The Inside-out of Masculinity: David Cronenberg's Visceral Pleasures", in Michele Aaron (ed), *The Body's Perilous Pleasures: Dangerous Desires and Contemporary Culture* (Edinburgh: Edinburgh University Press, 1999): 30-48.

Wood, Robin. "An Introduction to the American Horror Film", in Andrew Britton, Richard Lippe, Tony Williams and Robin Wood (eds), *American Nightmare: Essays on the Horror Film* (Toronto: Festival of Festivals, 1979): 7-28 [reprinted in Barry Keith Grant (ed), *Planks of Reason: Essays on the Horror Film* (Metuchen, NJ; London: The Scarecrow Press, 1984): 164-200; and in Bill Nichols (ed), *Movies and Methods Volume II: An Anthology* (Berkeley; Los Angeles; London: University of California Press, 1985): 195-220].

C: Selected reviews, articles and books about specific films

Stereo

Cart. "*Stereo*", *Variety* 316: 4 (22 August 1984): 17.

Rayns, Tony. "Stereo", *Monthly Film Bulletin* 38: 453 (October 1971): 204.

Crimes of the Future

Brigg, Peter. "*Crimes of the Future*", *Take One* 2: 6 (July-August 1969): 21.

Cart. "*Crimes Of The Future*", *Variety* 316: 4 (22 August 1984): 17.

Rayns, Tony. "Crimes of the Future", *Monthly Film Bulletin* 38: 454 (November 1971): 217-218.

Shivers

Bilbow, Marjorie. "Shivers", *Screen International* 20 (24 January 1976): 9.

Chesley, Stephen. "It'll bug you.", *Cinema Canada* 22 (October 1975): 23-25.

Combs, Richard. "Shivers", *Monthly Film Bulletin* 43: 506 (March 1976): 62.

C.V. "*The Parasite Murders*", *Positif* 171/172 (July-August 1975): 68.

Delaney, Marshall. "You Should Know How Bad This Film Is. After All, You Paid For It", *Saturday Night* (September 1975): 83-85.

Edwards, Natalie. "David Cronenberg's *The Parasite Murders*", *Cinema Canada* 22 (October 1975): 44-45.

J.L. "*Frissons (Parasite murders)*", *Image et Son* 320-321 (October 1977): 113.

Leayman, Charles D. "They Came From Within", *Cinefantastique* 5: 3 (winter 1976): 22-23.

Link, André. "Delaney's Dreary Denegration", *Cinema Canada* 22 (October 1975): 24.

Loyd. "They Came From Within", *Variety* 282: 7 (24 March 1976): 21.

MacMillan, Robert. "*Shivers*... Makes Your Flesh Creep!", *Cinema Canada* 72 (March 1981): 11-15.

Rouyer, Philippe. "'Frissons' et 'Rage'", *Positif* 410 (April 1995): 100-101.

Sanjek, David. "Dr. Hobbes's Parasites: Victims, Victimization, and Gender in David Cronenberg's *Shivers*", *Cinema Journal* 36: 1 (autumn 1996): 55-74.

Schupp, Patrick. "*Frissons (The Parasite Murders)*", *Séquences* 83 (January 1976): 35.

Shuster, Nat. "*Shivers*", *Motion* 5: 3 (1976): 47-48.

Taubin, Amy. "Back to the Future", *The Village Voice* 43: 2 (13 January 1998): 62.

Yacowar, Maurice. "You Shiver Because It's Good", *Cinema Canada* 34/35 (February 1977): 54-55.

Rabid

Allombert, Guy. "*Rage (Rabib)* [sic]", *La Revue du Cinéma/Image et Son* 322 (November 1977): 122.

Botting, Josephine. "*Rabid*", *Shivers* 57 (September 1998): 18-21.

Brown, Geoff. "Rabid", *Screen International* 109 (15 October 1977): 18.

Combs, Richard. "Rabid", *Monthly Film Bulletin* 44: 526 (November 1977): 240.

Hege. "Rabid", *Variety* 287: 8 (29 June 1977): 28.

Hofsess, John. "Fear and Loathing to Order", *The Canadian* 26 February 1977: 14-17.

Hurley, Kelly. "Reading like an Alien: Posthuman Identity in Ridley Scott's *Alien* and David Cronenberg's *Rabid*", in Judith Halberstam and Ira Livingston (eds),

Posthuman Bodies (Bloomington: Indiana University Press, 1995): 203-244.

Irving, Joan. "David Cronenberg's *Rabid*", *Cinema Canada* 37 (April/May 1977): 57.

Livingston, Ira. "The Traffic in Leeches: David Cronenberg's *Rabid* and the Semiotics of Parasitism", *American Imago* 50: 4 (winter 1993): 515-53.

Rolfe, Lee. "David Cronenberg on *Rabid*", *Cinefantastique* 6: 3 (winter 1977): 26.

Rouyer, Philippe. "'Frissons' et 'Rage'", *Positif* 410 (April 1995): 100-101.

Shuster, Nat. "Canadian Filmview", *Motion* 6: 4/5 (1977): 15.

Fast Company

Adil. "Fast Company", *Variety* 295: 3 (23 May 1979): 24.

Beard, Bill. "David Cronenberg's *Fast Company*", *Cinema Canada* 58 (September 1979): 32-33.

Jones, Martha J. "Fast Companies (2): Cronenberg on wheels", *Cinema Canada* 49-50 (September-October 1978): 17-19.

Taylor, Paul. "Fast Company", *Monthly Film Bulletin* 51: 605 (June 1984): 188 [review of video release].

The Brood

Bilbow, Marjorie. "The Brood", *Screen International* 229 (23 February 1980): 15.

Braun, Eric. "The Brood", *Films and Filming* 26: 6 (March 1980): 34-35.

Cart. "The Brood", *Variety* 295: 5 (6 June 1979): 20.

Creed, Barbara. "Woman as Monstrous Womb: *The Brood*", in *The Monstrous-Feminine: Film, feminism, psychoanalysis* (London; New York: Routledge, 1993): 43-58.

C.T. "Chromosome 3", *Cahiers du Cinéma* 306 (December 1979): 58.

Dowler, Andrew. "David Cronenberg's *The Brood*", *Cinema Canada* 58 (September 1979): 33-34.

Fox, Jordan R. "*The Brood*", *Cinefantastique* 8: 4 (1979): 23.

F.R. "Chromosome 3 (The Brood)", *Positif* 227 (February 1980): 88-89.

Guérif, François. "*Chromosome 3 (The brood)*", *La Revue du Cinéma/Image et Son* 345 (December 1979): 119.

Lucas, Tim. "*The Brood*", *Cinefantastique* 9: 1 (1979): 42.

McKellar, Don. "The Children of Canada", *Sight and Sound* 9: 7 (July 1999): 58-59.

Milne, Tom. "The Brood", *Monthly Film Bulletin* 47: 554 (March 1980): 44-45.

Paul, William. *Laughing Screaming: Modern Hollywood Horror and Comedy* (New York: Columbia University Press, 1994): 368-380.

Peary, Danny. "The Brood", in *Cult Movies: The Classics, the Sleepers, the Weird, and the Wonderful* (New York: Dell Publishing, 1981): 36-39.

Rabourdin, Dominique. "*Chromosome 3*", *Cinéma* 252 (November 1979): 88.

Schupp, Patrick. "Les monstres de l'été", *Séquences* 98 (October 1979): 27-32.

Scanners

A.G. "*Scanners*", *Positif* 242 (May 1981): 78-79.

Bilbow, Marjorie. "Scanners", *Screen International* 285 (28 March-4 April 1981): 13.

Braun, Eric. "Scanners", *Films* 1: 5 (April 1981): 36-37.

Cart. "*Scanners*", *Variety* 301: 12 (21 January 1981): 26.

Childs, Mike and Alan Jones. "*Scanners*", *Cinefantastique* 10: 1 (summer 1980): 35.

Chute, David. "He Came from Within", *Film Comment* 16: 2 (March-April 1980): 36-39, 42.

Cros, Jean-Louis. "*Scanners*", *La Revue du Cinéma/Image et Son/Écran* 360 (April 1981): 60-61.

Harkness, John G. "David Cronenberg's *Scanners*", *Cinema Canada* 72 (March 1981): 34-36.

Lofficier, Jean-Marc. "*Scanners*: Un frankenstein moderne", *L'Écran Fantastique* 16 (1980): 71.

Nacache, Jacqueline. "*Scanners*", *Cinéma* 269 (May 1981): 78-79.

Sammon, Paul M. "*Scanners*", *Cinefantastique* 10: 4 (spring 1981): 45.

Siegel, Lois. "Artists of illusion", *Cinema Canada* 63 (March 1980): 20-27.

Taylor, Paul. "Scanners", *Monthly Film Bulletin* 48: 567 (April 1981): 78.

Tesson, Charles. "Caïn et Abel Version S.F.", *Cahiers du Cinéma* 322 (April 1981): 57-58.

Videodrome

Bilbow, Marjorie. "Videodrome", *Screen International* 422 (26 November-3 December 1983): 17.

Bukatman, Scott. "Who Programs You? The Science Fiction of the Spectacle", in Annette Kuhn (ed), *Alien Zone: Cultural Theory and Contemporary Science Fiction Cinema* (London; New York: Verso, 1990): 196-213.

Chute, David. "David Cronenberg's Gore-Tech Visions", *Rolling Stone* 17 March 1983: 33, 36.

Dowler, Andrew. "David Cronenberg's *Videodrome*", *Cinema Canada* 93 (February 1983): 35.

Hill, Ian W. "*Videodrome*: TV or not TV?", *Video Watchdog* 36 (1996): 76-80 [letter from a reader giving a close and detailed analysis of the shortcomings of the MCA-TV version of *Videodrome*, plus an editorial response].

Jameson, Fredric. *The Geopolitical Aesthetic: Cinema and Space in the World*

System (Bloomington and Indiana: Indiana University Press; London: British Film Institute; 1992): 22-35.

Karani, Cathy. "*Videodrome*", *L'Écran Fantastique* 44 (April 1984): 24-29.

Klad. "Videodrome", *Variety* 310: 1 (2 February 1983): 18.

Lucas, Tim. "*Videodrome*", *Cinefantastique* 12: 2/3 (April 1982): 4-7.

――――――. "*Videodrome*", *Cinefantastique* 12: 5/6 (July/August 1982): 6-7.

――――――. "*Videodrome*", *Cinefantastique* 13: 4 (April-May 1983): 4-5.

――――――. "David Cronenberg's *Videodrome*", *Cinefantastique* 14: 2 (December 1983/January 1984): 32-49.

McKinnon, John P. "*Videodrome*: Insidious effects of high tech", *Cinema Canada* 81 (February 1982): 32.

Rickey, Carrie. "Make Mine Cronenberg", *The Village Voice* 1 February 1983: 62-65.

Roth, Marty. "*Videodrome* and the Revenge of Representation", *CineAction* 43 (July 1997): 58-61.

Taylor, Paul. "Videodrome", *Monthly Film Bulletin* 50: 598 (November 1983): 310-311.

Testa, Bart. "Panic Pornography: *Videodrome* From Production to Seduction", *Canadian Journal of Political and Social Theory* 13: 1-2 (1989): 56-72.

The Dead Zone

Ayscough, Susan. "David Cronenberg's The Dead Zone", *Cinema Canada* 102 (December 1983): 18.

Beard, William. "An Anatomy of Melancholy: Cronenberg's *The Dead Zone*", *Journal of Canadian Studies* 27: 4 (winter 1992-93): 169-179.

Binn. "The Dead Zone", *Variety* 312: 11 (12 October 1983): 20.

Edwards, Phil. "The Dead Zone", *Starburst* 70 (6: 10) (June 1984): 40-41.

Hogan, David J. "*The Dead Zone*", *Cinefantastique* 14: 2 (December 1983/January 1984): 51.

Jenkins, Steve. "The Dead Zone", *Monthly Film Bulletin* 51: 604 (May 1984): 147-148.

Lucas, Tim. "David Cronenberg's *The Dead Zone*", *Cinefantastique* 14: 2 (December 1983/January 1984): 24-31, 60-61.

Scotto, Daniel. "*The Dead Zone*", *L'Écran Fantastique* 43 (March 1984): 19-23.

Strick, Philip. "Uneasy lies the head: *Christine* and *The Dead Zone*", *Sight and Sound* 53: 2 (spring 1984): 150.

Tesson, Charles. "Main, Trop Humain", *Cahiers du Cinéma* 357 (March 1984): 50-51.

Verniere, James. "Screen Previews: *The Dead Zone*", *Twilight Zone Magazine* November/December 1983: 52-55.

The Fly

Cazals, Thierry. "Le Scénario Américain", *Cahiers du Cinéma* 391 (January 1987): 31-32.

Cook, Pam. "The Fly", *Monthly Film Bulletin* 54: 637 (February 1987): 45-46.

Doherty, Thomas. "*The Fly*", *Film Quarterly* 40: 3 (spring 1987): 38-41.

Dorland, Michael. "David Cronenberg's *The Fly*", *Cinema Canada* 135 (November 1986): 40.

Dowler, Andrew. "David Cronenberg's *The Fly*", *Cinema Canada* 135 (November 1986): 41.

Freeland, Cynthia A. "Feminist Frameworks for Horror Films", in David Bordwell and Noël Carroll (eds), *Post-Theory: Reconstructing Film Studies* (Madison; London: The University of Wisconsin Press, 1996): 195-218.

Jagr. "The Fly", *Variety* 324: 3 (13 August 1986): 11.

Kirkland, Bruce. "*The Fly*", *Cinefantastique* 16: 3 (July 1986): 15, 60.

Knee, Adam. "The Metamorphosis of the fly", *Wide Angle* 14: 1 (January 1992): 20-34.

Leayman, Charles D. "*The Fly*", *Cinefantastique* 17: 1 (January 1987): 46-47, 60.

Lucas, Tim. "*The Fly* – New Buzz on an Old Theme", *American Cinematographer* 67: 9 (September 1986): 60-67.

Magid, Ron. "More About *The Fly*", *American Cinematographer* 67: 9 (September 1986): 68-76.

Pharr, Mary Ferguson. "Pathos to Tragedy: The Two Versions of *The Fly*", *Journal of the Fantastic in the Arts* 2: 1 (spring 1989): 37-46.

QSF. "The Fly", *Screen International* 586 (7-14 February 1987): 60.

Rafferty, Terrence. "Out of the Blue: Letter from New York", *Sight and Sound* 56: 1 (winter 1986/87): 30-33.

Robbins, Helen W. "'More Human Than I Am Alone': Womb envy in David Cronenberg's *The Fly* and *Dead Ringers*", in Steven Cohan and Ina Rae Hark (eds), *Screening the Male: Exploring masculinities in Hollywood cinema* (London; New York: Routledge, 1993): 134-147.

Tesson, Charles. "Les yeux plus gros que le ventre", *Cahiers du Cinéma* 391 (January 1987): 25-27.

Dead Ringers

AD. "*Dead Ringers*", *Screen International* 673 (8-15 October 1988): 31.

Adil. "*Dead Ringers*", *Variety* 332: 7 (7 September 1988): 27.

Billson, Anne. "Cronenberg on Cronenberg: a career in stereo", *Monthly Film Bulletin* 56: 660 (January 1989): 4-6.

Bloch-Hansen, Peter. "Double Trouble", *Fangoria* 78 (October 1988): 52-55.

Cook, Pam. "Dead Ringers", *Monthly Film Bulletin* 56: 660 (January 1989): 3-4.

Creed, Barbara. "Phallic panic: male hysteria and *Dead Ringers*", *Screen* 31: 2 (summer 1990): 125-146.

Doherty, Thomas. "David Cronenberg's Dead Ringers", *Cinefantastique* 19: 3 (March 1989): 38-39.

Floyd, Nigel. "*Dead Ringers*", *Time Out* 959 (4-11 January 1989): 41.

Frank, Marcie. "The Camera and the Speculum: David Cronenberg's *Dead Ringers*", *PMLA* 106: 3 (May 1991): 459-470.

Gleiberman, Owen. "Double Meanings", *American Film* 14: 1 (October 1988): 38-43.

Jacobowitz, Florence and Richard Lippe. "*Dead Ringers*: The Joke's On Us", *CineAction!* spring 1989: 64-68.

Jaehne, Karen. "Double Trouble", *Film Comment* 24: 5 (September-October 1988): 20-22, 24, 26-27.

Jaworzyn, Stefan. "*Dead Ringers*", *Shock Xpress* 2: 5 (winter 1988/89): 37.

Katsahnias, Iannis. "La beauté intérieure", *Cahiers du Cinéma* 416 (February 1989): 4-7.

Kimber, Gary. "Dead Ringers", *Cinefantastique* 19: 1/2 (January 1989): 86-87, 120.

Lucas, Tim. "David Cronenberg's Dead Ringers: Part One", *Fangoria* 79 (December 1988): 26-29, 67 [continued in "Cronenberg Under the Knife: Part Two", *Fangoria* 80 (February 1989): 48-51, 68].

McGillivray, David. "Dead Ringers", *Films and Filming* 412 (February 1989): 32-33.

Moore, Suzanne. "A problem of identities", *New Statesman* 13 January 1989: 44.

Shaviro, Steven. "Bodies of Fear: David Cronenberg", in *The Cinematic Body* (Minneapolis; London: University of Minnesota Press, 1993): 127-156.

Shaw, Daniel. "Horror and the Problem of Personal Identity: *Dead Ringers*", *Film and Philosophy* 3 (1996): 14-23.

Shay, Don. "Double Vision", *Cinefex* 36 (November 1988): 33-49.

Stanbrook, Alan. "Cronenberg's Creative Cancers", *Sight and Sound* 58: 1 (winter 1988/89): 54-56.

Tesson, Charles. "Voyage au bout de l'envers", *Cahiers du Cinéma* 416 (February 1989): 8-11.

Tyrkus, Michael J. "*Dead Ringers*", in Nicolet V Elert and Aruna Vasudevan (eds), *International Dictionary of Films and Filmmakers – 1: Films*, third edition (Detroit; New York; Toronto; London: St. James Press, 1997): 260-262.

Walters, Margaret. "Albion Rovers", *The Listener* 12 January 1989: 31.

Naked Lunch

Beard, William. "Insect Poetics: Cronenberg's *Naked Lunch*", *Canadian Review of Comparative Literature/Revue Canadienne de Littérature Comparée* 23: 3 (September 1996): 823-852.

Downing, David L and Kim Kebris. "'Exterminate All Rational Thought': David Cronenberg's Filmic Version of William S. Burroughs's *Naked Lunch*", *The Psychoanalytic Review* 85: 5 (1998): 775-792.

Grünberg, Serge. "Humains trop humains", *Cahiers du Cinéma* 453 (March 1992): 12-14.

McCarthy, Todd. "Naked Lunch", *Variety* 345: 11 (23 December 1991): 43.

Moore, Oscar. "The Naked Lunch", *Screen International* 840 (17-23 January 1992): 24.

Murphy, Timothy S. *Wising up the marks: the amodern William Burroughs* (Berkeley; London: University of California Press, 1997): 67-72.

Silverberg, Ira (ed). *Everything is Permitted: The Making of Naked Lunch* (New York: Grove Weidenfeld, 1992).

Sinclair, Iain. "The Naked Diners Club", *Sight and Sound* 2: 1 (May 1992): 6.

Taubin, Amy. "The wrong body", *Sight and Sound* 1: 11 (March 1992): 8-10.

Thompson, David. "Naked Lunch", *Sight and Sound* 2: 1 (May 1992): 56-57.

Thrower, Stephen. "Literary Highs and Cinematic Lows: Problems, Pleasures, Imbalances in Cronenberg's *Naked Lunch*", *Eyeball* 3 (summer 1992): 26-29.

M. Butterfly

Chow, Rey. "The Dream of a Butterfly", in Diana Fuss (ed), *Human, All Too Human* (New York; London: Routledge, 1996): 61-92.

de Lauretis, Teresa. "Popular Culture, Public and Private Fantasies: Femininity and Fetishism in David Cronenberg's *M. Butterfly*", *Signs* 24: 1 (winter 1999): 303-334.

Ellis, Rose. "Dead gays society", *Gay Times* May 1994: 53-54.

Floyd, Nigel. "*M. Butterfly*", *Time Out* 4-10 May 1994: 60.

Harkness, John. "M. Butterfly", *Sight and Sound* 4: 5 (May 1994): 44-45.

Hoberman, James. "Phantom of the Opera", *The Village Voice* 5 October 1993: 49.

Johnston, Sheila. "*M. Butterfly*", *The Independent* 6 May 1994: 25.

McCarthy, Todd. "M. Butterfly", *Variety* 352: 5 (20 September 1993): 26.

Malcolm, Derek. "*M. Butterfly*", *The Guardian* 5 May 1994: Sec. 2: 6-7.

Newman, Kim. "M. Butterfly", *Empire* 60 (June 1994): 37.

Suner, Asuman. "Postmodern Double Cross: Reading David Cronenberg's *M. Butterfly* as a Horror Story", *Cinema Journal* 37: 2 (winter 1998): 49-64.

Tookey, Christopher. "*M. Butterfly*", *The Daily Mail* 6 May 1994: 36-37.

Walker, Alexander. "Of sex and spies", *Evening Standard* 5 May 1994: 4.

Crash

Amis, Martin. "Cronenberg's Monsters", *The Independent on Sunday (Review)* 10 November 1996: 8, 9.

Andrew, Geoff. "*Crash*", *Time Out* 4-11 June 1997: 78.

Andrews, Nigel. "Watch out, here comes *Crash*", *The Financial Times* 29 May 1997: 23.

Billson, Anne. "*Crash*", *The Sunday Telegraph (Review)* 8 June 1997: 7.

Bouquet, Stéphane. "Sweet movie", *Cahiers du Cinéma* 504 (July-August 1996): 24-25.

Brown, Geoff. "*Crash*", *The Times* 5 June 1997: 37.

"*Crash* (and burn)?: Special section: Cronenberg's auto eroticism", *FSAC/ACEC Newsletter (Association canadienne des études cinématographiques/Film Studies Association of Canada)* 21: 1 (autumn 1996): 15-20.
Contents: Bart Testa (15-16); Brian McIlroy (17); Barry Grant (17-18); William C Wees (18-19); Gene Walz (19); Jim Leach (19-20); Murray Pomerance (20) [the general heading of this section on the *Newsletter*'s contents page is: "FSAC members collide with Cronenberg"].

"Dangerous Driving", *Frieze* 34 (May 1997): 50 [J G Ballard interviewed by Ralph Rugoff].

Dick, Leslie. "Crash", *Sight and Sound* 7: 6 (June 1997): 48-49.

Dixon, Wheeler Winston. "The Moving Image in Crisis", in *Disaster and Memory: Celebrity Culture and the Crisis of Hollywood Cinema* (New York: Columbia University Press, 1999): 1-48.

Grundmann, Roy. "Plight of the Crash Fest Mummies: David Cronenberg's *Crash*", *Cineaste* 22: 4 (March 1997): 24-27.

Hensley, Dennis. "Crash: Test Dummy", *Premiere* 4: 12 (January 1997): 44-51.

Hoberman, James. "Body Work", *The Village Voice* 25 March 1997: 73.

Hunter, Allan. "Crash", *Screen International* 1060 (31 May-5 June 1996): 18.

Jenkins, Simon. "Morals of the postal code", *The Times* 24 May 1997: 22.

Kelly, Richard T. "'Crash' and car safety", *Sight and Sound* 7: 7 (July 1997): 64 [letter].

Kermode, Mark. "'Crash' course 1", *Sight and Sound* 7: 9 (September 1997): 64 [letter].

———————— and Julian Petley. "Road Rage", *Sight and Sound* 7: 6 (June 1997): 16-18.

Krips, Henry. *Fetish: An Erotics of Culture* (Ithaca; London: Cornell University Press, 1999): chapter 10.

Leith, William. "Any excuse to dress up as an insect and behave badly", *The Observer (Review)* 8 June 1997: 12.

Lim, Dennis. "Crash Course", *The Village Voice* 43: 11 (17 March 1998): 68.

Lucas, Tim. "*Crash*", *Video Watchdog* 42 (1997): 48-57.

McCarthy, Todd. "*Crash*", *Variety* 363: 3 (20 May 1996): 30-31.

Malcolm, Derek. "Navel-watching *Crash* bombs", *The Guardian* 18 May 1996.

—————————. "How was it for you?", *The Guardian* 6 June 1997: Sec. 2: 8.

Mars-Jones, Adam. "*Crash*", *The Independent* 5 June 1997: 3-4.

Musto, Michael. "*Crash*", *The Village Voice* 25 March 1997: 14.

Newman, Kim. "Crash", *Empire* 92 (February 1997): 28.

—————————. "Time machines", *Sight and Sound* 9: 4 (April 1999): 11.

Petley, Julian. "'Crash' course 2", *Sight and Sound* 7: 9 (September 1997): 64 [letter].

Reynolds, Nigel. "Violent, nasty and morally vacuous", *The Daily Telegraph* 9 November 1996: 3.

Rodley, Chris. "Crash", *Sight and Sound* 6: 6 (June 1996): 6-11.

—————————. "Game boy", *Sight and Sound* 9: 4 (April 1999): 8-10.

Romney, Jonathan. "Shock value", *The Guardian* 20 June 1996: Sec. 2: 8-9.

Russell, Jay. "Di/Crash", in Jane Stokes and Anna Reading (eds), *The Media in Britain* (London: Macmillan, 1999): 289-294.

Self, Will. "Thanks to the censors, it's a case of 'you haven't seen the movie – now read the book'", *The Observer (Review)* 24 November 1996: 15 [review of *Crash* novel by J G Ballard and *Crash* screenplay by David Cronenberg].

Shone, Tom. "Crashing bore not auto erotica", *The Sunday Times* 8 June 1997: Sec. 11: 5.

Smith, Marq. "Wound envy: touching Cronenberg's *Crash*", *Screen* 40: 2 (summer 1999): 193-202.

"Special Debate: *Crash*", *Screen* 39: 2 (summer 1998): 175-192. Contents: "Anal wounds, metallic kisses", by Barbara Creed (175-179); "Crimes of the future", by Michael Grant (180-185); "Automatic lover", by Fred Botting and Scott Wilson (186-192).

Stringer, Robin. "London debut for year's most shocking film", *Evening Standard* 26 September 1996: 17.

Suschitzky, Peter [interviewed by Allen Daviau and Fred Elmes]. "Auto Erotic", *American Cinematographer* 78: 4 (April 1997): 36-42.

Sutherland, John. "Crazy for Liz", *The Guardian* 29 May 1997: Sec. 2: 9.

Taylor, Chris. "'Crash' course 3", *Sight and Sound* 7: 9 (September 1997): 64 [letter].

Thompson, Ben. "*Crash*", *The Independent on Sunday* 8 June 1997: 11.

Tookey, Christopher. "Twisted wreck of a movie", *The Daily Mail* 6 June 1997: 44-45.

Walker, Alexander. "A movie beyond the bounds of depravity", *Evening*

Standard 3 June 1996: 16.

Walker, Alexander. "Porn goes into overdrive", *Evening Standard* 5 June 1997: 26-27.

—————————. "Teaching tolerance", *Sight and Sound* 7: 8 (August 1997): 64 [letter].

Waterman, Ivan. "Ballard makes a pile out of pile-ups", *The Independent on Sunday* 16 June 1996: 5.

Willett, Ralph. "'Crash' course 4", *Sight and Sound* 7: 9 (September 1997): 64 [letter].

eXistenZ

Adair, Gilbert. "Cronenberg unplugged", *The Independent on Sunday (Culture)* 2 May 1999: 5.

Andrew, Geoff. "*eXistenZ*", *Time Out* 28 May-5 June 1999: 71.

Billson, Anne. "You wanna play games in my bioport?", *The Sunday Telegraph (Review)* 2 May 1999: 9.

Boxer, Steve. "Organic gaming not coming soon to a console near you", *The Daily Telegraph (Connected)* 6 May 1999: 5.

Bradshaw, Peter. "In pod we trust", *The Guardian* 30 April 1999: Sec. 2: 4.

Calcutt, Ian. "*eXistenZ*", *Film Review* 581 (May 1999): 29.

Carrière, Christophe. "*eXistenZ*", *Première* 266 (May 1999): 58.

Charity, Tom. "Game boy", *Time Out* 1497 (28 April-5 May 1999): 14-16 [interview with Jude Law].

Christopher, James. "Cronenberg's tricks of the light", *The Times* 29 April 1999: 36.

"Cinéma chromosome", *Cahiers du Cinéma* 534 (April 1999): 63.

Curtis, Quentin. "A case of blandness leading the blind", *The Daily Telegraph* 30 April 1999: 25.

French, Philip. "Let's see what you're made of", *The Observer (Review)* 2 May 1999: 7.

Graham, Bob. "'eXistenZ' Is the Real Thing: Virtual thriller plays off fears, toys with expectations", *San Francisco Chronicle* 23 April 1999: C3.

Hoyle, Martin. "Cliché-clogged tosh disappoints", *The Financial Times* 29 April 1999: 24.

Jackson, Kevin. "eXistenZ", *Sight and Sound* 9: 5 (May 1999): 46-47.

Jean, Marcel. "L'A-réalité virtuelle", *24 Images* 97 (summer 1999): 48-49.

Johnston, Sheila. "Specialist in the really nasty jobs", *The Sunday Telegraph Review* 18 May 1999: 10.

Jolin, Dan. "Film of the Month: *eXistenZ*", *Film* 28 (May 1999): 82.

Lalanne, Jean-Marc. "Ceci n'est pas l'existence", *Cahiers du Cinéma* 534 (April

1999): 64-65.

Lopate, Philip. "*eXistenZ*", *Film Comment* 35: 3 (May-June 1999): 82.

Malcolm, Derek. "SFX on the brain", *The Guardian* 18 February 1999: Sec. 2: 11.

Morris, Wesley. "eXistenZialist", *San Francisco Examiner* 23 April 1999: B1.

Mullen, John. "Bio-degraded", *Select* June 1999: 97.

Newman, Kim. "*eXistenZ*", *Empire* 119 (May 1999): 29.

Norman, Neil. "Slithering into virtual banality", *Evening Standard* 29 April 1999.

Quinn, Anthony. "The games people play", *The Independent (Review)* 29 April 1999: 10.

Sardar, Ziauddin and Jonathan Romney. "Playing the game", *New Statesman* 26 May 1999: 35-36.

Shone, Tom. "Talking nonsense", *The Sunday Times (Culture)* 2 May 1999: 7.

Thompson, Ben. "Does this man think he's God?", *The Independent (Review)* 22 May 1999: 11.

Tookey, Christopher. "A touch of canal knowledge", *The Daily Mail* 30 April 1999: 44.

Index

Adams, Parveen 26, 27
Adventures of series of films 43
Aikin, A L 80
Aikin, J 80
Altered States 162
Ambrosio, or the Monk 172
American Cinematographer 20
Amityville Horror, The 42
Amplas, John 12
Andrews, Nigel 36, 39
Anger, Kenneth 20
Arabian Adventure, An 44
Argento, Dario 2, 22, 35
Aristophanes 87
Aristotle 79
Arquette, Rosanna 75, 97
"Ash-Wednesday" 161
Atalante, L' 155
Axel's Castle 27
Baker, Rick 36, 44, 46
Ballard, J G 97, 105, 132, 169
Barrett, Syd 46
Barrymore, Drew 59
Barthes, Roland 125, 134, 135
Bazin, André 138
BBFC **see** British Board of Film
 Censors
Beard, William 45
Beauty and the Beast (myth) 78
Beckett, Samuel 14
Beerbohm, Max 141
Beethoven, Ludwig van 126
Behind the Green Door 62
Benetton 65
Benjamin, Walter 130, 131
Benveniste, Emile 118
Bertolucci, Bernardo 132
Birds, The 61

Black Zero 20
Blake, William 131
Blanchot, Maurice
 7, 8, 13-15, 17, 19, 31, 143
Blasco, Joe 36, 44
Bordwell, David 168
Bosch, Hiëronymus 170
Bottin, Rob 46
Bouquet, Stéphane 105-107
Brahms, Johannes 31
Brakhage, Stan 20
Bresson, Robert
 27, 114-116, 118, 119, 141
Brien, Alan 38
British Board of Film Censors
 (BBFC) 40
Brood, The
 2, 3, 7, 23, 35-40, 43, 45, 51, 55,
  56, 61, 65, 66, 85, 176
Brooks, Mel 50
Brophy, Philip 2, 35, 44
Bujold, Geneviève 86, 99, 154, 155
"Burnt Norton" 28
Burroughs, William
 13, 20, 50, 75, 94, 95, 169
"Byzantium" 141
Cahiers du Cinéma 105, 170
Camera Obscura 114
Canada Council 21
Canadian Film Development
 Corporation 21, 22
Canadian Film-Makers Co-operative
 21
Canadian Motion Picture
 Equipment Company 20
Cannes Film Festival 180
Cannibal Girls 40
Carlson, Les 45

Carpenter, John   22, 35, 46, 53
Carrie   35
Carroll, Noël   79-81
Castell, David   38, 39, 44
Cavell, Stanley
    30, 126, 131, 132, 134, 142, 155,
                                       162
Chambers, Marilyn   62
Chaucer, Geoffrey   130
Christie, Ian   38
CineAction!   29
Cinecity   21
Cinefantastique   44
cinéma-vérité   179
Cinematic Body, The   28
Cinépix   21
Clark, Timothy   135
Classic cinema chain   40
Coleridge, Samuel Taylor   129, 133
Conrich, Ian   22, 23
Cook, Pam   86, 99, 149
Corben, Richard   46
Crane, Jonathan   23, 24
Crash
    3, 6, 9, 14, 15, 22-27, 69, 72, 73, 75,
    88, 97-99, 102-123, 132, 168, 170,
                             172, 180, 181
Craven, Wes   24, 35, 52
Crawford, Joan   162
Crazies, The   35
Creed, Barbara
    25, 26, 28-30, 37, 149, 151, 160-164
Crimes of the Future   35, 75, 179
Critchley, Simon   8
Cronenberg, Denise   19
Cronenberg, Esther   19
Cronenberg, Milton   19
Crucial Problems of Psychoanalysis
                                  112, 113
Crying Game, The   139
Curtis, Jamie Lee   62
Daily Express, The   38
Daily Mirror, The   22, 37
Dallas   42
Damisch, Hubert   114
Dark Victory   161, 162
Darwin, Charles   74
David, Pierre   43

Davie, Donald   18, 27, 28, 123, 137
Davis, Geena   74, 78
Davis, Judy   94, 95, 99
Dawn of the Dead   2, 35, 40
De Laurentiis, Dino   50
De Palma, Brian   22, 35
Dead Ringers
    6, 9, 25, 28, 29, 85-92, 97, 99, 123,
       148-167, 169, 174, 179, 180
Dead Zone, The   23, 50, 56, 65, 169
Dean, James   97, 106, 119
Deep Red   2, 35
Devils, The   40
Dixon, Wheeler Winston   60
Don't Look Now   61
Donne, John   160, 161
Dressed to Kill   42
Du Pré, John   40
Duel in the Sun   131
Eaten Alive   35
Edelman, Lee   89, 92
Edison, Thomas   53
Eggar, Samantha   45, 61
Electric Cinema, London   23, 41
Elements of Semiology   125
Elephant Man, The   69, 73
Eliot, T S
    13, 18, 27, 28, 123, 137, 138, 160,
                                       161
"Emerald Uthwart"   140
Empire Strikes Back, The   44
Essential Cinema Club, London   41
Evening Standard   180
eXistenZ
    15-19, 22, 169, 177, 179, 182
Exorcist, The   36, 40, 42
Fangoria   23, 35, 44-46
Fear   44
Film Canada   21
Financial Times, The   39
Fink, Bruce   103
"Flea, The"   160, 161
Flesh for Frankenstein   40
Flock of Seagulls, A   46
Fly, The
    1, 3, 6, 9, 11, 23-25, 30, 36, 50, 56,
    57, 61, 66, 73-75, 77, 79, 81, 84, 85,
       99, 127, 160, 162, 169, 174

Formalism 124, 128
Four Fundamental Concepts of Psychoanalysis, The see *Les quatre concepts fondamentaux de la psychanalyse*
Four Quartets 28
Franco, Jess (Jesús) 171
Frankenstein 23, 24, 30, 162
Frankenstein story 23, 53, 55-57, 61, 64
Freud, Sigmund 25, 70, 79, 84, 106, 107, 160, 161, 168, 170
Friday the 13th 59
From the Drain 21
Fulci, Lucio 44, 52
Fulford, Robert 21, 22, 69, 71
Fury, The 35
Future Life 44
Gap 65
Geasland, Jack 85
Gehr, Richard 45
General Electric 53
Getz, John 74
Ghost Busters 20
Glasgow Herald 38
Goldblum, Jeff 73, 78
Good, Janet 20
Gordon, Stuart 52
Gorezone 44
Gothicism 65, 172
Goya y Lucientes, Francisco José de 170
GPO Film Unit 22
Grande Illusion, La (Grand Illusion) 155
Grant, Cary 163
Grant, Michael 150, 152, 153, 157, 159-161, 164, 169, 172
Grierson, John 22
Guardian, The 38
Guild Home Video 42
Gunter, Barrie 42, 43
Halberstam, Judith 65
Hall, William 38, 44
Halloween 35, 59
Hanlon, Lindley 115

Harkness, John 129
Hawks, Howard 30, 162, 163
Heidegger, Martin 28, 129, 135-138, 142
Henley, Don 46
Hepburn, Katharine 163
Hills Have Eyes, The 35, 40
Hindson, Margaret 20, 22
Hirschhorn, Clive 38, 44
Hitchcock, Alfred 61
Hofsess, John 20
Hölderlin, Johann Christian Friedrich 7
Hollywood 29, 50, 131, 161, 169, 171, 182
Hooper, Tobe 22, 35, 53
Hughes, David 23, 38
Hunter, Holly 97, 99
Hutchinson, Tom 37
Independent Broadcasting Authority (IBA) 42
Intervision 42
"Introduction to the American Nightmare, An" 168
Irons, Jeremy 86, 89, 91, 133, 141, 149, 158, 159, 180
Ironside, Michael 46
Jacobowitz, Florence 28, 152-154, 156, 157, 159, 164
Jakobson, Roman 124, 125
James, Henry 11
Johnston, Paul 125
Kafka, Franz 12-14
Karloff, Boris 24
Keats, John 134, 136
Keller, Hans 31
Kelley, John P 45
Kennedy, John F 3
Kenner, Hugh 27
Kermode, Frank 140
Kermode, Mark 41, 44
Kierkegaard, Søren 142
King, Stephen 12, 46
Kipling, Rudyard 130
Klevan, Andrew 28-31
Koteas, Elias 75, 97
Kristeva, Julia 160, 161

Lacan, Jacques
  26, 27, 102-104, 107, 108, 112, 113,
    117, 134, 160, 161
Lancelot du Lac   114-119
"Landscape with a Boat"   7
Lear, Jonathan   6
Leavis, F R   30, 140
Lee, Arthur   46
Lee, Christopher   44
Leigh, Janet   62
Levinas, Emmanuel   8
Levy, Mark R   42, 43
Lewis, Herschell Gordon   46
Lewis, Jerry   30, 162
Lewis, Matthew Gregory   172
Lippe, Richard
  29, 152-154, 156, 157, 159, 164
Lone, John   91, 92, 132
Lovecraft, H P   46
Ludditism   62
Lukács, Georg   131
McGinn, Marie   4, 5
McLuhan, Marshall   182
McMasters University   20
M. Butterfly
  3, 9, 25, 27, 28, 50, 91-93, 95, 97,
    99, 123, 127-129, 131, 133, 134,
      138, 140-144, 169, 172
Machiavelli, Niccolò   53
Mad Movies   44
*Madama Butterfly (Madam
  Butterfly)*
    91, 138 **see also** *M. Butterfly*
*Magazine of Fantasy and Science
  Fiction*   19
Malcolm, Derek   38
Mallarmé, Stéphane   7, 18, 137
Mansfield, Jayne   97, 110
Marcus, Cyril   85
Marcus, Stewart   85
Martin   12, 35
Marxism   168-170, 178
Mattes, Jim   45
"Metamorphosis" **see** "Die
  Verwandlung"
Metro-Goldwyn-Mayer (MGM)
                         179, 183
Metz, Christian   114, 118, 119

Meyer, Russ   41
MGM **see** Metro-Goldwyn-Mayer
Miner, Steve   52
Monthly Film Bulletin   149
Monty Python's Flying Circus 46
Moore, Demi   171, 177
Moriarty, Michael   180
Motel Hell   45
Murdoch, Rupert   56
Murphy, Stephen   40
Naked Lunch
  9, 25, 88, 92, 94, 95, 97-99, 170
National Ballet of Canada   19
National Film Board of Canada 22
Nietzsche, Friedrich Wilhelm
                         172, 173
Night of the Living Dead 1, 35
"Nona"   12
North Toronto Collegiate Institute
                              19
"Ode on a Grecian Urn"   136
"Ode to Psyche"   135-137
"Ordinary Evening in New Haven,
  An"   124
Other Cinema, The   41
Pacteau, Francette   87
Parasite Murders, The **see** *Shivers*
Paris, Texas   161, 162
Pasternak, Boris   27
Pater, Walter   140, 141
Paul, William   63
Peary, Danny   42
Philosophical Investigations 5
Philosophy of Horror, The   79
Phoenix Cinema, London   23, 41
Plato   87, 90
Playboy   45
Plowright, Molly   38
Poe, Edgar Allan   8
Polan, Dana   114
Potocki, Jan   11
Pound Era, The   27
Powell, Dilys   23, 37
"Premature Burial, The"   8
psychoanalysis
  12, 25, 26, 79, 102, 108, 109, 112,
    113, 118, 162, 164, 169-171
Puccini, Giacomo 91, 127, 138, 143

punk 41
quatre concepts fondamentaux de la psychanalyse, Les (The Four Fundamental Concepts of Psychoanalysis) 109
Queen 46
Rabid 2, 22, 23, 35-40, 42, 43, 55, 61, 62, 66, 75, 85, 172, 176, 177, 179
Raimi, Sam 52
Random Harvest 161
Rank, Otto 160
Rebecca 42
Règle du Jeu, La (The Rules of the Game) 155
Reitman, Ivan 20, 40
Rękopis znaleziony w Saragossie (The Saragossa Manuscript) 11
Renaissance, The 140
Renoir, Jean 155
Robinson, David 36
Rodley, Chris 17, 19, 113, 127
Roeg, Nicolas 61
Romanticism 126-131, 134, 140, 142
Romero, George 1, 2, 12, 22, 35, 40, 41, 46, 52, 61
Rules of the Game, The **see** *La Règle du Jeu*
S/Z 134
Sade, Donatien Alphonse François, Comte de (Marquis) 103, 104
Santayana, George 61
Saragossa Manuscript, The **see** *Rękopis znaleziony w Saragossie*
Sarrasine 134
Sartre, Jean-Paul 13
Saturday Night 21
Saussure, Ferdinand de 125
Savini, Tom 46
Scala Cinema, London 23, 41, 42
Scanners 2, 6, 23, 35, 36, 38-46, 51, 55, 56, 61, 65, 75, 99, 127, 170, 183
Schrader, Paul 114, 115
Schreber, Daniel Paul 25, 84, 88, 94, 98
Schubert, Franz 31
Schwarzenegger, Arnold 162

Scream 24, 58, 59, 62
Screen 28
Scrimm, Angus 46
Searchers, The 18
Secter, David 20
Sedgwick, Eve Kosofsky 85
Sex Pistols 44
Shakespeare, William 160, 161
Shaviro, Steven 28, 29, 94, 99, 128, 157-159, 164
Shelley, Percy Bysshe 61, 131
Shivers 2, 6, 21-24, 35-40, 42-44, 50, 51, 55, 61, 62, 65, 66, 69-73, 75, 77, 79, 81, 85, 168, 172, 175, 176, 178
Shock Xpress 44
Shore, Howard 29, 152
Showalter, Elaine 160
Sight and Sound 129
Skeleton Crew 12
Smith, Dick 36, 44
Smith, Murray 24, 25
Smith, Richard, Jr 45
Sobchack, Vivian 51
Soloman, Robert C 70, 71, 80, 81
Some Like It Hot 162
Spader, James 72, 97
Spanish Festival of Fantasy Films 21
Spellbound 161
Spielberg, Steven 46
Spiral Staircase, The 161
Stallone, Sylvester 162
Star Trek: The Motion Picture 44
Starburst 44
Starlog 44
Steele, Barbara 62
Steiner, George 129, 135
Stereo 21, 35, 174, 179
Stevens, Wallace 7, 13, 27, 124, 144
"Storyteller, The" 130
Straw Dogs 40
Sunday Express, The 38
Sunday Mirror, The 38
Sunday People, The 40
Sunday Times, The 37, 38
Surrealism 20, 170
Suspiria 35
Symposium 87

Taylor, Charles 127
Telefilm Canada 21
Tempter, The 43
Texas Chain Saw Massacre, The 35
Theory of the Novel 131
They Came from Within see
  Shivers
Thirkell, Arthur 22, 37
Thomas l'Obscur (Thomas the
  Obscure) 8
Thompson, Kristin 124
Times, The 38
Todorov, Tzvetan 11-13
Toronto University 19-21
Transfer 20
Tudor, Andrew 52, 53
Turnbull, Randy 46
Turner, Ted 56
Twins 85
Unger, Deborah Kara 72, 99
Valéry, Paul 27, 123
Velvet Underground, The 46
"Verwandlung, Die"
  ("Metamorphosis") 12
Videodrome
  3, 6, 15, 23, 26, 36, 39, 45, 51, 55,
  56, 65, 66, 75, 85, 99, 170, 172
Walas, Chris 36

Walker, Alexander 39, 180
Wapshott, Nicholas 38
Warhol, Andy 41
Warner Bros 36
"Waste Land, The" 137
Waters, John 41
Weekender 38
Weller, Peter 94
Weston, Michael 126, 142
Wilde, Oscar 160
Williams, Linda Ruth 1-3, 7
Williams, Raymond 54
Wilson, Edmund 27
Wittgenstein, Ludwig
  3-6, 13, 17, 31, 125, 172, 173
Woman's Face, A 161, 162
Wood, Bari 85
Wood, Robin 69-72, 168, 178
World Viewed, The 155
Wrightson, Bernie 46
Yeats, W B 27, 123, 137, 141
Zeifman, Carolyn 19
Zéro de Conduite (Zero for
  Conduct) 155
Zettel 125
Zombi 2 44
Zombies see Dawn of the Dead

Notes on contributors

Parveen Adams is Senior Lecturer in the Department of Human Sciences at Brunel University, and Convenor of the MA in Psychoanalytic Studies. She co-founded and co-edited the psychoanalytic feminist journal, *m/f* (1978-86). Her books include *The Woman in Question* (with Elizabeth Cowie, 1990) and *The Emptiness of the Image* (1996).

Ian Conrich is a Lecturer in Media and Cultural Studies at Nottingham Trent University. He has contributed to *Sight and Sound* and the *Journal of Popular British Cinema*, and to a variety of books, including *The British Cinema Book* (1997) and *A Handbook to Gothic Literature* (1998).

Jonathan Crane is an Associate Professor of Communication Studies at the University of North Carolina-Charlotte. He is the author of *Terror and Everyday Life: Singular Moments in the History of the Horror Film* (1994), and has written on film and genre, and popular music.

Barbara Creed is Head of Cinema Studies at Melbourne University. She has published widely on feminism, psychoanalysis and the horror film, and is the author of *The Monstrous-Feminine: Film, feminism, psychoanalysis* (1993).

Michael Grant is Senior Lecturer in Film Studies at the University of Kent at Canterbury. His publications include *Dead Ringers* (Flicks Books) and *T.S. Eliot: The Critical Heritage*, as well as numerous articles on poetry, cinema and aesthetics.

Andrew Klevan is Lecturer in Film Studies at the University of Kent at Canterbury, and teaches a course entitled Film Style, Interpretation and Evaluation. His book *Disclosure of the Everyday: Undramatic Achievement in Narrative Film* was published in 2000 by Flicks Books.

Xavier Mendik is a Lecturer in Media and Popular Culture at Nene University College. He has co-edited *Unruly Pleasures* (2000), and is the author of *Bodies of Desire and Bodies in Distress: Sexuality and Death in 1970s Italian Horror* (1999). He is completing a study of Argento's *Tenebrae* for Flicks Books.

Murray Smith is Senior Lecturer and Chair of Film Studies at the University of Kent at Canterbury. He is the author of *Engaging Characters: Fiction, Emotion, and the Cinema* (1997) and co-editor of *Film Theory and Philosophy* (1995) and *Contemporary Hollywood Cinema* (1998).

ISBN 0-275-97058-2